PROFESSIONAL {and Personal} BRANDING from Scratch

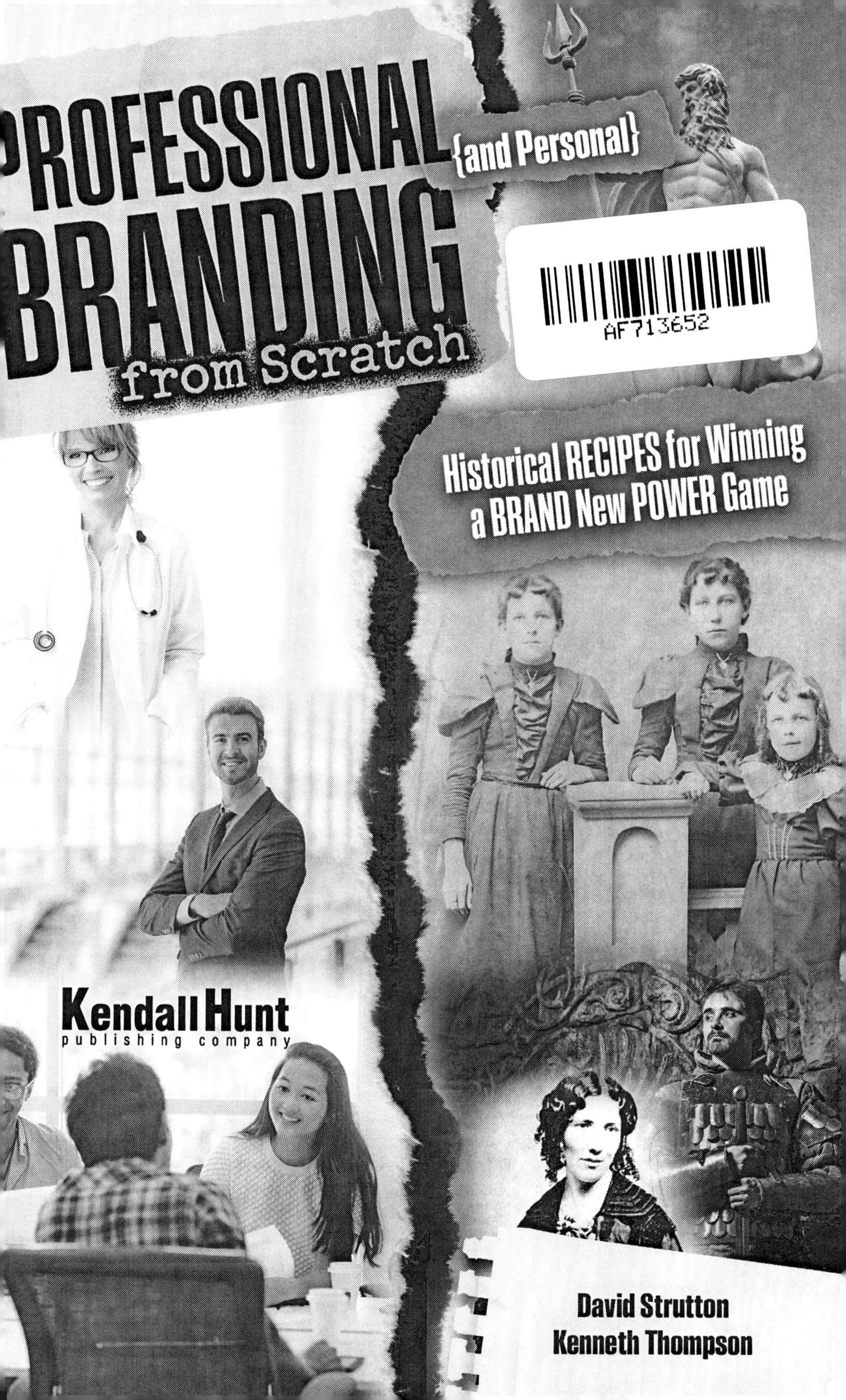

Historical RECIPES for Winning a BRAND New POWER Game

Kendall Hunt
publishing company

David Strutton
Kenneth Thompson

Kendall Hunt
publishing company

www.kendallhunt.com
Send all inquiries to:
4050 Westmark Drive
Dubuque, IA 52004-1840

ISBN 978-1-4652-9999-4

Printed in the United States of America

For Sherry – a beloved partner who has powerfully, persuasively, and permanently stamped her elegant brand into my life.

For Patricia – my partner and best friend without whose support this book and all else in life would be less meaningful.

Table of Contents

Introduction

Targeted Readers

Professional Branding, from Scratch delivers difference-making value for soon-to-begin professionals, soon-to-retire professionals, and people performing at any professional stage in-between. The branding principles and insights presented below were crafted to be universal in nature. The principles and insights delivered in *Professional Branding, from Scratch* will boost the success prospects of anyone seeking to identify and exploit socially responsible ways to accumulate more power and to exercise greater persuasiveness on whatever professional stage they perform.

How This Book Can Help You

Professional Branding, from Scratch will help you become or remain more successful by showing you how to increase your branding power and persuasiveness. Our premise is simple: Increase your ethically grounded power and persuasiveness, and your prospects for earning and sustaining leadership roles on whatever professional stage you occupy will materially expand.

In your struggle to succeed or sustain success inside increasingly turbulent, disruptive, and challenging professional sectors and markets, you can become overly immersed in today's news, trends, and theories. Yet these fashionable subjects are often here today and gone tomorrow. Fortunately, alternative and superior ways exist to acquire needed information and insights. Much that is valuable and timeless in its usefulness can be learned from experiences. From your own experiences, naturally. But more to this book's point from the historically successful or unsuccessful experiences of others. You will more likely succeed or sustain your professional success by exploring, learning, and integrating time-tested examples of how the right branding activities should be done right and devoting less attention to so-called latest and greatest buzzwords or other "get-powerful quickly" schemes.

The lessons embedded in the venerable struggles of others should help you identify and pursue historically proven paths toward more effectively branded positions on your specific stage. Your newly earned branding stature, in turn, will grow your power and persuasiveness among clients, potential or prospective partners, subordinates, peers, and individuals to whom you report. The opportunity to wield more power and exercise more influence in these settings surely appeals to you. Right? Don't worry. It's okay to "own the fact" that this opportunity appeals to you. Especially as long as your new power and persuasiveness is grounded in socially responsible sources and behaviors.

Ownership—acquiring and then leveraging an asset—is important. Throughout automotive history, few if any customers have ever washed a rented car. The reason: people only care about things they own. Given that you care about your professional future—an asset you could create, own and leverage (or ignore, merely rent, and endure)—you should READ THIS BOOK.

How to Read this Book

Dozens of actions must go right (or wrong) with the dynamics of a golf swing in order for players to hit a golf ball far and true (or into the woods). Similar descriptions apply to the complexity of the branding dynamics and outcomes you must generate and manage before branding initiatives can succeed. The inherent complexity of this activity, however, does not negate the fact that your branding acumen will prove critical to your present and future accomplishment.

Professional Branding, from Scratch was written as simply as possible. Books should be written to be read and understood rather than deciphered or interpreted. And this one was scripted, yes, from scratch, to be understood. However, the manageable fundamentals that will contribute most to your brand-management success are intricate, humanistic, nuanced, and not always uniformly logical or entirely self-evident in nature. But the inherent complexity of brand-management activities does not undermine the important role that the subject should play in your professional life. That is, if you learn how to execute the activities effectively. Especially in professional sectors being currently threatened by dynamically debilitating technological and global forces. That list includes all contemporary professions, by the way.

Still, *Professional Branding, from Scratch* is not always easy to read. Perhaps especially for younger professionals or current students. The potential pain of this reality is compounded in a world where reading and writing no more than 140 characters at a time is now more rule than exception for many of the same people who most need the following ideas, insights, and lessons. How should you respond to this book's occasional complexity?

Consider reading only one chapter a day. Reading with highlighter, a piece of paper, and note-taking pen in hand. Doing these latter three things alone will help you think more clearly and learn more easily. You should also read driven by the goal of capturing and prioritizing the specific insights most germane to successful branding performance on your stage. Permit any new concepts and insights you discover to sink in … slowly. Pivot toward "old school" in a digital world. "Going Old School"—entirely consistent with *Professional Branding, from Scratch's* historical underpinnings. Finally, work hard at personalizing your branding/rebranding initiatives as one concept builds on another. Work motivated by knowing and embracing words that Hall of Fame professional football coach Vince Lombardi offered about the ideal and natural relationship that does and should exist between success and work:

- "The only place where Success comes before Work is in the dictionary."[1]

Presumably, you already understand one core message Coach Lombardi sought to convey through these words: "Work hard." Because you've worked extremely hard to earn the status and prestige you currently or soon will enjoy. Why squander an opportunity to squeeze greater value for yourself and your family from the professional standing you've already created or are about to create for yourself?

Preface

A Problem: Once Fertile Fields are Currently Withering

A book called *The Professions* was published during the pit of the Great Depression. In this book British sociologists Alexander Carr-Saunders and Paul Wilson hailed the strength, value, and perseverance of professionals and the professional fields. Professionals were celebrated as "stable elements" in a turbulent world. Lauded as stalwarts poised to "inherit, preserve, and pass along traditions common to their respective professions." The authors proposed that professionals would function as "stable centers of resistance to 'crude environmental forces' which threaten steady and peaceful evolution."[2]

High praise, indeed, because the 1930s world was exceedingly tumultuous. Stability was sorely needed during this time. Because beyond question, stability and a sense of permanence were each in short supply. Surely we're not the only ones seeing a parallel between that era and the one we're currently living out. Lest you failed to recognize the trends, which is unlikely, all sort of professional fields are currently encountering turmoil generated by crude environmental forces.

The professional fields traditionally resisted "crude environmental forces" by establishing and rigorously enforcing high barriers-to-entry. These barriers-to-entry effectively capped the quantity of people qualified to deliver the specific, highly valued problem-solving services that have always defined respective professional fields. And made most fields financially and psychologically rewarding. Such fields include experts performing in business, management, entrepreneurial, and consulting; medical; engineering; legal; scientific, technological, and analytical; creative, artistic, and architectural; academic, educational, and administrative domains. And others we unintentionally overlooked.

Professions routinely constrain recruiting efforts to people holding advanced degrees. Generally, the more prestigious the degree-granting institution, the better. Many professions require postgraduate licensing and ongoing training as prerequisites for initial or continued membership. Membership in exclusive associations are "musts" rather than "nice-to-haves" for some professions. Lengthy apprenticeships are required in others. Anyone, for example, can brand herself a management consultant. But top-end consultancies require years of extensive training, experience, and sustained success as precursors for promotion to partner. Other ancient but still functioning professions emphasize the importance of tradition and extensive education. Academic professionals don medieval garb to celebrate ceremonial occasions; British barristers still wear wigs inside courtrooms. Physicians spend multiple challenging, stress-inducing postdoctorate years acquiring and refining knowledge and skill sets related to medical specialties. Accountants and financial advisors are certified and must be recertified.

You likewise probably paid a high price to enter your field. The time, money, stress, and effort you expended was substantial. But the price of admission was worth it. Right? Especially if you consider the security, prestige and opportunity to accumulate wealth that you now or soon will enjoy due to your status. If you're feeling good about your accomplishment, demonstrated abilities, and elevated status within in a now-global socioeconomic hierarchy, good for you. "You Got That Right," as rockers Lynyrd Skynyrd sang in the 1970s. You deserve to feel satisfied because you worked hard to plant seeds that birthed fruit you now enjoy.

Your authors similarly feel satisfied about our status and earned accomplishments in our academic field. We are satisfied. But hardly complacent. Because perhaps like you, we're increasingly sensing certain material threats rising inside our profession. Experiencing convergent pressures emanating from uncontrollable sources that threaten to slowly degrade our professional power. Soon enough, it appears, the same pressures may suddenly and substantially degrade our power. But we don't plan on letting this happen. We're doing whatever is possible, reasonable, and ethical to consciously and continuously strengthen our professional brand.

That's our plan. What's yours? You should have one. Because the sorts of pressures that are impacting almost all other professions and individual professionals today are also conspiring to drag down our prestige, pricing power, and perhaps our future employability. This process is likely already underway in your profession. We know we don't know your profession. Doesn't matter. Trends similar to the ones that threaten us are present within every contemporary US profession.

Threats Began on Farms—Yes, Really

Agricultural technology birthed the idea and reality of the farm as an industry. During less than 150 years, the birth of cotton gins, 1793; internal combustion engines, early 1800s; pasteurization processes, 1863; nitrogen fixation, leading to fertilizers, 1918; scientific plant breeding, 1920s; and combine harvesters, 1930, created a world in which two or three people could perform farming functions that formerly required hundreds. The ensuing industrial revolution moved American workers into factories. Never-ending but ever-accelerating globalization and automation effects eventually moved many workers back out of their factories as they migrated to offices. Throughout this evolutionary process American consumers generally benefitted from the steady emergence of a service-based, professionally-oriented economy. As did the individual professionals who drove this now-historical marketplace.

Time passed. The US economy and its professional classes increasingly prospered as separate but interdependent "entities" built on the provision and receipt of "comparatively scarce" professional services. Comparatively scarce, because services were inevitably delivered by domestically based professional providers. And because the economic law known as "supply and demand" works, those services along with their professional providers became and remained highly valued. The total number of jobs, however, also always grew. Especially jobs in sectors providing professional services.[3] Until recently.

The challenges to the professions that are materializing today differ radically from preceding threats. A new era, a new paradigm, new threats and most tellingly, new opportunities for individuals who manage, and mediate those challenges effectively to prevail, has arrived. An era in which technological-based professional employment will grow. But one where those same software and computer engineers and technologists will increasingly innovate legions of other professionals and nonprofessionals out of work or to lower status positions. The net:

- The total quantity of well-paying and prestigious jobs available in developed nations, including positions currently manned by professionals, has and will continue to persistently decline. This dire condition will continue to abide for at least a generation, and perhaps far longer.

Publications as august, reserved, and progress-oriented as the *Wall Street Journal* issue breathless bylines admonishing readers to stand up and recognize that: "Artificial intelligence is still in its infancy—and that should scare us."[4]

Clichés often merit the ink that they receive. Even platitudes rarely enter cultural consciousness absent a basis in fact. The following assertion is clichéd: Technology is a one-way street, and traffic on this street never stops moving forward. But this statement is not just true. It is also rife with associated implications.

And now technology, and the good-news, bad-news consequences it delivers, are evolving faster than ever. Many individuals, including professionals, struggle to understand these technologies. Others experience anxiety because they cannot or feel they cannot keep up with the changes. Still other professionals understandably sense they're losing ground to technological forces they can neither control nor influence. We cannot envision the near-term arrival of any brake that might tamp down technology's increasing velocity or impact on entire professional sectors arrayed across the domestic economy.

Instead, whatever can be done to mitigate and manage the often vicious consequences that technology is imposing on the traditional professions will usually be best executed on an individual basis. Individuals like you. Your professional brand is one logical place to begin doing what can be done to blunt and eventually overcome the negative consequences technology and globalization otherwise may impose on your status.

Your brand: An asset you should understand, manage, control, influence, and, ultimately, leverage in ways that benefit you. And yes, leverage to benefit clients, prospects and other key audience members around you! This latter set of benefits is "huge," riffing a word co-opted by Democratic Presidential candidate Bernie Sanders during the 2015/2016 election cycle. If you're not thinking about how better to satisfy the needs and solve the problems of clients/customers as a primary reason why you're doing things, such as creating or managing your brand more effectively, you'll find trouble from the start.

Further *Rise of the Machines:* No, Not Referencing *Terminator III*

Technology, mere machines, is continuously degrading the professions' two strongest claims to an exalted standing. Professionals' initial claim to fortune, fame, and security derived from their ability to expand the body of knowledge in their particular field. Their second claim derived from professionals' license to deliver, typically on a relatively exclusive basis, their particular expertise to unordained, often actually grateful client groups. But now, the impact of these two sources of professional prestige, power, and "pricing power" is waning.

IBM and the Baylor College of Medicine recently developed a system called Knowledge Integration Toolkit (KNIT).[5] KNIT scans the medical literature and generates innovative research questions to drive solutions for pressing medical problems. Takes some edge off the intellectual luster currently associated with bleeding-edge medical research, doesn't it? Meanwhile, the entire anesthesiology is under actual technology assault. Who needs to pay a physician professional wages when a machine performs the same function at 20% of the cost?

Israeli computer scientists, themselves accomplished professionals, recently developed a process that uses facial recognition techniques to solve a puzzle. The problem has flummoxed Torah scholars for decades. The algorithm pieces together 300,000 ancient Jewish manuscripts that were discovered, torn and tattered, in the attic of an old Cairo synagogue.

Various software programs now regularly outperform legal experts in predicting the outcome of court decisions involving patent disputes being argued before the US Supreme Court. In trends reminiscent of what happened to farmers computers can already manage millions of legal documents, sorting, and prioritizing them for relevance. Soon enough one such machine will complete the work of 500 attorneys. There's probably a lawyer joke in there somewhere.

Technology is equipping machines and para-professionals to coopt the performance of many routine but absolutely necessary professional tasks. Computers already sort troves of data and offer high-quality financial advice.

Computers are never motivated by fear or afflicted by greed or bias. Could anyone claim, straight-faced, that similar descriptions apply universally to financial professionals employed by Fidelity Investments or Edward D. Jones?

How much time will pass before machine-generated professional-like insights and solutions prove superior to the insights and solutions delivered by actual professionals? The answer is probably "not much"... time. A startup firm called Kensho already provides accurate responses to questions sophisticated enough that Fidelity's or Edward D. Jones' financial advisors might be loath to attempt to answer them. Questions such as what happens to technology stock prices when privacy or piracy scares arise. Or when terrorism strikes, again, at another major airport?

Nurses and physician assistants, lacking M.D.-level training and experience but armed with computers and other highly efficient diagnostic devices, do far more work formerly reserved exclusively for doctors. At far lower prices, of course.

"Simple" smartphone apps and online services sometimes permit laypeople to dispense with some such professionals entirely. Or, at the least, to ratchet the "Pros" down a full measure or two from their traditional pricey pedestals. Approximately 4,000,000 patients visited WebMD each month during 2015, exceeding the numbers of patients who visited regular US doctors during the same periods.

Consider the professoriate. Sitting in their ivory towers, tenured or tenure-track English, History or Business professors are inexorably being displaced by clinical instructors, likely to few people's regret save themselves and their families. Clinical instructors are often fine teachers. More importantly in the new academic paradigm; however, these clinical instructors happily teach at 25%–50% or less pay than actual professors in particular fields normally receive. More threats are arriving. Apart from games, educational apps are the second most popular product category in Apple's app catalog. Massive Open Online Courses (MOOC'S) attract millions of new "college" students, and further threaten the professorate's prestige and status.

Accounting, architectural or various managerial professionals are hardly immune to similar assaults. Nor, as noted, are professionals plying their values in legal domains safe. Judges and attorneys increasingly turn, frequently at the behest of clients, to small claims resolutions through "e-adjudication." The technique is already employed by e-Bay to resolve more than 60,000 litigious-worthy disputes that arose among its customers.

People smart enough to turn professional in the first place should also be wise enough to deal in reality rather than an idealized version of the world that probably never existed. But even if an ideal world once existed the fact is that jobs; employees, of any ilk, always drag down profits. This is especially true when the same value that a professional has produced can be generated by nonprofessional people or machines that cost less. And companies will pursue any even tolerably moral alternative that can lessen their costs. As they should ... this is how competition, capitalism, and capital work. These cost-cutting measures include outsourcing (resulting in lost jobs), transferring manufacturing to foreign locales (again, more lost jobs), and replacing more expensive human capital with less expensive technological capital (more jobs losses still).

Classic Laws; Contemporary Consequences

Economic laws almost always exercise their will. The relative scarcity of the problem-solving services provided by professionals performing in specific fields has traditionally elevated the value, prestige, and power of individual professionals. All due to the consequences of the first economic law.

Adam Smith's pivotal law of supply and demand was born in 1776, the year in which the great philosopher published the first economics book, called *The Wealth of Nations*.[6] Great philosopher? Absolutely, Adam Smith was not an economist. Instead he invented the profession now known as "economics." Amazingly, Thomas Jefferson's *Declaration of Independence* and Thomas Paine's *Common Sense* were also published during 1776. This was clearly a time for creating history-changing documents and for establishing perpetually prominent professional brands.

The traditional law of supply and demand materially influences prices for products or services in any market. As supply expands, meaning as the "value" provided by any product or service becomes more widely available, prices for those products or services decrease. Value, professional or otherwise, can be described in various ways. But you would benefit from viewing value as your problem-solving capacity—as perceived by actual or potential clients, or superiors, peers, or subordinates. Your professional value exists as an genuine or "imagined" reality in eyes of others. Others whose approval or acquiescence is crucial to your success. Your professional value is an entity—an asset—that you can choose to manage. Or, sadly, choose to ignore.

Until recently, the law of supply and demand always worked to protect and actually elevate the best interests of the professions and individual professionals. Today, however, the consequences of another historical economic law are rapidly supplanting the favorable consequences that the professions' adroit management of "supply and demand" once generated for individual professionals. The law is called "creative destruction."[7]

Creative destruction, as a concept and an increasingly "predatory" fact of contemporary professional life, was developed by Austrian economist Joseph Schumpeter during the late 1940s. Actually, creative destruction unfolds either as a "predatory" or "opportunistic" fact of contemporary professional life. Your "point of view" regarding whether the predatory or opportunistic qualifier applies depends, like many things, on your "point of viewing."

Creative destruction exists or arrives when newly created products, things, and/or ideas destroy the established products, things, and/or ideas that preceded them. Situations, marketplaces or professional sectors arise in which newer things or ideas disrupt and debilitate established things and idea. In such situations, markets or sectors, proverbs such as "the big eat the small" no hold water. To the contrary, "the fast" (who are generally powerfully branded) destroy "the slow" (generally weakly branded, if at all). The music publishing industry has profoundly experienced the "slash and burn-like" effects of creative destruction's slash for the last 20 or so years. As have myriad other fields, to lesser or greater degrees.

The entwined convergence and power of uncontrollable environmental factors such as globalization, digitization, commoditization, and better-informed clients are concurrently "juicing" these Schumpeterian-like creative destruction effects. Juicing as if those consolidated environmental "effects" were on steroids. The pace of this destruction is accelerating and likely won't abate for generations, if ever.

The uber-successful professionals and firms who are destructively creating—although destruction is not their intention—this "brave new world" often emerge from obscure places. Such as, for example, Estonia (Skype). Or the city of Galicia, in rural northwestern Spain (Inditex). Internet-based technologies permit fledgling ventures to grow huge seemingly overnight. Which is wonderful unless you're the professional whose traditional firm just got shallowed whole or is being eaten piece by piece—the way one eats an elephant. The velocity and scale of these success stories is understandably disconcerting and disruptive to older orders.

Entrepreneurial professionals who champion and drive these successes generally employ minimal human capital and physical resources. This is partially due to the fact that digital services are highly automated and party due to outsourcing. Blockbuster boasted more than 9,000 US stores and 83,000 employees as recently as 20006.[8] Netflix, along with Red Box the original Blockbuster buster, employs only 2000 or so workers and actually rents the computing power for its streaming videos from Amazon.[9] Apple employs only some 93,000 workers worldwide. A smallish number that makes sense once you understand that Apple does not actually manufacturer or distribute the products it markets. Apple, instead, mostly manages its brand and the designs and technological advantages that drive the creativity of its brand.

The University of Michigan recently reported that the 1250 or so firms that have gone public in the United States since the year 2000 employ, on average, only 700 employees worldwide. The current professional paradigm operates without pity, not "that there is anything wrong with that"—as George Constanza might suggest. Champion firms operating within this paradigm constantly reinvent, reconfigure and reposition themselves to delay the fates that befell once new but now seemingly antiquated parentage firms such as AOL, Nokia, or HP.

By the way, we are not knocking creative destruction. The same creatively destructive forces that led 1950s-era medical savant Jonas Salk to develop the polio vaccine also obsoleted the iron lung. No one can criticize that result. (Younger readers can Google "iron lung." But trust us, this life-saving technology was simultaneously terrific and horrific.) Our legitimate concern, instead, is that technologically-induced and accelerated creative destruction is increasingly making large numbers of professionals tools to the machine. Anyone reading this now interested in becoming a tool to the machine in their future?

A Jobless Future

A jobless future is coming. Truth be written that future has already arrived in many geographic and professional precincts across the United States. No rash of empty, exaggerated or deceptive political or business promises will preclude this future's arrival. You would be wrong to believe otherwise. And now that you know, you would be wrong—to a degree approaching an instance of "voluntary self-destruction"—to not do what is possible, professional branding-wise, to prepare for soon-to-arrive future. Unless you are okay with an economy in which everyone is either a barista at Starbucks or driving *each other* around in Uber vehicles.

What will millions of workers do in an America where "capital" no longer requires "labor," channeling Karl Marx's *Communist Manifesto*?[10] Written in 1848! we might add. Robots and other technological forms will take over. Uneducated, unskilled, or unmotivated—for goodness sake, how much Pokemon Go can one play?—people will find it impossible to prosper in the face of this onslaught. Which may merit a big so-what from some haughty individuals. But even the arrogant should understand that these millions will no longer be able to afford their professional services.

What will likely occur in a world without work but with universal health care? Untold numbers of people freed up to create a second Renaissance? Or millions more poorly motivated citizens living vicariously through celebrity gossip and often silly electronic diversions that permit them to create mini-worlds-of-me? The answers are playing out around us right now.

But these dire words and sour warnings don't apply to you, right? Surely you're protected against these sorts of threatening trends? Of course you're protected, until you're not. Or more predictably, you're protected unless and until the formerly differentiated values associated with your professional status are incrementally and eventually more materially degraded. All because the formerly differentiated value that once accrued naturally to the professions and individuals professionals is increasingly being commoditized. You either already know this, are experiencing these effects yourself, or know someone who, riffing the 1960s guitar god Jimi Hendrix, is already "experienced" in such dissolute matters. And like Mr. Hendrix, he or she may not long survive the dissolute experience.

Even high-end service provider firms are ruthlessly becoming more efficiency oriented. Managerial consulting giant Accenture, for example, now contracts huge chunks of formerly professional work to third-party employees living in the developing world. Well-qualified third-party employees, but individuals who willingly work for dimes on your salary dollar. Meanwhile, Accenture abandoned its traditional partnership model and is now a public firm.

This result is attributable to consequences associated with ever-encroaching globalization and outsourcing trends. Globalization, coupled with technology, has remade the domestic economy. The question is settled. For now and into anyone's foreseeable future.

The American marketplace long ago evolved into a service-based economy. But today, even high-end service providers are far less protected. People who occupy many professional positions are no longer primed for formerly traditional, almost guaranteed, success. Instead, the future presence of many professional jobs is hardly guaranteed.

Individual clients are concurrently becoming more efficiency minded as they gain greater insights about their providers' true costs from Internet technologies. Larger organizational clients no longer engage with consultancies who court them with partners but send in junior varsity to perform the consultation. Can anyone blame them?

What Makes You the Professional You?

Professional fields and individual professionals merely survive or absolutely thrive largely based how well they solve the problems that the profession and its professionals presumably are uniquely qualified to solve. At an core level any profession exists because certain problems exist that can only be solved by the highly skilled people who inhabit the field. Educational problems, related generally to the ills that the presence of ignorance foments throughout modern societies. Design problems, principally related to the "bad outcomes" that arise when the form and function of products don't come together in ways that suggest desirable meaning to customers. Health problems, related directly to the onset of death if cancer, recently branded as the "*Emperor of All Maladies*," is not treated properly.

Things can and have changed, however. The welfare of many professions is increasingly being threatened. These threats typically arise because a given profession is suddenly or slowly no longer recognized as the only or even the best game in town. Which represents a huge challenge the subject relates to "individual professionals-solving-problems" previously "owned" by the particular professional in which they perform. This trend—this fact—should not surprise. History reveals that few ways of understanding, thinking about, or solving client or customer problems are eternally "good to go." The displacement of one professional paradigm—a paradigm is simply a broadly accepted way of thinking about and solving problems—with a new and superior set of solutions is normal, natural, and desirable. Unless you are the professional and your profession is the one being disrupted or displaced. These descriptions apply to every profession that has ever existed, currently exist, or one day will exist.

Known, broadly-accepted solutions always work well–until better solutions come along. This is why people now ride horses for pleasure and drive cars to work. Or why travelers almost always use airborne rather than waterborne solutions to travel from Baltimore, Maryland to London, England—even though each solution gets you there. No one should be surprised to read that old paradigms are displaced by fresher alternatives. The same theme has played out across millennia.

One major difference is in play today, however. A big, hairy, audacious, "should-be-scaring-you" and "motivating-you-to-strategically-react" difference. These displacements used to unfold at glacial rates. No longer. Changes across and within the professions are currently playing out at "baud" paces. Baud, or the speed at which information travels across the globe along the internet. The unprecedented speed of these transformations is the primary reason why many professionals need new ways of thinking about and managing the perceptions that key others—we call them "audiences"—develop about the problem-solving values they create and deliver. When we write unprecedented, we mean it. Contemporary Americans take more photographs during every 2 minute period than were shot during the entire nineteenth century. A fact rendered more meaningful once one realizes photography was introduced commercially in 1839![11]

Daniel and Richard Susskind recently predicted that an intractable convergence of technological; globalization; commoditization, particularly of professional services; and democratization of knowledge trends may facilitate a "dismantling of traditional professions."[12] As stated, professionals traditionally offered the best solution, often the only game in town, to legions of clients. This is no longer true in many sectors. Clients historically lacked the understanding to tread even tentatively into the specific areas over which professionals previously wielded monopoly power. Again, this no longer holds true. Across sectors, technology permits now-former clients to acquire the understanding and thus the solutions they need when they need them through nontraditional sources. Think WebMD, LegalZoom or Google. Of course, when better-informed individuals now opt to acquire actual professional solutions, they often do so at heavily discounted rates.

Many former havens of security are being hammered by inexorable outside forces. Pounded-upon to degrees that the professions have never experienced. These "inexorable hammers" are increasing in their scale and potential impact on individual professionals. These three facts are, well, facts. Not in doubt. But one issue remains up for grabs:

- How will you countermand these threats to your and your family's future wellbeing?

We're Not Luddites

A seemingly interminably soured global economy is partially responsible for these threatening trends. But information technology, the most destructive of all contemporary creators, is the primary culprit.

This book does not address what we are or should be doing with new technologies, or what new technologies are doing to us. Instead *Professional branding, from Scratch* addresses what you can do to not just fend off but rise above technology's power-negating impact on your profession or individual professional value. Nor are we are thinking from a Luddite-like perspective when labeling technology the "primary culprit." The term "luddite," infamously, was the brand ascribed to early 19th century English workers who destroyed labor-saving machinery as a protest against the threats that then-new technologies were imposing on their livelihood. The brand "luddite" is often used more broadly today to describe people who futilely oppose technological change.

We're not Luddites. This book does not demonize technology's evolution and power. Or for that matter globalization processes. We wrote this book at various times during a roughly 12-month period while typing on keyboards located in 5 different American states and 13 foreign nations. By name: Australia, Austria, Slovenia, Canada, Costa Rica, Croatia, Egypt, Germany, Greece, Italy, Mexico, New Zealand, and Turkey. The technological and globalization trends we write about each represent progress. And who can, should, or would fight progress?

Technology and globalization processes are likely already huge parts of your present. As noted, our futures too. Each factor is poised to play even more dominant, likely power-draining roles in our futures. This book does not pushback against that future. Nor, in our view, should you. But you should prepare for this future's otherwise professionally-punishing arrival. This book is here to help you prepare.

Gentle Response to Possible Pushback

Many professionals had best get ready. Probably even you. Your previously well-ordered professional world soon may begin unraveling. Some people reading this may already be experiencing vibrations from these seismic-like shifts. Others may only be sensing the nearness of impending threats. Which makes sense. After all, some animals can discern earthquakes before they actually arrive. Such animals include catfish, snakes, and weasels—no negative insinuations intended!

Let's assume you're intelligent, self-reliant, and justifiably cynical individual. Given this, you logically might disagree with general "doom & gloom" assessment outlined in the Preface. You might counter, sure, these negative trends and facts were interesting. But what about your profession's power to manage complexity? An argument like this: Americans will always hand over Federal tax forms and records to Certified Public Accountants or other tax preparers because the process are too complicated to fuss with. But technology is increasingly managing certain types of complexity more deftly than humans. Turbo Tax, anyone?

Or you might counter with an emotion-based argument: Wouldn't patients or clients rather be informed about potentially deadly illnesses or bankruptcy by fellow humans? Perhaps. In fact, likely. But extreme expertise and personal empathy rarely arrive in the same human package. Bad news probably is best delivered by individuals who excel in sympathy and empathy. But investors might not want grandma advising them that the expiration date for getting rid of the dog investment or upping their monthly retirement ante is rapidly approaching.

Technology is not just getting smarter at systems-type analyses. Machines are improving at rates human intelligence cannot match. You merely deciding to improve your cognitive skills or technical training—while obviously valuable and desirable—may longer suffice. It will be impossible for you to outthink the analytical power that technologist masters are rapidly developing and disseminating. Simply developing more genetic human capital may not suffice to ensure your prosperity and success proves sustainable in the coming economy.

Something more may be needed for most professionals to establish or sustain success in increasingly challenging fields. We believe that a substantial part of that "something more" is your brand, and how well you manage this brand for purposes of differentiating your value and growing your power and influence in ways that help your clients, yourself, and your family.

Two Questions: Ask One, Not the Other

Don't ask: What functions can I perform that technology cannot? Don't bother. Machines are becoming increasingly dexterous at performing disparate, highly complicated tasks at rates—and "prices"—you cannot match. Consider accounting. Or financial, marketing, engineering, architectural, design, or data management analytics. Or even the activities that formerly drove lucrative billing and high employment throughout legal fields. These activities are obsoleting at unprecedented yet still rising rates.

Instead, you should ask:

- What activities will human beings, driven by their deepest psychological natures or the realities of daily life, simply insist must be performed by other humans?

The answer is that the nature of such activities will be mostly relational. This is a good thing for people reading this book. That's because relational activities are generally "brand-able." Relational activities are thus differentiable. Brand-able identities and images of the sort that would be reflected in your seeming or genuine ability to comfortably occupy positions of authority, responsibility, expertise, and/or accountability while also solving the problems of others. A branded image as a "pro" who can wisely provide care, counsel, solace, encourage, or kicks-in-pants in near-equal-measures, on as-needed-bases might come to mind. Or a branded image as a "pro" who powerfully and persuasively projects the willingness and capacity to perform effectively as part or more likely the leader of teams.

The prospects for transactional-oriented professionals are declining in most fields. The prospects for effectively branded relational-oriented individuals are simultaneously growing. Empathy, for example, is emerging as an essential professional skill. Empathy entails the ability to sense what another person is feeling or thinking and responding in accordance with what the other wants or needs. Empathy, classically described as the power to understand others as if you had "walked a mile in their shoes." The patients of high-empathy physicians heal better than those served by low-empathy medical providers.

The ability to function empathically—with empathy—in groups is more important than ever.[13] Functioning empathically as either group leader or member. Knowing how to tell powerful branding narratives, at times even using words, as part of distinctive professional identities, stories, images, or capabilities that facilitate understanding of the exact key points that should impressed on important people. These sorts of relationally based branding skills are now emerging as fundamental precursors to sustainable success.

Powerful brands might emerge from the demonstrated ability to lead others to your way of thinking. Powerful brands likewise might emerge from knowing how best to mix diverse people together in ways that produce new and useful results. And when you possess earned branding power and persuasiveness that you can leverage, ensuring that diversity does not, worse case, tear a team, organization, or even a nation apart. (About that last "national" reference, look around if you are skeptical.) Or, more likely, render the diverse entity less efficient than should be the case. How great would it be if the contemporary professional politician class could learn to leverage diversity in ways that bring citizens together rather than rip them apart?

(Indulge us a brief but useful digression. Diversity rarely comes naturally. Social systems—which include all teams, organizations, and nations—innately seek to reproduce themselves. Yet "reproduction of self" is antithetical to diversity. As is well-known, diverse groups perform more effectively, but only if they can be lead effectively. Diverse units, however, are always more challenging to work in and difficult to lead. The reason: diverse views lead to more disagreement and conflict. Thus while the results are better people are less happy with the experience. Meanwhile, diversity is increasing on every domestic stage on which professionals develop and deliver their solutions. Beyond question, an earned reputation for managing and leading diversity effectively will prove a strong brand identifier for generations to come. For what is worth, which is lot, experts are fortunately coalescing around the idea that an ability to create "psychological safety" is a key to successfully managing diverse groups. When psychological safety prevails across diverse team teammates believe they can express exactly what they are thinking or feeling absent fear of reproach, criticism, or sanction.)

The most secure and successful professionals in this rapidly approaching future will generally combine technological awareness and proficiency with social awareness, personal power, and relationship acumen. The most successful individuals will likewise understand how to integrate ethical values, social responsiveness, relationship acumen and personal power into clear, consistent, and compelling professional brands. Powerfully persuasive professional of the sort that only you can create and therefore should consciously cultivate for yourself.

Notes

1 Quotation Dictionary (1972). *Quotation Dictionary*. Boston, MA: Career Institute, Inc.

2 Schumpeter, Joseph (2015). Professor Dr. Robot QC: Once Regarded as Safe Havens, the Professions are Now in the Eye of the Storm. *The Economist*. 74. October 17, 2015.

3 Fallows, James (2013. The 50 Greatest Breakthroughs Since the Wheel. *The Atlantic*. November, 23–32.

4 Gelernter, David (2016). Machines that Will Think and Feel. *Wall Street Journal*. C1. March 19/20.

5 EurekAlert (2014). Study Shows Promise in Automated Reasoning, Hypotheses Generation Over Complete Medical Literature (2014). *EurekAlert: The Global Source for Science News*. August 14, 2014.

6 Smith, Adam (1776). *The Wealth of Nations: A Landmark Classic*. New York, NY: Harper & Row Publishers.

7 Schumpeter, Joseph (1950). *Capitalism, Socialism and Democracy*. New York, NY: Harper & Row Publishers.

8 Fritz, Ben (2011). Dish Network Wins Bidding for Assets of Bankrupt Blockbuster. *Los Angeles Times*. May 29, C1.

9 The Economist (2012). The Woes of Netflix: Looks Bleak. *The Economist*. October 27, 2012, pp. 37.

10 Steger, Manfred B. (1997). *The Quest for Evolutionary Socialism: Eduard Bernstein And Social Democracy*. Cambridge, UK; New York, NY: Cambridge University Press. 236–237.

11 Plagens, Peter (2016). Don't Look Now. *The Wall Street Journal*. C-16. April 9, 2016.

12 Susskind, Richard and Daniel Susskind (2016) *The Future of Professions: How Technology will Transform the Work of Human Experts*. Oxford, UK: Oxford University Press.

13 Bellet, Paul S. and Michael J. Maloney (1991). "The Importance of Empathy as an Interviewing Skill in Medicine." *Journal of the American Medical Association*, 226(13): 1832–1832.

PART I

Key Ingredients

Chapter 1
Setting Your Table

"There is no work like early work" ...
because ... "Good managers look ahead"

– Isabella Breton (1837–1865).

Readers are leaders and leaders are readers. This statement has been true at least since Johannes Gutenberg perfected the printing press around 1436. Do you want to become or remain a powerful leader in your professional field? Would you welcome an opportunity to become or remain more persuasive in the same arena?

If you answered yes to either or both questions, read on. Why? Because this book was designed, from scratch, with two purposes in mind. The first purpose: To explain how you can secure a more powerfully persuasive professional leadership position. The second: To show you how to sustain that position post-arrival. The historically grounded lessons delivered by *Professional Branding, from Scratch* are timeless in their value and universal in their applicability. The lessons provide actionable insights about how best to increase your power and persuasiveness by creating and sustaining a stronger brand. How strong a brand? One strong enough to practically ossify your reputation.

In her nineteenth century book *Everyday Cooking*, Isabella Breton offered 28 Kitchen Maxims. In the opening quote that frames this chapter, we combined her first two adages. Mrs. Breton asserted that "if the novice will commit them to memory she will have before her the fundamental truths of the art of cookery." The book before you offers a slight variation on her assertion. "Commit its core messages to memory" and you "will have before [you] the fundamental truths of the art" of professional branding. And these "fundamental truths" will apply regardless of whether you are a novice or experienced professional.

Your professional brand simultaneously captures and projects sets of beliefs, values, and assets that "key others" perceive are associated with you. If properly managed, your brand should confer differentiation and added value to you. These two outcomes, in turn, will enhance your power. As your power rises your ability to influence the behavior of "key others" with whom you interact as you perform in your profession grows in lockstep. "Key others" include actual or prospective clients and customers (hereafter, the term "clients" is generally used); actual or potential partners, associates, or cohorts; and individuals reporting to you, managing you, or working as peers with you in professional settings.

Martin Luther King, Jr. described power as the ability to effect change through vigor, energy, stamina, and moral behavior.[1] You should manage your brand such that your branded professional identity evolves into a core source of strength from which you draw and project greater power through ethical means.

If you're a professional, you already have a "brand." Doesn't matter whether you've managed or chose to ignore your brand. Or even knew your brand existed. There is one universal, intriguing, and potentially threatening characteristic associated with your brand, however. Specifically: if you don't create and/or manage the beliefs, values, and assets that others formulate about you, then other people will control the branding process for you. Your brand will evolve or devolve into whatever identity that various audiences establish for you if you don't preemptively your brand for them.

Principles only become recognized as principles after they have been proven to work across situations, contexts, and time. "Work," as in routinely produce desirable outcomes. The same basic professional branding principles that would enhance the power and persuasiveness of legal, accounting, or health care professionals would also elevate the power and persuasiveness of professionals performing in engineering; logistical, supply chain, financial and investment, human resource, or marketing management; creative, innovative, or artistic; architectural, technological, or analytical; educational, academic, or training; governmental, administrative, or nonprofit and public interest; consultative or entrepreneurial sectors—in brief, across all professions.

Becoming Successful; Remaining Successful

The power and persuasiveness of effectively managed professional brands can prove enduring. While exceptions exist, Lance Armstrong or Bill Cosby come to mind, effectively managed brands typically hang tough even when encountering well-founded, well-funded, and concentrated attacks from various media, legal, personal and professional peer-group quarters. To illustrate, consider another extremely well-managed brand, one that has similarly experienced extensive attacks from various governmental, media, medical, legal, and even entertainment sources.

Beyond question, the assaults confronted by particular brand are legitimate. Legitimate insofar as many of the profession's most prominent employees and senior leaders recently have been either convicted of spousal, partner, and child abuse or accused of engaging in transparent cover-ups of these criminal behaviors. Well-founded assaults, insofar as numerous convictions of murderers, murderer-suicides, drug-induced serial rapes, and other forms of physical assault have emanated from the profession's limited pool of permanent employees. You see, this global profession has less than 2000 full-time—lets label them "in the trenches"—employees during any given year. Well-founded assaults, insofar as the profession's employees have routinely been found guilty of pervasive illegal performance-enhancing drug use and of inside- or outside-the-rules workplace infliction of permanent brain damage, that is, chronic traumatic encephalitis; or other bodily harm on fellow employees, as well as on themselves. Well-founded assaults, insofar as the profession's middle- and senior-level management has been accused and often convicted of overt acts of spying; various types of cheating; and fraudulent cover-ups of one or more of the previously listed front-line employee offenses.

Wow, what a brand this must be! The ability to retain its power and persuasiveness despite these beatdowns is remarkable. Or as we say, welcome to the National Football League. "The League's" globally iconic branding acronym *NFL* is also known by those who know for denoting *N*ot *F*or *L*ong. "Not For Long," given the average career life expectancy for the profession's employees; that is, 3.3 years. Yet despite the persistent assaults it has experienced for the worst of reasons, the NFL brand remains powerful. So powerful that "The League" still "owns" an entire day of the week plus part of Monday, Thursday, and even Saturday, during play-off season. That's how powerful a powerful brand can be and remain even in the face of withering external attacks.

Obvious and Less Obvious Paths to Professional Success

Stay mindful of the powerfully positive consequences that successful brands can generate as you *work* through this book. "Work" will prove necessary for you to benefit materially from this book because *Professional Branding, from Scratch* tackles three *inherently complicated* and *interrelated* subjects:

- Professional brands.
- Professional brand management.
- The human foibles, rationales, and irrationalities; traits, attitudes, and beliefs; and decisions and resulting behaviors that affect and are affected by how and how effectively you manage your brand.

Two words, "work" and "interrelated," and one phrase, "inherently complicated," were *italicized* above. The highlights underscore the reality that even the simplest possible explanations can become difficult to understand when an issue as complicated as branding is addressed. And the branding ideas and principles developed below are frequently far more challenging than the dumbed-down, lowest-common-denominator books, texts, and tweets that many people limit themselves to today.

But we believe you are smart enough, willing, and able to dig deeper than that. We're likewise confident that your hard work; that is, the diligence with which you approach this book and its professional branding insights will payoff for you.

Paying off immediately by elevating your near-term power and persuasiveness. Paying off longer term by showing how to retain this newly earned branding power and persuasiveness throughout your career.

The most obvious path to success in any professional setting is one marked by regimen, structure, and persistence. That is, your own ... Regimen, structure, and persistence. Because the presence of these three qualities and values in your workaday lives will, capture, and directly or indirectly facilitate outcomes that in turn will function as universal precursors to successful performance across professional sectors. You first should develop, then assimilate into your problem-solving core, and ultimately deliver each of these three values on whatever professional you perform. Presumably you've already integrated regimen, structure, and persistence into your work life. True professionals cannot expect to succeed or sustain success unless they inculcate each value into their preparation and execution. There are no shortcuts to long-term professional success.

Two additional less obvious, narrower, and less heavily traveled paths also exist along which you can earn and sustain professional success. The first path relates to the quality of ideas that you create or adopt and integrate into your professional life. One extremely "high-quality" idea drives this book: do whatever is necessary, possible, and ethical to elevate the power and persuasiveness of your brand. Ideas, like behaviors, have consequences. The consequences that will result should you adopt and live out this idea to the max across your career will prove profoundly positive.

The second path to earned success relates to the quality of ideas that you select as "guideposts" in your work life. Guideposts function simultaneously as boundaries and benchmarks. Boundaries should constrain and govern our professional and personal decision making. In effect, they direct our behaviors. Boundaries also exist to keep your branding efforts inbounds. Benchmarks, meanwhile, prescribe exactly how you should execute the ongoing branding activities you've designed to ethically enhance the power and persuasiveness of your brand. Benchmarks also provide measures against which you assess progress toward your professional goals.

Neither path could ever displace the acute value that the presence of regimen, structure, and persistence will confer to you. But not surprisingly, the presence of each "governing value"—regimen, structure, persistence—would undoubtedly uniformly complement and amplify the value of each brand-based recommendation we offer below.

Integrate this Story into Your Brand Narrative

Professional Branding, from Scratch tells the story of professional branding. A brand-new-to-world story; one that has never before been fully explained. Stories about personal branding have been written for quite a while. Stories about professional branding? To date, there are none. This book is the first that tells the story about how best to brand your professional self.

The first rule of storytelling:

- "Make me care" about the story being told.
  You should care deeply about the following story because it was created for and is about you.
  A second rule of storytelling, especially when a particular type of story is being told:
- Create an impending sense of danger or possible catastrophe.
  Fear makes people care. Care intensely, in fact. Presumably about the story being told.

Few people have ever jolted awake at 2:15 am because they were experiencing Jackson Browne-like "Peaceful Easy Feelings."[2] (Mr. Browne wrote the song; country rockers "The Eagles" made it famous.) Fear of the whip once drove slaves to work. Fear of dismissal, failure, or pending irrelevance still drives free professionals to work. Existential fears about encroaching obsolescence or the prospect that some combination of technology and less expensive foreign providers might displace them or degrade their value to the point where their wages drop might similarly drive readers to initiate appropriate actions aimed at mitigating the factors causing their fears. At least we hope so. You should care deeply about this story. Because many, perhaps most, of you should be concerned about the future you had planned to build and enjoy. A future now being threatened in ways you likely never anticipated.

A third plausible storytelling rule: If their stories make readers "care due to a scare," the storytellers themselves should also provide workable solutions that mediate, alleviate, and sometimes eliminate the imminent threat. Everyone loves stories that have happy endings, right? Yet due to converging and uniformly negative environmental trends that few can control many professionals increasingly need to create new and navigable paths to their own happy endings.

Fortunately, this book is not just a "wag-our-figure"; "point-out-all-the-problems-all-the-time"; "we're-so-screwed" tome. *Professional Branding, from Scratch* instead offers unique solutions to these genuinely pressing "professional" problems that absolutely merit your careful consideration. Most tellingly, this book provides brand-driven stories that demonstrate why and how neophyte or experienced professionals alike should develop and implement a distinct yet universally applicable solution to the problematic challenges that are or soon will visit their professions. A solution designed to mollify your reasonable fears and materially improve your professional future.

Professional Branding Success: Born or Created?

Certain people appear to enjoy advantageous brand-able capabilities essentially from birth. Some people actually have won highly specific genetic lotteries. National Basketball Association (NBA) power forwards, for example, were born to grow into a particular body type and potentially elite level of athleticism. But even these genetically gifted humans can only succeed at the top of their extremely exclusive profession if they carefully nurture their body type and athletic potential. Stated differently, even genetically blessed NBA players become genuinely successful only after they have grittily cultivated their natural talents. Take, for example, three-point shooting savant Stephen Curry. He is undoubtedly a graceful, fast-twitch athlete. By NBA standards, however, his physical gifts are rather pedestrian. But he is now branded as the G.O.A.T. (*G*reatest *o*f *A*ll *T*ime), shooting wise. Simply, nor not so simply, because he engaged in 22-plus years of diligent preparation before arriving at this juncture, at the epitome of his professional preparation, at the still tender age of 28.

Professionals performing on any court or stage should similarly cultivate distinguishing capabilities on which they can brand themselves as being different from and better than others who occupy the same professional stage. First, by widening their repertoire of skills through reading and reflection. Second, through willingly doing the hard work necessary to learn the right new things in the right ways from the right sources. Right things, ways, and sources with the descriptor "right" itself being defined by what constitutes "right" in specific professional sectors. Descriptions of what constitutes "right," branding wise, in accountancy settings obviously might diverge from what constitutes "right" in advertising agencies.

This book is the "right source" for you. *Professional Branding, from Scratch* is uniquely positioned to make the complicated task of developing and managing your brand successfully as simple as possible. Hopefully you're willing to work hard enough to understand its branding lessons.

We all intend to grow older. With aging, our useful experience presumably grows. As time passes and experience grows, we should mature and grow in wisdom. The value of your brand similarly should grow. Reading this book will decrease the likelihood that you end up "too-soon-old" but "too-late-smart" in your chosen profession. And "too-weakly branded" along the way as a consequence. Professional life, even during challenging times, should be about more than just merely surviving. Your career, which we presume is a big part of your life, should also be about absolutely thriving. If not, why did you work so hard to arrive at your current station?

A Genuine Solution

How can you de-commoditize the hard-earned value of your skills in an increasingly challenging world? Truth told, the best way to mediate and manage these nagging threats entails unleashing your powers of creativity and innovativeness. Bet you did anticipate that response right here? Especially since this book is not fundamentally about creativity—although it does feature one chapter (9) that exclusively addresses the topic. But this book does offer another genuine, personalized, and customized (one size would never fit all) way to de-commoditize your value. The solution relates to your brand, and how to develop and leverage its value as you learn how to play brand new power games. And play them very, very well. Are we really offering a total solution to the potentially prestige-swallowing, spirit-crushing, income-siphoning, and uncontrollable environmental trends introduced earlier? Of course not. One-size-fits-all solutions to such universal and malevolent problems could ever exist.

But does *Professional Branding, from Scratch* offer a solution? Yes, absolutely. Which is fortunate, insofar as an irresistible compression of their power, prestige, and pricing purview has increasingly made it more difficult for individual professionals to enjoy the perks of power and privilege that only recently was there for their ready taking. The historically based, time-tested, and consequently high-quality ideas and advice provided below will permit you to enhance your power and persuasiveness inside your profession by managing your brand more effectively.

Why are the core new ideas present in this book historically based? First, because past events and knowledge is always useful as a framing and contextualizing device. Second, because historical details can reveal large contemporary truths and generate actionable insights. The means, motive, and opportunity for the ideas and insights provided in this historically grounded branding book to change the arc of your life for the better have cohered. Third, actionable insights about the best of history can be leveraged to bring out the best in us. Often, even the worst of history can similarly be leveraged to bring out the best in us.

What happens in your future is largely determined by what you do now. Given this three-headed rationale, and the fact that the threats described in the Preface will inevitably grow in scale and scope, the time is right for this book. This book does not just provide insights you should want. The book provides insights you should crave. Even if you never realized how much you need the following solutions—until now.

Professional Branding, from Scratch Addresses ...

The future is unknown, chaotic, and threatening across almost every contemporary professional field. Applying specific predictions or prescriptive remedies to chaotic systems is difficult. *Professional Branding, from Scratch* is not about technology or globalization, the effects each factor will engender for the professions in the future, or the increasingly tumultuous professional worlds that result. The book instead provides advice and counsel about how to manage your "present" better in order to succeed more fully in your "future." A well-managed brand can mitigate much of the uncertainty, chaos, and threats that many professionals are poised to confront now and in their future.

Some things can be learned on the job. Yard-work, community organizing, bartending come to mind. The best way to develop and execute value-enhancing professional branding strategies is a different matter. Developing a powerful brand is not something most people learn on the job.

Your training has presumably taught you how to make effective decisions in your chosen field. You're probably already "hell-on-wheels" efficient when it comes to decision making in your professional silo. Nothing but praise be unto you for that hard-earned accomplishment. But your earned acumen likely has done little to augment your ability to make effective decisions in professional domains outside your field of expertise. Decisions about how best to brand yourself professionally, for example.

Why? Because, paraphrasing former Secretary of State Henry Kissinger, being a professional generally consumes rather than creates the sort of intellectual capital that can be wielded to good effect in other fields.[3] Full disclosure: Dr. Kissinger was opining about high national office holders. By the way, we believe that economists or attorneys generally may be exempt from this general rule.

If you are new gal or guy just entering your professional battleground, you don't want find yourself in situations where you make up your branding strategy as your career is being launched. You really might get your metaphorically or not metaphorically "blown-off." Nor do you want to ignore opportunities to develop branding strategies as your "years-in-rank" tick off sans sufficient professional advancement. Yet to their financial, emotional, and psychological detriment, many professionals are doing the one thing; that is, making crap up as they go along—or experiencing the other; that is, a stalled career.

What about you? What's your plan for earning or sustaining a branded reputation as a professional performer who develops and delivers value—read, "solutions"—perceived as different from and better than the values being developed and delivered by your competitors or colleagues?

Given today's "crude [environmental] forces," you would need to bring incredible quantities of intellectual capital to your stage to successfully differentiate your brand successfully on your own. Or get really lucky? Or read *Professional Branding, from Scratch* to acquire actionable insight about:

- How you can to develop more professional *power*.
- How you can develop more professional *persuasiveness*.
- How you can create more power and persuasiveness by developing and executing your branding assets in ethical and socially responsible ways.

The story unfolding below has the power to inform and transform you. Eventually, after you learn more about how to manage the right things right insofar as those things relate to your brand, others around you and who merely know you by reputation will define you and your value less by your actions than by their reactions to your brand. That's a good thing … for you!

This is exactly what happened, on a global scale, with the recently deceased Muhammed Ali and his era-shaping professional brand. Because from 1964 to

1967, Ali destroyed the indestructible, twice (Sonny Liston); changed his name (Cassius Clay to Muhammed Ali); and did the inconceivable before the majority of Americans deemed the decision credible, by refusing to fight in Vietnam (Man, I ain't got no quarrel with them Vietcong). The "Champ" did this before antiwar protests were cool. As he was told would happen, Ali then was stripped of his World Heavyweight Championship title. But primarily because Ali boldly lived out his core values, the power and persuasiveness of his brand grew and grew, and then grew more. The power of the Ali brand has not abated across five decades.

There was and only will be one Muhammed Ali, an influential, powerful, global brand one-half century in the making. Few readers would ever enjoy the opportunities or endure the challenges that the self-proclaimed G.O.A.T. experienced while creating his brand. But you are surely smart enough to ethically manage your brands for purposes of achieving worthy ends. Ends that benefit your clients, you, and your family. You need this book, assuming you're committed to helping others and winning competitions in increasingly challenging professional sectors.

A Paradox to Learn and Leverage

During the same era in which these threats to the professions and professionals have steadily emerged your world has probably paradoxically evolved in certain ways into an easier place in which to succeed. Let's assume, first, you can or have mastered the technology. Fortunately, a subject addressed in other books. And honestly, mastering technology is not that difficult. Bright and not-so-bright 12-year olds around the world already possess said mastery. Second, let's assume you are actually do work hard and with focused purpose. Frankly, again not a difficult assumption to make at all, not if you are the type of person who self-selectively choose to read this book.

Assuming technological mastery and the right work ethic/focus, the only other thing besides profession-specific skills—and clearly, you've acquired them—that you must master to succeed entails learning how to:

- Present yourself and thus your brand to others in ways that consistently redound, over time, to their and your own best interests.
  Not coincidentally, not just learning how to:
- "Treat others not just how you would want to be treated" but also learning to "treat others the way they would want you to treat them" will aid and abet your success, as well.

The notion of treating others as you would want to be treated, of course, is the Golden Rule. This rule was originally expressed nearly 2000 years ago in Luke's Gospel [6:31]. Luke admonishes: "And as you would that men should do to you, do you also to them likewise."[4]

The second quoted counsel ensues from the lesser known but more relevant, in today's world, Platinum Rule. Fortuitously but not coincidentally, individuals who concurrently honor the Golden and Platinum Rules will also bring both and good fortune to their brands.

Notes

1 Abernathy Ralph (1989). *And the Walls Came Tumbling Down: An Autobiography.* New York, NY: Harper & Row.

2 Masley, Ed (September 30, 2014). 10/1: 5 Essential Eagles Albums: Hotel to Border. *The Arizona Republic.* Retrieved November 23, 2015. http://azcentral.com/story/entertainment.

3 Kissinger Henry (2014)., *World Order.* New York, NY: Penguin Press.

4 *The Holy Bible (2006). New Revised Standard Version.* Nashville, TN: Thomas Nelson Publishers.

Chapter 2
Can You Handle the Truth?

"Place your iron hand inside a velvet grove"

—Napoleon Bonaparte (1769–1821).

*While being cross-examined in the 1992 film **A Few Good Men**, the fierce U.S. Marine Corps Colonel Nathan Jessup inexplicably lost his imposing self-possession, shouting throughout the courtroom, "You cannot handle the truth!" "Inexplicably," because the attorney of middling ability, played by Tom Cruise, would never have broken the powerful Jack Nicholson character in real life. Truly powerful and persuasive professionals, operating in any sector, don't break easy.*

Powerful people typically experience little need to break others, either. They don't need to, because their reputations proceed them. Individuals whom others have "branded" as powerful instead exercise power with comparative ease, almost naturally, seemingly as an endowed right. A right you one day could earn from the reputational value embedded in and disseminated by your brand on any stage on which you perform.

Colonel Jessup's five fateful words about who or who could not "handle the truth" triggered a rant. His own. An outburst that portentously began with the bold assertion that his prosecutor "has the luxury of not knowing what I know." That is, Jessup's prosecutor had never been exposed to essentially insoluble problems. Nor had he had to think deeply, incessantly and obsessively about; or actually solve, truly wicked problems. The sort of problems for which any solution, if one is even possible, likely will prove neither completely right nor wrong. Problems of the sort everyone knows about but rarely opt to discuss openly or in polite company. Problems so multifaceted that only professionals operating in the relevant field – on this stage, the United States Marine Corp – can fathom their full implications.

Colonel Jessup's tirade culminated with the famous shout-out "You want me on that wall. You need me on that wall." (The "wall", by the way, was build at the Guantanamo Bay Naval Base, located on U.S. territory shielded inside the nation of Cuba. The naval base also houses the Guantanamo Bay Detention Camp, now more infamously-branded as the prison that has housed hundreds of captured terrorists since 2001.) Here, Jessup again spoke unvarnished truth. He was referencing the darker sides of professional life as it might unfold in any challenging sector. Referencing the sort of challenging, disturbing, routinely arising events, behaviors, circumstances, threats or high-end glitches that people who navigate increasingly difficult passages successfully must first understand and eventually master. That is, if those professionals plan to succeed and sustain their success over the long-term through ethical means.

The fictional but factual Jessup was likewise directly and indirectly referencing things that perceptive professionals know happen and occasionally do themselves. Through just a few good words, the Colonel underscored the extent to which even supposedly sanguine settings, like professional workplaces, are often subtly or overtly nasty places. Unforgiving places. Places characterized by dog-eat-dog encounters in which dueling professionals struggle competitively and collaboratively to secure solid grips on *the next rung up organizational ladders. And only one person at a time can hang onto that rung. Places where professionals not bringing their "A" games every day when it comes to client acquisition or customer relationship management face genuine prospects of being ejected from the game. Places where even "A" gamers must deal directly and/or harshly to the realities of the moment. Places where the demonstrably best way to achieve victory and then secure your peace is to be prepared for war. And not just prepared metaphorically.*

The Guilt-Free Acquisition of Power and Persuasion

Can you handle the truth that it is appropriate, desirable, and indeed ethical to:

- Learn the ways and means to secure more branding power and persuasiveness as you ascend perilous, by-no-means-secure ladders up and over the walls and barriers that separate you from where you now are to the level of success that will satisfy you?
- Learn these ways and means for purposes of lessening or mediating the risks that you will encounter when confronting other professionals who already occupy strong positions on their own walls—and who naturally aim to retain their power? Individuals who, through no fault other than their human nature, seek to keep you on the lower end of the wall you share. Fellow professionals who have, to date, learned to play branding power and persuasion games better than you.
- Learn, understand, and apply the lessons that follow for purposes of building a more powerfully persuasive brand?

People often pass through their professional lives unaware that they are imbued with opportunities and surrounded by factors that make it easier for them to influence, manage, or manipulate the decisions of others around them. Or unaware that the phrase "manage or manipulate" should not evoke uncomfortable reactions within you. You're a professional, after all. Educated and trained, in many instances oathsworn to solve big hairy audacious problems of a sort only professionals can solve, all while helping others, even in contexts where not every problem has a solution.

The act of "helping" others—a group that could include organizations or society—likely resides at or near the core of what you do, or are supposed to do, in your professorial life. You thus should always brand yourself as an effective problem solver. Especially after you have grown into actually being extremely successful at problem solving.

You alternatively might brand yourself as the sort of person who brings out the best in others or manages others' problems such that they would then enjoy the opportunity to bring out the best in themselves.

In a best possible world that you could create for yourself, you might brand yourself along each branding dimension. As was the case with former NBA Coach Phil Jackson. Jackson leveraged his Zen Master brand to coach the Chicago Bulls to six world titles, then followed up by leading the Los Angeles Lakers to five additional titles. During his reign of power, Coach Jackson really did simultaneously solve the difficult (persuading the luminescent Michael Jordan to sublimate his transcendent game for the good of the team) and bring out the best in his other players.

This book tells stories explaining how you can grow more powerful and persuasive by managing your brand more effectively. Stories worth your attention because they addresses one problem nearly every professional routinely confronts. The problem: no matter how much or little power you currently possess, you would welcome an opportunity to secure more. But only for ethical purposes, of course!

A sense of having too little influence over people or events can feel intolerable. When people feel ineffectual or weak, they feel miserable. Few people who are honest with themselves would admit to wanting less or the same amount of power that they currently possess. (Just like all honest people must admit they would like at least one of their body parts be larger or smaller.) No reason exists to feel guilty about this desire. Instead, let's just acknowledge that almost everyone seeks more power. Some people's desire for greater power is only surpassed by their lack of insight about how to attain it.[2] Hopefully, those ranks will not include you. Not after you have completed this book.

Some people pursue power more successfully than others. Perhaps, in fact probably, because they created a plan to grow their brand's persuasiveness. What about you?

Prospects for acquiring power and persuasiveness can be endangered whenever you appear too greedy in your attempts to secure either. Even highly assertive people typically advance more rapidly when persuading key others they are reasonable and respectable by acting in subtle, ostensibly balanced, fashions. Or when they present themselves and impress others that they are fair, decent people who combine the effectively assertive actions with judicious thought. Like it or not, occasions arise when avid strivers who consciously pursue power succeed in part because they have built brand identities suggesting they are congenial, not crafty; democratic, not duplicitous; and straightforward, not sly. Even when these branded depictions do not represent their true self.

The Real World

There is an ideal world. We all covet the ideal. Ideal places that are peaceful and fair, that are equitable. History is very much the opposite. For example, past results demonstrate clearly that some effective leaders are often exceptionally good liars. Insert your favorite professional politician suspects here. The opposite of what one would hope would happen. The opposite of anyone's ideal world.

Which brings us to the real world, the one in which you perform out various professional roles. A world you may have rode into on a dream and learned was a nightmare. This book unfolds in the real world; that is, the venues in which you work. Places, collectively, where, as noted, crafty (shrewd); duplicitous (two-faced) and sly (artful) tactics undeniably *are* part of other professionals' self-presentation and resulting rise or fall. Real worlds where, when coupled with legitimate talents and drive, the ability to exercise branding skills effectively has smoothed many individuals' elevation to genuinely high and mighty positions where great opportunity to exercise power and persuasion exists. You want to ascend that wall, too.

The decision making and resulting actions of most successfully branded professionals usually must impress others as civilized, equitable, and objective. Today's politically correct world outwardly and actively subscribes to these (civilized, equitable, and objective) values. Today's "politically correct" workplace settings accept nothing else and nothing but. Yet individuals who operate exclusively within the boundaries of such restrictive guidelines may prove vulnerable to the predations of their peers, superiors, or even clients who are not similarly constrained.[3] Recommendation:

- Don't worry so much about being politically correct. When it comes to branding yourself, worry more about simply being correct.

Real-world emotions such as *incivility*, *prejudiced*, and *subjectivity (one-sidedness)* often lurk just below the outwardly benevolent surfaces of "players" who supposedly subscribe to political correctness. As they likewise reside, undoubtedly, right below the surface of whatever stages on which you ply your skills. And these real-world emotions, unchecked, arrive attached to predictably negative consequences. For you, of course.

This bleak but realistic take on genuine life inside professional organizations and other settings should not surprise anyone reading this now. Should you be surprised if the same selfish human instincts that govern your decision making also dominate everyone else's? After all, we humans are all, in the Protestant reformers Martin Luther's immortal words: *incurvtus in se*, a Latin phrase. These words mean, in English, humans are all instinctively and selfishly "bent-inward" in service to ourselves and own needs rather than outwardly in service to God and the needs of others.

Outwardly, branding professionals who yearn for greater power and persuasion in route to leadership positions surely understand that they should respect niceties of the sort introduced earlier. They know they should present, or brand, themselves as congenial, democratic, straightforward, civilized, equitable, objective, and so forth. But inwardly, unless they are inexplicably naive, branding professionals should also discern the need to be sensible, prudent, and occasionally a bit circumspect in their private decisions and public actions. Branding professionals should likewise learn the art of deftly outmaneuvering peers while subtly administering to superiors while servicing their own desire to skillfully build and subsequently manage successful brands. Individuals who master this skill will more quickly attain branded positions that confer greater clout and opportunity to persuade.[4] If these actions appear devious, they should, because they may be. But only devious if you initiate these actions with the wrong purposes in mind, for reasons explained below.

When the French General and Emperor Napoleon Bonaparte wrote "Place your iron hand inside a velvet glove" he was expressing these general ideas.[5] A contemporary Napoleon, who surely would be concerned about his brand, might have added that when the goals you pursue are worthy, arrive on the field prepared to exercise either device: your iron hands and/or your velvet gloves.

This book examines each possibility: iron hands or velvet gloves. The book does this by advocating a real politick approach to securing greater more brand-based power and persuasiveness. For advisory purposes, few holds are barred. As should be the case. After all, true power players are rarely weak in spirit or purpose. As rare: weak-in-spirit or purposeless professionals who are able to play branding power games effectively.

Justifying the Unjustifiable

There is nothing wrong with actively pursuing greater power and persuasion within any organization or inside the professional sector where you perform. Instead, the purposes for which you intend to use any acquired power make your pursuit of greater branding power and persuasion right or wrong. Your ability to perceive branding situations as just that, simple circumstances, rather than episodes of good or evil behavior is a perspective, a virtue, and inexhaustible value that you should aspire to acquire.

We recommend that you view acquired branding power; that is, the earned ability to more easily persuade others to, shall we say, see things your way, as an "opportunity" to do well for yourself. Because newly acquired branding power clearly is. But we likewise recommend that you view acquired branding power as an earned opportunity for you to create greater good for others. Again, because it truly is. Pursuit of either end, or result, will always complement pursuit of the other. Stated more plainly: If you simply concentrate intently on doing good for others, far more than your fair share of good will inevitably migrate back to you.

Me, a Power Player?

The notion of strategically playing branding power games may stimulate public expressions of disgust among some professionals. A road to persuasiveness that, for them, is best not taken. Perhaps, you similarly believe you can opt out of these "power games" by managing your brand in ways having nothing to do with power. Our suspicion, though, is that the class of professionals who *truly* subscribe to such guilelessness can be tallied on a short roll. And among those who've *actually earned* substantial stores of power, the roster of *non-believers* would be smaller still. Nonetheless, the possibility of powerless-brand influence-acquisition strategies should be considered. That is, if the actual concept of such a branding strategy is not too oxymoronic.

Still, if such professional sectors exist at all, purportedly non-power players might be identifiable based on their publically espoused claims and highly refined sense of:

- **Moral Equivalence.** A morally equivalent branding tactic might involve advocating that everyone should be treated fairly—and alike. An examination of the classical liberal versus conservative worldview may illustrate the point here. Conservatives and liberals, after all, differ fundamentally in their definition of fairness. In liberal minds, fairness means that everyone, in the end, should get the same thing, or outcomes. In conservative minds, fairness means that everyone should "get" in accordance with what they put in. Or, in accord with the value they have created. That is, people should get what they have earned, get what they deserve.

Moral equivalence should be respected. Why? Because some people clearly do execute certain valued tasks differently and better than others. Therefore, we would argue those people should be rewarded differently. We strongly suspect moral equivalence generally does not exist in the real world in which you work. Across time people do and largely should earn returns in proportion to the value they have created and introduced to the world. We believe everyone with whom you interact should be treated fairly. We harbor no illusions that everyone with whom you interact should be treated the same. Nor, almost certainly, do you. People should be treated in accord with how they deserve to be treated. Consequently, you should always play brand-based power games, assuming you always play in ways that are ethical and socially responsible.

- **Perfect Honesty/Transparency.** Another associated non-power branding tactic might entail public pronouncements that perfect honesty or complete straightforwardness will prevail in all dealings with others. Yea, right, maybe in some other version of planet Earth. This exact promotional tactic was employed by the 2007/2008 "Hope and Change" Presidential campaign initiated by then-candidate Barrack Obama. Mr. Obama repeatedly announced, sparing no fanfare, that his administration would be the most transparent in history.

The facts are in. As well-branded pop psychologist Dr. Phil might ask: "How'd that work out for you?" Notwithstanding the fact that utter honesty and complete straightforwardness often hurt many people, including honest-broker branders, this tactic is difficult to execute in real world settings. Beyond this, few perceptive people view such behaviors as completely objective or free from personal motivations.

- **Naiveté.** While genuinely guileless or naive individuals conceivably might wrangle for control and persuasion, those who make overt shows of their naiveté may be more sophisticated than anyone. Or perhaps they are the most transparently manipulative branders of all. To be certain, branding professionals have been known to play a selective "ignorance" card as a deceptive means of protecting themselves against allegations that they are seeking unearned advantage or influence.

Our thoughts: Never fall for this tactic. Avoid the mistake of having an experience but missing its meaning or the opportunity to learn that is embedded in it.

The truth is that even genuinely non-power players might lapse intermittently into power-based branding tactics of their own. They may belong to the small faction of professionals who can skillfully employ less-than-direct maneuvers to secure greater power and persuasiveness. After all, even the unenlightened use of the right branding tactics may prove effective.

Should You Play Power Games?

Do most professionals play brand-based power games? Should they? Absent empirical evidence, the first question cannot be conclusively answered. But for two reasons the latter question merits a unqualified yes. Reason one is that much can be lost—financially, personally, familial wise—when individuals opt out of professional brand-based power games. History, anecdote, and probably your personal experience is replete with examples revealing how persons quickly experienced severe power deficits by not playing brand games or by playing them poorly. Their prospects for immediate or longer-term success or at times even survival were also often imperiled.

Reason two is that choosing to not play branding power games would represent a voluntary misfortune—a self-inflicted wound—for most professionals. As would not acquiring the requisite skills to play them effectively. Moreover, nothing is inherently unethical about choosing to pursue, acquire, and exercise branding power as a means of earning socially responsible, client-enhancing ends. Even when your earned branding power generates greater professional persuasiveness for you as an ancillary but not unintended consequence.

Presumably, these justifications comfort you. But truth be written, the presence or absence of your comfort is irrelevant. Branding power games will still be played out through whatever means are available in pursuit of good and bad ends anyway. Human nature is such that many people instinctively thirst for formal and informal authority and the concomitant opportunities to exercise persuasion or secure the leadership values that are derived from authority. Some individuals are simply more or less transparent in their attempts to satisfy such needs. Certain people are also more or less successful in their branding efforts. Surprised?

As for you:

- Learn to play brand new power games, if you do not already do so. Learn how to play these games better. Play your power game, however, only in pursuit of ethical ends.

Any reference to *means and ends* naturally introduces thoughts of Machiavellian behaviors. This association may trouble you. Your angst, however, is probably misplaced. The great counselor, Niccolo Machiavelli, was actually highly moral.[6] His timeless masterpiece, *The Prince,* was crafted for leaders' eyes only and should be evaluated and criticized only in the proper historical context (circa 1513 AD). With good cause, Machiavelli believed his leaders' primary duties were to keep foreigners out and to create an organized state in which law-abiding citizens could freely conduct their business and social affairs. Worthy goals, each, insofar as the achievement of these ends ensured that the state's women, children, and property rights would remain inviolate. Such were the *written* ends Machiavelli sought for his leaders and, consequently, for his leaders' people. He never argued that *all ends justified any means.* Machiavelli instead contended that those specific, limited ends justified any means.

This discussion about the right or wrong of Machiavelli's means/ends continuum is comparable to contemporary thinking about the sort of leadership/subordinate relationship that ideally should exist. Leadership guru Warren Bennis proposed the valuable distinction that effective managers "*do things right*" whereas effective leaders "*do the right things right.*"[7] These statements imply that the development and subsequent execution of power in pursuit of reasonable corporate or personal ends; doing the right thing, is not just appropriate. Doing the right thing is also your moral imperative.

Our take:

- As a professional you face an actual obligation to exercise power effectively. Otherwise, no one could or should assign the honorific title "professional" to you. Developing and exploiting your branding power is wrong only if you exploit while pursuing improper ends.

This discussion is not intended to discount the importance of socially responsible behavior. To remain effective across periods longer than the shortest short runs, you must be ethical. Suggesting that the pursuit of power-based branded persuasiveness and leadership is all about technique, and that branding technique is all that matters, is simply wrong. Just like suggestions that branding power is morally neutral is wrong. The purposes for which brand based power is used determines its morality.

Adolf Hitler brilliantly managed his brand from about 1929 until the winter of 1942/3. The preceding statement is neither a joke nor a stretch but rather whole truth. During the winter of 1942/3, Hitler's *Thousand Year Reich* spanned a historically unprecedented geographic span. Hitler was also a monstrous leader. The ends he sought through his power were beyond indefensible. Less than two and one-half years later, he controlled nothing but a bunkered hole deep in the ground. Not surprisingly, his *Reich* had only lasted 12 years. Evil brands usually cannot stand. For long.

Remember: When questions arise regarding how best to acquire long-term branding power, morality is an indispensable part of the answer.

Power-Enhancing Perspectives

Rather than struggling against inevitable feelings of premediated remorse (should I power-brand myself?) and inevitably falling short (because you usually brand yourself, poorly, anyway), you should learn three fundamental perspectives. Each perspective should inform your branding efforts. Each perspective is adopted from Machiavelli's *The Prince*.[8]

Understand That Power Is Amoral

Our initial brand power-enhancing perspective follows from the need to understand that power is amoral. The purposes for which acquired or retained branding power is executed makes its application moral or immoral. The role played by branding power and persuasiveness should be neither denigrated nor venerated. Power, at its core, is a brand-based game. A game played vigorously for high stakes. But only a game, in the end. One you should learn to play, if you don't currently participate. One you should learn to play better if you are currently burdened by a mediocre or worse brand.

In arenas, where games of sport play out, players rarely judge competitors based on their intentions. Nor should they. Each team, or competitor, is merely trying to win. Actions are what count. Your external and internal competitors, and even your clients, should similarly be judged based on the effectiveness and morality of their decisions and behaviors. After all, competitors are merely trying to win the same professional game as you.

Pay attention to the consequences of your client's or competitor's actions, rather than any presumed intentions; take nothing personally; manage all branding impressions you make; and execute based on certain fundamental and nearly universally applicable branding power rules. Do these four things and you will command marked advantages as you pursue branding power. Easier said than done, of course. Especially "taking-nothing-personally."

Master Your Emotions

The second brand power-enhancing perspective follows from the need that professional power players will encounter to master emotions—their own. Emotional responses to challenging or threatening circumstances will pose substantial barriers to your ability to acquire, exercise, or maintain brand power and persuasiveness. In what a nod toward modern-day "emotional intelligence,"[9] Machiavelli taught leaders to master their emotions. This specific leadership virtue can provide a core foundation from which substantial branding power can eventuate.

Repetitive emotional outbursts or decisions generally cost prospective power players far more in the long run that any presumed short-term psychological benefits they might yield. Emotions blur logic and blunt reason. Fail to visualize situations accurately, and bad outcomes are likely to result. Specifically, the likelihood that you will respond appropriately with the requisite control to pressing problems, opportunities, or threats radically diminishes.

There are seven basic human emotions: anger, fear, disgust, contempt, joy, sadness, and surprise.[10] Re-examine the list. Five emotions are emphatically negative. A sixth, surprise, can occasion harm. Contempt is every bit as much human nature as is love. But power players' decision to harbor contempt for anyone or anything is like them drinking the poison and hoping the target of their enmity dies.

Anger is probably the most debilitating emotion for professionals seeking to build their branding power. Anger clouds vision. Anger's arrival makes any situation or performance less subject to your control. Anger's presence typically strengthens the tenacity and purpose of antagonists you might confront or create. Double negatives best avoided by power-brand performers. When trying to outshine or counter the forays of rivals, it's often better to keep them off guard by affecting pleasantness and approachability rather than anger.

Machiavelli advocated using patience as a shield. Patient responses routinely trump emotional reactions in most settings. Patience, in particular, should trump anger. Unless, of course, occasionally unsheathe genuine or feigned anger on chosen stages for unstated tactical branding purposes. When you're thrust into trying circumstances, perhaps against your will or best judgment, patience protects you from unforced errors. By contrast, demonstrated impatience may brand you as weak-willed, foolish, or overly assertive.

Ancient Greek and Roman rulers and courtiers learned how to wield patience as a metaphorical battering ram. Each community was taught the value of steadfast perseverance. A Latin phrase expresses this genre of patience: *Ne te terant molari*; that is, "Wear the bastards down."

Patience is not natural, meaning it rarely rises easily, in challenging settings. Ancient Greeks, according to Thucydides, hailed patience as a distinctive virtue of the Gods. Gods, of course, enjoy singular advantages versus mere mortals—gods possess endless time. Even in real time, however, many challenging situations or opportunities for brand-driven self-enhancement are more easily approached, reconciled, and exploited when you address them with sufficient patience. Beyond question, one of the most relevant branding-building virtues in any setting derives from the ability to simply, consciously, and persistently recognize the need to avoid impatience. Can you cultivate this virtue?

Friederich Nietzsche wrote, "The value of anything lies not in what one attains with it, but in what it *costs*."[11] The philosopher's passage spoke directly to our need to exercise appropriate restraint as we execute branding initiatives. Value entails "a quantifiable assessment of the benefits and costs derived from exchange offerings and exchange itself".[12] Had Machiavelli reconciled the associated professional brand-management implications featured in each definition, he might have written:

- "Perhaps you achieve your branding goals, but at what cost?"

When you are branding, which should be always, evaluate estimated costs and never jump preemptively into any important decision, action, or written/spoken word. Aspiring or active branders should judge important decisions that their strategies or current contexts are forcing them to make based on one criterion:

- What will this choice cost me?

There is usually more than one criterion to consider, of course. But the personal cost criterion often should be considered first.

Had branding activities been overtly recognized or discussed as such during his era, Machiavelli would have understood that substantial portions of your earned branding power derives from decisions or actions you choose to not pursue or be dragged into. Your career may be long or short. The branding arc of your professional life may prove propitiously or perilously steep. Rapidly up, or rapidly down, in plainer written English. But the fact remains that opportunities to create truly differentiating brands are rare—unless you learn how to consciously cultivate them yourself. Only finite amounts of time, energy, or talent are available from which any branding power player can make withdrawals. Scarce resources should not be squandered on any branding actions that do not yield material differentiating value.

Engage with the Present through Pragmatic Distancing

The third brand-based power-enhancing perspective follows from the need to exercise pragmatic distancing. Foster, as in develop, the ability to uncouple from current circumstances and to speculate objectively about a known past and possible branding future you could create. For yourself. Machiavelli referenced Janus, a two-faced Roman deity assigned to guard gates and doorways, in *The Prince*. Machiavelli used his contemporary readership's knowledge of Janus as a means of reminding his Renaissance-age readership, who understood Roman history, to look constantly toward both the past and the future.

Forward-looking professionals, as a brand identifier the word "proactive" comes to mind, should constantly visualize imminent problems that may injure their brands or generate opportunities to enhance their brands. Dependent, obviously on how you strategically respond to those problems. Such players are less likely to be caught by surprise or miss opportunities. Backward-looking professionals, perhaps the dismal brand identifier "reactive" would attach to them, should never see the past only as opportunity rather than as another way to revisit old injuries or reinforce grudges.

Machiavelli encouraged leaders to scrutinize the past to educate themselves about lessons embedded in the prior successes and failures of others, as well as their own. His advice should extend to branding professionals who first should seek to develop and thereafter sustain desirable personal branding images. You should leverage the opportunity to reevaluate your own and others' mistakes. Then you should determine how best to avoid similarly negative consequences for your future brand identities. In contemporary professional settings, Machiavelli's principle might extend to the notion that sometimes when branding or rebranding you may need to ignore sunk costs—despite real or imagined losses that may be experienced. Decision makers typically should not allow prior "investment" failures or troubles to prevent them from making pragmatic assessments of future benefits.

Believe in Progress—Your Own

Throughout history most pf humanity did not readily accept the possibility of human progress. Essentially, not until the Scientific Revolution. Before this time, cultures almost invariably assumed that the Golden Age was in the past. People believed, at best, the world was moribund, if not burdened by inevitable decline. Simple human know-how, leaders and followers alike assumed, could never resolve the world's most pressing problems. The learned and unschooled multitudes who comprised cultures cast across the world "understood" that if Buddha, Confucius, Jesus, and Muhammad—beings who knew everything that was important to know—offered no remedy for disease, poverty, scarcity, or war then there was no hope.[13] How could simple human beings be expected to cope and solve these deities or demigods could not?

Then the Scientific Revolution began, in 1543, with the publication of two books. One book was about astronomy; the other, anatomy. Aha, one must suppose, the power of a few good books is revealed. Because, post-revolution, things began changing for the better. Once the world's sentient population slowly realized there were many important things that humanity did not know, and melded this ignorance to the idea that incremental scientific progress still could grant new powers to humanity, people increasingly understood things could improve. More people began to believe that certain recipes involving appropriate portions of devotion to past wisdom and motivated, in-the-moment creativity could inspire a new Golden Age. As they should have believed—because this is true. And humanity began to understand that through their focused will and informed efforts motivated individuals can improve various aspects of their daily life and performance.

As we hope you now also understand and believe.

A Historical Take on Branding Power

Aside from the few who inherit power, the journey toward "earning" powerful and influential brands is hazardous. For many, the passage likely inspires more fear than hope. Opportunities to fail, as well as impediments to success, abound. But those seeking to develop more powerful brands should understand the need to man-up, woman-up, or human-up, if you will. Brand-power players should likewise understand the need to be or become aware of and resolutely committed to overcoming all obstacles that impede their paths.

Think about the path toward historical branding power followed by Abraham Lincoln. The now iconic leader who lost numerous local, regional, or statewide before winning the Presidency. Or Thomas Edison, who "invented" the lightbulb hundreds of times. Or Kemmons Wilson, the serially entrepreneurial founder of Holiday Inn, who responded to a 1983 Harvard M.B.A. student's intimation that his success had been a cakewalk by asserting, "I've failed more times than you've tried."[14] We bet an entrepreneur like Mr. Wilson knew how to lose. Which is useful, because successful professional branders usually must learn how to lose, so long as losing does not become accepted habit. How should professionally branded power players respond to a loss? For starters, never whine, complain, or act like anyone's rhymes with rich. Confront failure face-to-face, respond with grace, and walk forward.

Any branding professional can win with grace and style. Branding champions, or people destined to ascend to this hallowed station and remain there also know how to lose. How much can anyone learn from winning, especially in comparison to how much one can learn from failure? Especially when erstwhile losers embrace failure as an opportunity to learn and to renew their commitment do whatever is necessary and appropriate to ultimately achieve professional success.

Still you might logically respond: Lincoln, Edison, and Wilson were exceptional people characterized by uncommon vision. This argument would be valid and relevant. The possession of uncommon vision, after all, indeed is associated with one's potential ability for acquiring clout. Another American luminary, no less than Thomas Jefferson, wrote that a natural aristocracy exists amongst men (today, Jefferson surely would have included women). If Jefferson was right, and history suggests he was, the vast proportion of the population not naturally endowed with similar characteristics appear destined to struggle in their efforts to play power games.

Though these masses may struggle, the fact remains that many competencies and capabilities associated with the task of securing branding power are broadly understood. They are certainly available to be learned and used by motivated people who possess reasonable ability. But another solution is available to professionals seeking inside information about how to attain and retain greater power and persuasiveness in modern settings. This solution entails learning from time-tested "power and persuasion" leadership principles that once were applied with great success or failure on now largely bygone historical contexts. Time-tested, because time is the truest test of the value of anything. An anything that might include a work of art, theatrical performance, song, building or other human-made artifice, leader, or your brand. Thus, our use of historical examples should cast greater and more illuminating light on the path that contemporary professionals who aspire to create and leverage more powerful brands might take. Such patterns should serve, metaphorically, as recipes for success.

Confucius wrote: "Study the past to divine the future."[15] Shakespeare similarly suggested: "The past is prologue."[16] Proposing that lessons learned from struggles to acquire power and exercise persuasion that were waged on various historical stages should apply to similar struggles played out on contemporary stages is logical. The past is not a true compass. But it can function as a map. History charts human experience, stops at the present, and gives no clear sense of direction. The past does not repeat itself, not exactly, nor does it proceed in predictable rhythms or patterns. Unforeseen events disrupt known trends. Everything, as in all future occurrences or events ensuing from any present event, is subject to what Edward Gibbon called the "vicissitudes of fortune."[17] Each factor is a historical "limitation." More precisely, a limitation that might preclude using history as guide. But what else do we have? History is demonstrably the best of several less than perfect guides to what will likely will happen in your future if, for some inexplicable and frankly indefensible reason, you choose not to brand or branded badly.

One final point unifies and clarifies a useful relationship between history, time, and experience. The combination of time and experience—that is, the marriage of your time and experience with that of historical others—will not make you infinitely wise. But this marriage of your and their time and experience, once understood and exploited, will make you more intimately knowledgeable. "Knowledgeable" in ways you can leverage for your branding benefit.

Notes

1 Rotten Tomatoes (2011). A Few Good Men. Flixster. Retrieved February 29, 2016. http://www.rottentomatoes.com/m/few_good_men/
2 Green, Robert (1998). *The 48 Rules of Power*. New York, NY: Penguin Press.
3 Scheibe, Karl E. (1979). *Masks, Lies and Secrets*. New York, NY: Prager.
4 Strutton, David (2004). "The Courtly Path to Managerial Leadership." *Business Horizons*, 47: 7-18.
5 Senger, Harro von (1991). *The Book of Stratagems: Tactics for Triumph and Survival.* New York, NY: Penguin Books.
6 Scharfstein, Ben-Ami (1995). *Amoral Politics*. Albany, NY: State University of New York.
7 Bennis, Warren (1985). *Leaders: Strategies for taking charge*. New York: Harper-Collins.
8 Machiavelli, Niccolo (1940). *The Prince and the Discourses. Trans. Luigi Ricci and Christian Demond.* New York, NY: Modern Library.
9 Petrides, K.V., R. Pita, and F. Kokkinaki (2007). "The Location of Trait Emotional Intelligence in Personality Factor Space." *British Journal of Social Psychology*, 98: 273-289.
10 Graham, Michael C. (2014). *Facts of Life: Ten Issues of Contentment*. Denver, CO: Outskirts Press.
11 Green, Michael S. (2002). *Nietzsche and the Transcendental Tradition*. Champaign-Urbana, IL: University of Illinois Press.
12 Pelton, Lou, David Strutton, and James R. Lumpkin (2001). *Marketing Channels: A Relationship Marketing Approach*. New York, NY: McGraw-Hill.
13 Harrari, Yuval Noah (2015). *Sapiens: A Brief History of Humankind.* New York, NY: Harper Collins Publishers.
14 Snyder, Neil H. and Michele Graves (1994). "Leadership and Vision," *Business Horizons*, 37(1): 1-7.
15 Rainey, Lee Dian (2010). *Confucius and Confucianism: The Essentials*. Oxford, UK: Wiley-Blackwell.
16 Ackroyd, Peter (2006). *Shakespeare: The Biography*. London: Vintage.
17 Porter, Roy (1989). *Gibbon: Making History*. New York, NY: St. Martin's Press.

Chapter 3

Professional Brands, Described

> The best branders carefully craft desired personae; portray those personalities publically; and polish them for posterity—
>
> David Strutton and Kenneth Thompson (2016).

Historians are confident that brands and branding have existed as far back as a time when medieval craft guilds wielded brands as badges to signify product quality and distinguish their work. And probably further back than that. In fact, to an atrocious era when ancient Romans first employed advertising to promote individually branded "professional" competitors who were poised to fight each other to one's death in gladiatorial arenas. Each historical example speaks directly to why professional branding initiatives should still be pursued today.

The term brand was originally used in a prominent fashion in the U.S. for purposes of designating and distinguishing one owner of horses or cattle from other owners. Imagine any branding scene you've seen in cowboy movies or television programs. There, you've got it. The purpose for which branding efforts were initiated then – identifying living products as belonging to one ranch and not another – remains a primary reason why branding is used today. The other reason: To distinguish the quality of a product or of one's personal or professional value. Again, each historical example speaks directly to why you should considering branding – think, *favorably-distinguishing – the quality of you, as a product, and of your work.*

Was that sweater made by Merona or Brioni? The answer influences how much you're willing to pay and how you feel about yourself after buying the sweater.

Is that cancer treatment, a brand-able professional service, delivered by a practitioner associated with Houston's nationally-renowned M.D. Anderson Cancer Research Center? Or is the medical professional affiliated the Presbyterian Hospital located in Denton, TX? The services provided at each health care facility is, to our knowledge and in our direct experience, outstanding. But here, the far more prestigious brand of one institution; that would be M.D. Anderson, migrates to the brands of the health care professionals delivering their medical solutions there. Cancer patients would surely migrate to the more powerfully branded institution, too.

Professional Brands Deliver Eternal Stories

The term "brand" captures all meanings, images, sensations and responses, experiences, and content that customers perceive is associated with particular products or services. "Brands" are gaseous in their ability to expand or contract to fill any space. Brands are promises, lies, reputations, prestige-enhancing devices, or TED talk buzzwords.

Or for that matter brands, your brand, is represented by the hats, tattoos, haircuts, or bowties you choose to wear, display, or reject. While the norms and values that prevail in your precise professional sphere may constrain your choices, your brand still can generally evolve into whatever you as a discerning "marketing" tactician elect to make it. Yes, everyone is a marketer. Insofar as everyone has something of value that they seek to sell. Primarily, yourself. Logically, then, the term "professional brand" encompasses the set of beliefs, values, and assets that others perceive are associated, again, with you.

If properly managed, brands can create differentiation. At net, your development, possession, and execution of a powerful professional brand can decisively and favorably influence the decisions made and behaviors displayed by prospects, your clients, or other important audiences. Others who might include superiors, peers, subordinates, investors, investigators, members of the media, anyone else exposed to you.

Professional brands are also psychological constructs. They exist inside client's minds. Brands likewise function as signals, good or bad. Your branded signals influence proximate or distant individuals' decisions to view or "position" you as formidable or insignificant; as powerful or powerless; as one who merits attention or can safely be ignored.

Successful brands may tell eternal tales. Horatio Alger-like stories that feature "rags to riches" accomplishment. Alfred Lord Tennyson's immortal yet sadly too mortal "Light Brigade" dauntlessly entering the valley of Death ... "rode the 600." Or perhaps, George Washington, who "never told a lie." The best branding stories generate alternative worlds in which you metaphorically reside and prevail.

Stories are not just arguments or collections of facts. Stories contain multiple meanings that can be discussed, questioned, and reinterpreted by others—"audience members"—who engage and interact with the stories. Countermanding the power of compelling stories that have been performed out effectively on appropriate professional stages is difficult. Unless you tell, or perform out, superior stories on the same stage.

You should strive to be or become the first, best, professionally branded storyteller on your stage. Sometimes you should even use words when telling your branding tale. But not necessarily? Have you ever heard anyone say "the best sermon I ever heard was the one I saw?" We have, and the underlying implications apply here.

Have you considered what your story is, or should be?

Professional Branding Stories Build Reputations

Branding stories, in turn, drive *reputations*. Your branded reputation will be embodied and reflected in how audience members predict, explain, and generally accept or reject; that is, "review" your judgment, knowledge, and behaviors on the stages that are most relevant to your profession. You can opt-in and mindfully earn a reputation. Or opt-out and still earn a reputation, mindlessly. Thereafter, however, you can enjoy or you must endure whatever reputation your behaviors or nonbehaviors wrought.

When identifying the self-branding stories that you eventually will seek to intentionally create, choose carefully. Successful branding narratives can create reputations that permit you to work in fireproof offices in fireproof neighborhoods. Successful branding stories, in other words, can better position you to take measured risks that might further elevate the prestige, power, and persuasiveness of your brand. Often, as you will learn, even if you fail while taking these measured risks.

You should willingly take measured risks, as appropriate to your profession or career stage, as you seek to brand yourself. Because often there are no wholly right or wrong branding answers. Instead, there are just options, each accompanied by specific risks and rewards. Often, those differences are difficult to quantify in monetary terms. With the exception of two absolutely quantifiable and predictable outcomes:

- The demand for and prices charged for the values generated by your professional performance will rise or fall in lockstep with the trust, value, liking, and preference engendered among clients and individuals with and for whom you work by your reputation and through your branded story.

When creating your brand identity, never pursue reputational distinctions unless those differences feature decisive, or determinant, differences. Managerial or legal professionals performing in shark-eat-shark worlds, for example, might seek branding reputations exemplifying the degree to which they never complain and never explain. Professionals occupying new-age managerial stages, we're feeling something.com, alternatively might seek branded reputations that underscore the extent to which they understand and accept that people working for them enjoy undeniable rights to their chaotic, self-absorbed anxieties and complaints, as well as the right to occupy their own sovereign space. Nerf ball and flextime for everyone. As long as, that is, their sovereign space does not encroach too freely or overly deeply into yours. In so many words, a brand based reputation as a nice guy or gal who nonetheless possesses and imposes hard boundaries.

You should ask: What sort of reputation would best serve your goals with audiences who "review" your performances on the professional stages that you plan to dominate? Hardball, yes? A difficult question to answer, for certain. But answer it best you can. You plan to run with and eventually lead the big dogs, right?

The Role Played by Authenticity

For better or worse you perform during an age in which your clients can instantly "learn" truths or lies about most important things they are considering buying. "Things" that certainly include you and your services. Or, as importantly, about the professional providers with whom they currently engage, but soon may abandon. And why not, if any hint of dissatisfaction arises among your clients—or other key audiences... Other attractive professional options, after all, are almost always available. Which represents another reason why the professional you should brand and brand better.

Contemporary professionals work and perform in worlds in which online reviews and friend or coworker comments on social media help clients and other audience members discover and disseminate information about a product's actual underlying flaws or shortfalls at the speed of baud. (Baud: the unit measuring the speed at which information is transmitted by computer-mediated technologies.) The ease with which clients or prospective clients can access or spread impartial information today makes them more willing to abandon habitual brands. Or, perhaps more likely, never engage at all. Simply because they learned about some shiny new performer, or discovered another professional provider offering the same quality solutions as you but for lower prices.

This type of Internet-based or face-to-face "word-of-mouth" information is deemed impartial; that is, "unbiased" by current or prospective clients. Consequently, world-of-mouth information is extremely persuasive. Clients or prospects know their friends, family members, or coworkers are not shilling for you. These folks are absolved from an original sin from which branding professionals can never earn absolution. Friends, family members, or coworkers never say what they say about your brand, either good or bad, "for the money." By contrast almost anything the "professional you" says to prospects or clients can be construed, logically, as being at least partially "about the money." And audiences with whom you share your stage know this. No one should be surprised that the value of "old-time marketing" magic is fading in this world. The presence of traditional brand loyalty is slipping in lockstep. And likely will ebb further.

Your "authenticity" is one sure cure for declining brand loyalty. Authenticity, best described as client perceptions, hopefully shared widely among their fellows, that you are genuine, sincere, and legitimate. Your "brand" is, in so many word, the "real deal." As clients become better informed about the underlying qualities of products, you!, and more cynical about any overt marketing gimmicks, they are poised to become more attracted and loyal to any brand that they deem more honest and real. This could and should be the authentic you. As long as you, as product, also display other determinant brand identities.

This hard-earned result would portend huge future wins for you and your brand. But this outcome is possible only if you actually possess and legitimately bring authentic differences to the professional stages on which you perform.

Woe be until you and your brand, if you cannot. Authenticity is more easily achieved when your brand features real-world qualities and differences that competitors currently lack and perhaps could never muster. If your brand displays and delivers the right skillsets, attitudes, and socially responsible personae; desirable verbal and nonverbal messaging; and you couple those characteristics with an attractive stage presence and artefactual presentation your authenticity will grow. It will grow because you'll genuinely be more authentic.

A task easier described than done. But one that is still imminently doable. Particularly, if you are discerning and wise enough to follow the paths laid out below. And a branding goal so important that you should resolutely set your mind and shoulder to the task of executing it. Just like Luke's Gospel reports "Jesus set his face like flint" on his way to Jerusalem and His splitting history-in-two destiny. "Splitting history" as in BC and AD.

Apple remains a textbook example of authentically effective corporate branding. The superior design and ease of use associated with Apple's smart products makes its brand ineffably powerful in an increasingly commoditized personal device market. During 2014, Apple only generated 6% of total revenues in the personal computer market. Yet, the firm claimed 28% of all profits. Apple's extraordinary share of profits underscores the tangible power and persuasiveness generated by authentic brands.

The Role Played by Professional Brand Equity

Beloved, respected, and/or feared brands become more valuable, powerful, and persuasive as a consequence of the effectively differentiated meanings that key others, again think clients or your boss or peers, assign to them. Or perhaps all three descriptors, assuming your brand could become authentic enough to achieve this trifecta, given that client "fear" might occasionally serve your ends? Which is not a farfetched prospect. The added value and newfound branding power that accrues to well-branded products is called brand equity. Or, in this context, professional brand equity.

Traditional brand equity captures customers' entire sets of perceptions and feelings about associated products, services, places, organizations, or ideas. Or, for that matter, individual professionals. Brand equity perceptions and feelings generally lean strongly toward the positive. Traditional brand equity also captures the extent to which customers willingly pay more to own or use one brand rather than another brand from the same product category. Apple phones, as noted, command higher prices than Android phones. This "pricing power" results from the brand equity Apple has developed and leveraged across the years. Whenever "brands" earn "equity," they generally develop greater "top-of-the-mind" awareness among critical audiences, including clients. "Top-of-the-mind" awareness means that whenever a problem arises that might be solved by a specific product or professional service provider the brand that enjoys greater "equity" comes to mind, first. You could be delivering tax preparation, advertising messaging, engineering, or Lasik solutions, for example. Once you earn "first place" in client or prospective client minds you can usually secure "first place" in their wallet.

In classic marketing settings, brand equity and consequently branding power are developed through the skillful administration of a "marketing mix." (Administering the marketing mix entails managing a product, and its price, promotion and distribution in ways that create uniquely desirable value in the collective minds of customers or prospective customers.) Branding power can emerge quickly as a result of earned brand equity, as happened with Google and Facebook. Or, the power of brand equity can take years to develop. Then, seemingly suddenly, things "blow up." This occurred with the Hyundai brand in the United States around 2008. The automotive brand was first introduced to the US marketplace in 1986. Then, all those years later, the Hyundai brand earned huge equity seemingly overnight because it was first to promise a 100,000 mile/ 10 year bumper-to-bumper warranty. This new branding identify, this new difference, this promise, delivering a compelling story that spoke directly to the actual quality of the Hyundai product proved determinant.

As a professional you can earn greater brand equity and more persuasive power by skillfully managing your brand identifiers. (The meaning and implications of "branding identifier" is discussed below.) When this happens, the propensity of clients to think first about you and your brand when encountering problems for which other professionals also offer solutions is high. You will succeed or fail based on your demonstrated or perceived ability to solve client problems effectively.

Your branded "identity" also might provide emotionally based values to clients or to superiors, peers, or subordinates for whom or with whom you work. The abstract meaning of these emotional values extend beyond the values associated with any routine benefits that any other less-well branded professional from your field might generate.

The Role Played by Brand Identifiers

The term "brand" was traditionally defined as a name, word, symbol, or other characteristic such as color (brown; UPS), shape (Jaguar automobiles' "appearance"), or design (Apple touchscreens, which proved not just the shape of things to come but the shape of things to covet) that targeted audiences perceive is distinctly different from those offered by marketers selling the same products.

Branding symbols, in particular, matter greatly. Identifying symbols can say in an instant what words cannot. Symbols can capture and reflect an audience's deepest beliefs and aspirations. They can invoke client faith or fears. Symbols can gin up customer prejudices or honor customer preferences.

In and of themselves, however, symbols possess no intrinsic value. Nor do symbols naturally manifest or capture any intrinsic or meaning. Their meaning, their value, derives from how we use them. The meaning and value of symbols consequently may evolve over time in concert with a given, professional brand's behaviors or actions. Consider, for example, the plethora of symbolic meanings that various conflicting groups have assigned to the Confederate battle flag. Or to the swastika, the branding identifier of Nazism that originated in India as a Hindu artifact. The symbol meant, simply, good fortune, luck, and well being.

Brand identifiers are anything that make it possible to distinguish particular brands from their branding counterparts. Professional identifiers uniquely identify the solutions created or delivered by you from the solutions created or delivered by your competitors. After establishing your brand identifiers, do you want to be perceived (identified) as an approachable and down-to-earth regular guy or gal? As an aloof or a take-no-prisoners authoritative specialist? Perhaps, you perform on a stage where an aura of carefully cultivated mystery might confer power. Or, in a professional setting where projecting a studied distance would confer charisma to you and your values. Only you know this. Depending on your profession or the clients you target, you alternatively might seek to project one, none, all or some of these identifiers to elevate your brand's persuasive power.

You should answer three questions successfully before choosing the brand identifiers and image that you will seek create:

- What do I, as a brand, do?
- Who do I, as a brand, do it for?

- What difference will I make in the world?
- And will that difference be enough to favorably distinguish my professional brand? If the answer to this question is no, return to the third bulleted item and begin upgrading your branding game. Time to generate more brand-able value as you execute your professional tasks.

Choosing Effective Brand Identifying Messages

Certain guidelines appear relevant regardless of the brand identifiers you select to differentiate yourself. To begin with, brand messages should emphasize the most important client benefit or solution that you can deliver that you would also want to be associated with your brand. Keeping the main thing the main thing, as explained below. This specific brand message-building approach involves the development of a "Big Idea." The term "Big Idea" is the actual phrase advertisers have always used to label the randing principal that is being discussed. The Nike branding message that insisted customers "Just Do It" is a classic Big Idea. As was and is Michelin's "You've Got a Lot Riding on Your Tires" message. The Big Idea should be able to bring the brand message, and its value and problem-solving capability, to life in memorable ways.

Across time your "big branding idea" should function metaphorically as a sturdy hook on which additional incrementally different branding messages could be hung going forward throughout your career. Burger King's simple but memorable "Have It Your Way" branding identifier operated as a sustainable and self-perpetuating hook on which subsequent brand messages were hung for almost 25 years. Consider the beauty of Master Card's "Priceless," a branding identifier that signals to customers, "buy what you want, through Master Card's assistance, and damn the price"... "because the value accumulated in terms of your life experiences and memories is worth any price!"). Or Miller Lite's "Tastes Great, Less Filling" brand identifier. The brand message signaled to drinkers in a light hearted fashion that they can simultaneously "have more fun and imbibe fewer calories." Finally, Intel's classic "Intel Inside" brand identifier offers the promise and value of a well-branded guarantee of performance.

Each "big idea" succeeded because it provided as a highly successful durable platform upon which decades of successful advertising campaigns were launched. As has been true of Walmart's EDLP, that is, Every Day Low Prices, coupled with a smiley face, which provides additionally welcome friendly assurance of savings! And each firm, except Burger King, was strategically wise enough to not fix what was not broken with the "big ideas" that drove their successful brand messaging across decades.

When creating effective branding identities you also must identify the type of *message appeal* to use. Most brand messages simultaneously include informative and persuasive contents. These two elements are often so entangled in advertising messages that it is difficult to tell them apart. Basic informative messaging content typically include the brand name, presentations of principal features and benefits, and possibly a mention of price. Even highly persuasive messages generally must contain informative elements in order to succeed. Any bundle of message informativeness and persuasiveness that you create presumably should grab and retain client attention in noisy, crowded, and competitive sectors. Your same informative and persuasive content should coalesce in message appeals that deliver rationales that "explain and justify" why clients should purchase and remain loyal to your particular brand, as opposed to buying or remaining loyal to another brand, or buying nothing at all.

Brand Identifier Messaging Should ...

Regardless of the brand identifiers you decide to feature in your branding message, the messages themselves ideally should be:

- Memorable, or easy for clients and key others to recall and remember.
- Believable.
- Distinctive, from similar messages offered by competing professionals.
- Focused on some "determinant" feature, aspect, benefit, or problem-solving capability that you alone can deliver that also gets associated with your professional brand. Time to generate more brand-able value as you execute your professional tasks.

The content delivered in this paragraph is extremely important. For any branding message to prove determinant in client or prospect minds, the feature, function, or benefit emphasized in your branding message must be different from and better than what your competitors are saying or offer in their messages. Or, in a best case scenario for you, not discussing at all. Regardless of what professional brand identifier dominates, your message first must establish a memorable *point of differentiation or point of difference, or POD,* to become determinant. Second, any audience that you target your brand identifier message toward view your POD as important as it engages in the decision-making processes that eventually allow prospective or actual clients to choose between competing professional alternatives.

The word "believable," as related to branding identifiers, likewise merits its distinguishing quotation marks. This is because advertising message "believability" often must be taken with a large grain of salt. A grain of salt generically known as *puffery,* that is. Puffery is a promotional statement or claim that is based more on subjective rather than objective claims. Puffery, in an advertising context, includes messages that knowingly offer exaggerated claims about brands. Claims can be exaggerated to the point where they make assertions that no reasonable person would take seriously. But these embellished assertions still function to meaningfully differentiate your brand in increasingly strident and congested fields, if they are delivered "properly." Puffed-up branding claims, you see, might distinguish you as being different and better in ways that simultaneously entertain and capture the attention of people exposed to them. Such claims would typically be accompanied by the unselfconscious, knowing use of humor. Puffery has been around a long time, and that's no exaggeration. However, given your professional status, puffery should be used judiciously.

Context and Perspective Matter

Love stories unfolding in Dallas, Texas, may differ materially from those evolving in Detroit, Michigan, or Dijon, France. Okay, as Tina Turner famously sang: "What's Love Got to Do with It?" Our answer is, nothing. The point made above relates to the impact of context, not love. As in, context matters greatly. Consequently, whatever branding identifiers you pursue when developing your brand should be appropriate for the context in which you perform and execute your professional services and responsibilities. Context matters; context and circumstance must be accounted for as you build your branding power. Your brand speaks directly to your story, right?

When developing and managing your brand identity you should understand, accept, and make accommodations for the cultural norms of the "others" whose perceptions and impressions you are seeking to manage. Geographic, ethnic, and corporate cultural differences proliferate across the United States and the world. For example, what constitutes polite or aggressive behavior in New York City or Beijing may be viewed entirely differently in Dallas, TX, or Charlotte, NC. America and Americans themselves have always been simultaneously egalitarian and snooty. Big cities look down on small towns. The North, inexplicably, on the South. Inexplicable because so many Northerners appear hell-bent on "going south"—moving there—as soon as possible. Right and Left Coast habitués literally look down on the interior middle during their flyovers.

However, reciprocity, like exchange, is a phenomena that makes the world go round. Being what it is, reciprocity inspires each object of disdain to look back toward its critic with their own reverse snobbery. Read on to learn how better to mindfully manage, leverage, and play these "hungering for respect" games more effectively than others who essentially are playing them mindlessly.

You are not and should not narrowly view yourself only as a learned and/or experienced entity who exists merely to make and deliver professional services or products. Instead, view yourself as a differentiable and marketable human brand that solves the problems of important audiences. You create and deliver highly valued branded solutions to others. What you do is important.

Desirable circles still exist in which financial success is not the be-all and end-all. But the list of such settings are thinning in highly globalized and commoditized *professional* sectors. So without money, you had best bring other sorts of value to the table, or your "stage." Charm, wit, beauty or attractiveness, talent, kindness, and generosity certainly help. These qualities and are valued. But these things are valued mostly to the extent that they complement other characteristics that are ready made for easier, near-term conversion into social or financial capital. This social and financial capital could include a compellingly distinctive professional brand. We guarantee it. Indeed, without having big financial nut, its getting more difficult to hang around without being supplanted by other folks who already have their branding mojos working. Not an ideal depiction of the world, to be sure, but realistically a depiction of the world as it is.

Some folks have their branding mojo working so well that their branded identities say without saying, "yes, I would be jealous of me, too, were I not already me!" Obnoxious, yes; indeed the statement purposefully reflects a nasty, evocative, and mischievous sentiment. The nature of this sentiment, however, does not negate the fact that you should aspire to create a similar branded identity for yourself. But only when you execute branding efforts through ethical and socially responsible methods. Yes, we know, this is a branding qualifier that we have already made several times. Which should underscore how important the principal is.

CHAPTER 4
Creating Ethical Brands

"Be nice to people you are passing on your way up. You may see those same people on your way down"

—Wilson Mizner (1876–1933).

The world's great religions share much in common. Each advocates, for example, that "better-off" individuals, say, professionals, should care for rather than people who are "worse-off." In professional settings, these "people" would often include less well-informed and comparatively weaker clients.

The Jewish Old Testament suggests 46 times that "haves," after every harvest, should leave some grain behind in the corners of the field for "have-nots." "Have-nots" are colloquially described as "widows and orphans." Biblical. shorthand for weak, dispossessed or poor people. The Christian Apostle Paul famously wrote a letter to the newly formed church at Philippi. This epistle admonished the Philippians: "Let each of you look not just toward your own interests, but also to the interests of others" (Philippians 2:4). The first Gospel likewise speaks to the continuous imperative that professionals face to bend toward the truth in all their affairs, brand-related or not. Matthew 5:37 prescribes: "Simply let your 'yes' be 'yes' and your 'no, no'; anything beyond this comes from the evil one."

Islam offers another compelling rationale regarding why professionals should act ethically when building or maintaining their brand. The religion states: "He who brings a good deed shall have better than it; but those who bring an evil shall be thrown on their face in the fire" (Sura XXVIL).

We can construct no better advice than these three religious tenents for professionals who seek to develop sustainable reputations as ethical players. Professionals should build their brands on nothing less than broadly-accepted religious or other broadly-accepted ethical standards. Naturally, what is ethical is also almost inevitably socially responsible. And professionals who behave in "socially-responsible" ways are inevitably better prepared to succeed as they seek to favorably brand their values. Again, especially over the long run.

Professional Branding Truths

Most of us live, play, and perform in an age of choreographed reality. Do you share all or only the best of your life on Facebook? Instagram posts? Many professionals live highly choreographed public lives: politicians, lawyers, physicians, marketers and salespeople, or architects come to mind. Certified Public Accountants (CPAs) during tax season, perhaps? Many suggest, with self-evident good reason, this is an age where symbolism triumphs over substance. How did Paris Hilton become famous, again? The "what are their first names" Kardashian women? Others characterize this age as one where narrative frequently prevails over fact. Or one in which truth matters only to the extent that certain people want it to matter. Or finally, an age where cynicism logically reigns? One assertion that surely makes sense. Who can you trust, after all? Priests or ministers? Political leaders? Media or corporate moguls?

Is this actually the perfect time to learn how to "fake sincerity" yourself? Might be, insofar as effective fakes and feigns have surely bolster the power of many brands, right? Of course, you don't know for certain whether or not in writing this we just "faked sincerity" ourselves?

The answer is that we did. We actually believe genuine truth is incontrovertible. That only one version of truth exists. And that the truth will abide, over the longer run. One abiding truth is that speaking, doing, and acting out the truth is fundamental to sustainable branding success regardless of the sector in which any professional performs. Philosophers long ago concluded that the world is too small for anything but truth. This decision was settled millennia before the Internet made possible 24/7/365 free-flowing global banter about actual lies, supposed lies, or mere rumors about lying began spreading at a speed only the Internet can provide.

Fast or not, old school former National Football League coach and current ESPN analyst Tony Dungy clearly understands the branding power that the presence or absence of the truth can impose. Speaking on ESPN's *Mike & Mike* show days after Tiger Wood's carefully cultivated, at that point decades-old branding reputation imploded one fateful Easter evening, Dungy said: "Remember, what is done in the dark usually eventually comes to light." And when sunlight, the world's strongest disinfectant, appears, your brand's standing likely will be permanently damaged if you have not been walking in the truth. Even if, as presumably would be the case, you perform on stages far less visible than the ones once dominated by Tiger Woods'—or sadly, Lance Armstrong and Bill Cosby's—now utterly devalued professional brands.

You should live, speak, and perform as if your every action and word was issued under a klieg light. When you act or speak less than truthfully, particularly over the longer run, your reputation and branding valuation will likely be badly injured. Just ask former American British Petroleum CEO Anthony "Tony" Hayward what happened when he failed to quickly or fully accept responsibility for the 2010 Gulf Coast oil spill. Instead, he whined (and this is verbatim) "I just want to get my life back." We would note, Hayward said these wprds sais any apparent concern for the tens of thousands whose actual welfare was badly disrupted by the oil spill. Or the Toyota, General Motors, or Volkswagen brands; automobile manufacturers who recently baldly misrepresented the truth about their gas pedals, ignitions, and emissions, respectively.

Consider Martin Shkerali, CEO of Turing Pharmaceutical. Acting on its CEO's instructions, the firm purchased the right to market Daraprim, a lifesaving human immunodeficiency virus drug. Turing Pharmaceutical then raised the drugs' price from $13.50 a pill to $750.00, a 4000% bump. Mr. Shkerali' malevolent pricing strategy came to light during late 2015. Let's call it now. Shkerali's branding power, his ability to prevail persuasively upon others' behaviors, is permanently diminished.

Truth-telling entails fully and accurately disclosing all relevant facts. Sounds simple. But it is not. Because truth-telling can prove challenging. When you speak truth, or your sincere interpretation of the truth, because multiple versions exist in certain settings, you're often second-guessed and denigrated by somebody. You should feel comfortable doing what you know is the right thing if for no other reason than the right thing is always the right thing to do. But you can also derive comfort, along with enhanced reputational value, from knowing that truth usually helps branding images over the long run as it elevates the power and persuasiveness of those brands identified as truthful.

The long run is always important. That's where the future in which you will eventually perform professionally always dwells.

Professional Ethics Is ...

Ethics entail moral principles that govern individual or group decision making and their subsequent behaviors. Ethics provide insights about the sorts of issues that professional decision-makers should evaluate when seeking to identify right (moral) or wrong (immoral) branding decisions. When present in our lives, ethical standards function as mirrors that reflect our imperfections, if we choose to act unethically. Ethical standards act as curbs against our inherently arising moral faults—we are all born sinners. In effect, ethical standards keep our lives on the straight and narrow. Or at least that is the purpose of ethics. Ethics function similar to how child bumpers function to keep children's bowling balls on the straight and narrow. Ethical standards, finally, offer snapshots of how a moral life should look.

Ethical standards provide higher baselines for morality than legal standards. Legal standards, while important, simply reflect society's agreement about what represents a moral or immoral act. Consider how difficult it is to secure societal agreement about anything. Talk about the law representing the lowest common denominator or the need for political-like compromise that often devalues the role, letter and spirit of truth. You could engage in branding decision making and subsequent activities that exist well within the bounds of the law and still participate in unethical decision making and activities that, if revealed, would degrade the value of your brand. To develop and sustain an ethical professional brand, surpass the letter and spirit of the law.

"Can You Think ...

... of a reason why you should piss into a well you may need to drink from tomorrow," as a Russian proverb asks? Probably not. Assuming you answered "no," hold this singular thought in mind.

Can you identify, with assurance, the three factors that will and have contributed most directly to your success? Again, probably not. No shame in that. But now that we have your attention the three factors contributing most to most professionals' success are:

- The family circumstances into which they were born.
- Their intelligence quotients (IQs).
- Their self-control.

Now, an easy question. Which factor can you control? No one has ever selected their birth parents. So that possibility is out. Additionally, experts agree: about 50% of IQ is inherited. The other 50% is environmental. This is, of course, the timeless nature versus nurture argument. Yet you cannot control your childhood environment, or the nurturing you experienced, while growing up, either. Even "dedicated-to-learn-whatever-it-takes-to-succeed" professionals' ceiling IQs levels lock-in early.[1] Which leaves one conclusion:

- The success-facilitating factor that you can most control is your self-control. Good news, at last. After all, you should be able to control your ethical or unethical choices, right? Especially when engaged in a task as important as developing and executing your professional branding identity.

But how do people improve their self-control? Isn't this tendency something one either possesses or lacks quite early in life? In part, the sentiment embedded in the last question is accurate and true. In terms of their ability to exercise self-control People are close to fully formed early in life. Statements such as "first 3 years of life last forever," in terms of the lifelong consequences wrought by those first 3 years, apply here. The 1970s song titled "Teach Your Children" (Well), written and sang by Graham Nash, apparently offered good advice.

One means to achieve self-improvement and, ultimately, develop more powerfully persuasive brands ... entails, hold the presses, simply resisting unethical temptations. In other words, by deliberately avoiding situations that test your self-control. To whatever extent you can exercise control, you might strategically structure the stages on which you perform out and deliver your solutions in ways that minimize unethical distractions and temptations.

Consequently, you should understand the sorts of situations and performance stages that are likely to challenge your sense of self-control. This is the best insight we can provide right now. Because unfortunately, you often cannot eliminate or avoid situations that test your self-control. Nor, despite the recommendation just offered, can many professionals structure their performance stages in ways that would fully eliminate unethical distractions.

Most professionals are smart enough to understand the difference between right and wrong. Even when vigorously attempting to differentiate your branding value, you should still be able to tell. Right? The truth is that you are smart enough to understand this difference. Were this not so, you would not have been bright enough to turn "pro" in the first place. Why then, do we often experience so much trouble choosing or behaving right rather than wrong in branding-management situations that feature opportunities to deceive or engage in other morally questionable behaviors?

Here, the answer is simple. Human beings routinely struggle to choose right, all the time, because we are incredibly selfish. Human beings are too self-centered, self-absorbed, self-serving, egoistic, greedy, or oriented toward "me-first" to act otherwise. Seek proof? Conduct the following experiment. First, birth or borrow two happy healthy 2-year olds. Mix in one safe and seemingly empty but actually closely adult-supervised room. Then place the kids, seemingly by themselves, in the room. Add one highly desirable toy. A toy with which only one child at a time can play. How long before a sinner arises among this otherwise innocent and distinctly nonprofessional pair?

Sinners? Weren't we discussing ethics and branding? Actually, all three topics have been in play for some time. Sin, the word, derives from the ancient Hebrew. It means "missing the mark." Unethical professionals are human beings who somehow "missed the mark." So is every other human being. Sinners have missed the mark because they violated norms, rules, customs, mores, guidelines, *values*, or moral standards prevailing within their relevant cultures.

Narcissistic Thought Disorder

Why are humans so selfish? One answer resides inside the Latin phrase, incurvitus in se. The concept, made famous by Martin Luther, captures the degree to which humans are inherently wired to oxymoronically live-out their lives "inwardly."[2] This means humans are built from birth to focus intently on serving themselves, first, rather than focusing "outwardly" in service toward or for others. Not everyone does this, of course. But self-centeredness is the default human condition unless some intervening factor or factors impose their will.

Luther argued that humans are selfish because their Creator made them that way. Martin Luther once was a Catholic priest. In 1517, he reformed Catholicism by founding a Lutheran sect. Luther's "extension" of the original Roman Catholic Church brand has since evolved into the various differentially branded Protestant religious sects that exist today.

People Are Really Selfish

Human beings generally feature three traits that branding professionals should understand. After acquiring these insights, leverage them in ways that promote your branding advantage—when doing so is socially responsible. Trait one: Nearly everyone wants to be the center of the universe. And in our own minds, the only place where anyone actually lives, we are. Trait two: Indeed, many people assume and act as if they already were (the center of the universe). Trait three: Everyone wants to see the value of every asset they own to grow in value over time, every time. Now that you know these essentially universal self-centered human motivations exist, you should learn how to leverage them in ways that enhance your branding power.

But first there is something else to learn. Because two pairs of motivations drive most client decision-making processes for better or worse. These same two sets of motivations also generally drive your decision making. Including decisions you make that will elevate choices that elevate or degrade the value and persuasiveness of your brand over time.

The first set of client motivations derives from humanity's innate self-centeredness and desire to have more than their fellow humans. The net consequence: Almost everyone desires all they can get all the time. Moreover, most humans seemingly instinctively want to acquire more than others have. The second set of client motivations derives from humanity's natural desire to acquire more pleasure or avoid any pain. Either or, as it were. One, the other, or both sets of motivations materially influence many of the most important decisions that your clients make.

Being only human, professionals also want more for themselves. We professionals also similarly want to avoid all possible pain or secure more pleasure. However, usually after the passage of time, accumulation of experience, or realization of hard-earned success, some professionals actually learn that sometimes enough actually is enough. Or, learn that too much pursuit of pleasure often proves painful. These two motivations often influence decisions that in turn influence the long-term success or failure of your brand. Indeed, the interaction of these two motivational sets is the primary reason why professional decision-making is rarely drive exclusively by ethical or moral guidelines. Even decisions clearly destined to favorably or unfavorably the power and persuasiveness of our brand identities.

People are Naturally Born to …

… cheat. Professionals, like everyone else, are natural born cheaters. Most people cheat, some if not most of the time. That is, if two "cheat-facilitating" conditions are present. According to the book Freakonomics,[3] the first enabling condition under which nearly everyone cheats is when they believe the stakes or rewards rewards that redound to "cheaters" are sufficiently high. Assuming they get away with the cheat, obviously. The second condition that promotes cheating is when prospective "cheaters" perceive their risk of getting caught is sufficiently low. When these conditions intersect, watch out.

We hope you're currently thinking if not feeling something like: "Wow, I knew but really did not know all this stuff!" The phrase "a little knowledge can be a dangerous thing" is well-known. Also well-known, this condition misleads people into thinking they are more expert than is actually the case. But you are an expert in your chosen professional field. You understand that substantive portions of right type of knowledge can be a powerful thing. And you've just been exposed to powerful insights about basic human nature. You should learn how to exploit these insights, or how to avoid being exploited by them, as you script an ethical plan to improve your brand.

Knowledge is an asset whose value should grow across the span of a career. Particularly, if you intentionally initiate measures designed to build your actionable insights. Knowledge, particularly that which enhances your decision-making acumen, is a core source of power. Ethical power, once earned, can be managed in ways that elevate the power and persuasiveness of your brand.

What Would Abraham, Jesus, Buddha, and so on, Do?

Meanwhile, returning to that often uncomfortable subject, religion ... Listed alphabetically, the world's five great religions are Buddhism, Christianity, Hinduism, Islam, and Judaism. As inferred in the opening vignette, each of these five philosophies speaks directly and expansively about ethics. Fact is, each religion's leading thinkers and doers have always written and spoken more about the ideal (read: ethical) sort of relationship that human beings should cultivate with each other (read: clients, superiors, peers and subordinates) than about humanity's spiritual connection with the higher power variously identified as God by four of these five religions. (Buddhists do not believe in a god). Most of what philosophers and ethicists believe is true, relevant, and useful about ethical decision making in professional settings is rooted directly or indirectly in one or more religious philosophies.

The Ten Commandants, the well-known summary of the Jewish Law, concentrates more attention on the ideal relationship that faithful Jews should create with each other than about the relationship they should create with God. Six Commandments directly address how people should behave toward each other. The other four prescribe the sort of relationship that people should cultivate with God.

Our eighth and final initial framing question: Does any of this have anything to do with professional ethics? The answer is yes: All of this chapter's preceding discussion has everything to do with professional ethics and social responsibility, and with the opportunity you enjoy to create a more powerful and persuasive brand.

Only Your Fair Share

Religions generally counsel that humans should "strive" to make the world a better place. "Striving" is synonymous with "struggling," which is telling. Because the Greek root for the word struggle is combat. Yes, the implication is that you should fight, when appropriate, to make the world a better place. Full stop. We doubt whether any formal ethical code has ever provided a superior ethical guideline. You presumably occupy a role in which you are well-positioned to make the world a better place. That's because you perform on a professional stage on which you able to create value for others.

When you create value for others (a "get" for clients or others), you rightfully expect to take away value from them as part of a hopefully ongoing exchange process. This "getting and giving" of value forms the basis for exchange relationships. Exchange is the process that makes the provision and receipt of professional services possible.

Your brand-able value is created through your actual or perceived usefulness to clients. Perceived usefulness, as reflected in your ability to solve clients' problems successfully. In due course, your perceived usefulness would also be reflected in your branding reputation. Your branded reputation likewise would benefit materially when you spread incremental value throughout clients' worlds and never take away excessive value for yourself. Even, and perhaps especially, in situations where you had the power to take away more than your fair share.

We synopsize this advice into one idea:

- Never take more than your fair share of value off the table, even when you can. That's it. Do this, and the reputational value that will accrue to your brand over time might astound. Because across time as you develop, strengthen, sustain, and ultimately accumulate broadly networked webs of successful relationships with others by reflexively treating each client, partner, associate or report fairly you'll evolve into a professional problem-solver who enjoys an ethical reputation. Congratulations: No matter what else you do professionally you just materially enhanced your ability to win a brand new power game.

Branding Takeaway

Right now you could be excused for thinking: Really, that's all you got? My stage, my professional world, is too large. Full of too many real power players. My stage is absolutely full of cynicism but utterly devoid of morality. The world as a whole is too burdened with insoluble problems for such simplistic counsel to work. Where would I begin? Actually, following Mother Teresa's counsel, begin with the next client you see. That is, if you're not already universally acting in a strictly ethical fashion.

Consider how Mother Teresa responded when a critic called her out about the fact there were too many lepers living in Calcutta for her team to possibly cure them all. The situation was clearly insoluble. But Mother Teresa replied to her critic:

- [Yes, you're right. But still] "I'll start with this one. Never worry about numbers [she said]. Help one person at a time. Always start with the person nearest you."[4] Ethically minded and ethically guided professionals perform on stages on which the means, motive and opportunity to act in a similarly moral manner coalesce. Ethical professionals should leverage this opportunity to, in John Lennon's famous lyrics, "come together, right now," with their clients. How? By ethically satisfying the problems of their clients.

This is how individual human progress toward being, becoming, or remaining a more ethical professional in a generally unethical world could and should happen. Few people are able to become more ethical merely through good intentions or force of will. Just as few people stop smoking or lose weight just because they know these are the right things to do. Instead, people who become more ethical, or for that matter lost weight or stopped smoking, have successfully exploited their intelligence. They used their intelligence and did what they knew beyond any question was in their best self-interests to do. As Aristotle recognized long ago, one thing fascinating about human beings is our capacity for reason and our ability to ignore it (logic). But reason should reign over all, the great thinker counseled.[5] You surely agree. Right?

Accordingly, when the subjects are ethics and its relationship with branding, we advise:

- Be reasonable and do what is clearly in your best interests to do. If you create more value for than you take away from the clients that you serve you have done enough to ensure that one day, and likely sooner rather than later, you will enjoy a powerfully persuasive brand. This simple logical act will permit you to master the intrinsically unethical pull of your innate human selfishness.

At the same time, you would soon enjoy greater value in your lives. Entirely because you acted reasonably by logically focusing on generating and providing morally grounded value to the audiences you professionally serve.

Humans should not primarily be takers. We should also be makers. And most professionals are also *creators*. The mere ability to create, however, is not inherently valuable. You can create solutions that add value or produce outcomes that subtract value from the world. Your ethical responsibility as a creative professional is to leave some added value on the table that you could have taken away. Over time, nothing but good would gravitate to your brand identity when you choose this path.

Ironically, the opportunity just described might be viewed as onerous by highly creative professionals. After all, it is the most creative professionals who are actually best positioned to take more value from tables in the long run. Let's talk more about this issue ....

Professionals Enjoy the Power to Create ... the Right Stuff

The power to create is accompanied by the responsibility to create ethical stuff; that is, things, outcomes, and solutions. When you focus solely on creating value and sharing it with others, you end up becoming and being more creative, productive, and emotionally satisfied than if you turn your attention toward extracting value from the world. In a world as globalized and technologically transparent as this one now is, the days of strip-mining value out of others, even when you enjoy the power to do so, should end. Strip-mining, as a professional behavior, worked better when clients and others had less knowledge or fewer professional options from which to choose.

Contemporary clients can quickly identify, vet and turn toward other professionals who engage with them through less coercive behaviors. And once they do, your client is lost forever. Worse still, they may knowingly disparage your brand through negative messaging.

Negative messages, in turn, are often replicated rapidly by others engaging on social networking sites. They consequently spread exponentially. Negative brand messages, often tantamount to gossip, are much more fun to send and receive than positive messages. Branding gossip is like receiving forbidden stolen goods. Gossip, think of two or more people telling things about a third entity that the "third person" would prefer not be known, clearly appeals more to most people. Eliminate gossip from the world, and the numbers of texts or subscriptions to twitter would precipitously decline.

Professionals should rarely give things away for free or less than they are worth, pro bono efforts notwithstanding. Giving away valuable stuff is unsustainable and counterproductive in other than charitable contexts. Giving away free value likely "cheapens" anyone's brand and branding power, and is illogical. A digression, but one that is extremely useful in this branding context:

- "Cheap," "cheaper," or "cheapen"—as labels potentially identified with your brand—are bad words. Why? The answer is simple: Would you ever want anyone to describe you or your behaviors as cheap? Embracing a professional brand identify as one who is affordable, inexpensive, value based, or even reasonably priced is acceptable. Cheap? Never.

Take care of your family, and colleagues or employees first before taking care of others. This is the core of traditional capitalism. Then, after taking care of first things first, you can begin to take care of others.

An Atheist Take on the Same Principles

Some readers may be uncomfortable with the religious tenor that has dominated the discussion to this point. Perhaps you'll secure comfort, confidence, and stronger ethical conviction from learning that a prominent atheist expressed views highly similar to those advocated above. The atheist in question was the Russian emigrant Ayn Rand, author of *Atlas Shrugged* and *The Fountainhead*, two of the twentieth century's most influential books.

Ms. Rand advocated an ethical philosophy called Enlightened Self-Interest in her writing. The philosophy suggests:

- People who intentionally act to further the interests of "others" are ultimately serving their "branding" self-interests. Here, "others" would include the professional cohort to which you belong or audience members you seek to serve and satisfy. Stated more diabolically: A sure way to secure selfish branding gains is by apparently selflessly serving the interests—by satisfying the wants and needs and/or solving the problems—of key "others."

Deciding to act in ways that promote enlightened self-interests is generally desirable. The act usually strengthens one's brand and is entirely ethical. Enlightened self-interests, as a guiding ethical philosophy, is consistent with another deceptively self-serving ethical branding principle. The principle is called "Doing Well by Doing Good." Doing well by doing good entails, simply, "doing well" for one's branding interests by "doing good" [things] that help, say, clients solve their problems or satisfy their wants and needs. Professional acts through which you could "do well for yourself" and your brand by "doing good for others" include:

- Supporting moral causes with professional time, talent, and treasure.
- Doing exactly what you say you will do, every time; conducting your professional affairs not just as a branding promise "maker" but also as a branding promise "keeper."
- Performing professionally in social responsible fashions by being environmentally neutral, at worst, or ideally, by acting in ways that generate net environmental gain.
- Legitimately following each guideline associated with enlightened self-interests as a governing personal philosophy, or alternatively, "never taking more than your fair share of value off the table," if when you can.

Follow these guidelines and your brand will love you. So will your clients.

Acting Out Enlightened Self-Interests

You can become a more enlightened brand, an entity capable of creating greater good for yourself by first doing well for others, by following with three accessible paths. These follow.

- First, to brand yourself as ethical you should be or become extremely client focused.

The leadership of Panera Bread apparently bought into this principle. During the bottom of the Great Recession, the restaurant chain adopted a "pay what you can" branding and pricing strategy in its St. Louis region stores. Even folks who had lost or could not find a job still enjoy eating a meal out. Knowing this, Panera Bread promoted the fact that customers who could not pay full price should still come, order, pay what they could afford, or nothing at all—and then eat. As part of its branding play, Panera simultaneously asked customers who could comfortably pay a little extra to do so. This strategy worked, in fact, quite well. Restaurants who offered this deal enjoyed higher traffic, generated higher revenues, and earned greater profits.[6] And years later, Panera still reaps enhanced reputational value power from this decision to do well for itself by doing good for others by focusing intensively on customer needs.

- Second, to brand yourself as ethical become extremely value focused in whatever problem-solving solutions you develop and deliver. Being or becoming extremely "value focused" does not imply you should discount your price. In fact, the opposite outcome will likely emerge. Professionals who earn reputations as high-value performers are better positioned to command premium prices for their services.

The recent proliferation of autism among American children has understandably attracted substantial media attention. Autistic children often act out vociferously when excited, engaging in behaviors that would often upset others who do not know the child. This makes it difficult to take autistic children to the movies, even for films targeted at their age group. Recognizing this, AMC Movie Theatres developed and executed a "value-focused" branding strategy. The plan set-aside one screen on a "one-time-a-day" "once-a-week" basis exclusively for autistic kids. Then, autistic children, and their families and friends, could watch child-appropriate films with each other. Attendance and profits on a per-screen basis grew materially.[7] AMC secured all manner of favorable publicity for its brand. Which only seems right, doesn't it?

- Three, to brand yourself as an ethical professional you should remain perpetually socially focused.

When developing and executing branding strategies, you generally should hold client needs, society's long-term needs, and your need to perform profitably foremost in your mind. (Professionals should always dance close to revenue lines.) And then set about satisfying all three core need sets. Again, these often inherently conflicting outcomes are difficult to balance. But it can be done.

For example, most people would prefer to eat healthier food. Many consumers also would prefer eating food that is less harmful, or not harmful at all, to the environment. Knowing this, fast-food entrepreneur Steve Ells, founder of Chipotle, sought to destroy fast food as America knew it by serving pasture-raised pork burritos and steroid/antibiotic-free chicken tacos. By targeting audiences seeking healthier, "greener" food, Chipotle scored huge brand equity and customer loyalty, earned higher revenues and secured record-breaking profits.

This success story continued until 2015/16, when a tainted food scandal broke extremely bad for Chipotle. Unsurprisingly, the firm's branding power—along with its level of patronage, profits, and market valuation—fail precipitously as a consequence.[8] Still, Chipotle's founding story illustrates how a professionally managed firm "did well for itself" by "doing good for others" who valued and benefitted from the good works of the firm. Until those good works, and a branding reputation largely based on those good works, went astray. Which, we would hasten to add, did not have to happen. The ethical path, pursued persistently across time, consistently works out well for professional branders. Until and unless, they either perceptually or actually veer off the path.

Can Professionals Learn to be More Ethical?

You might logically assume the answer to this question is yes. If not, why discuss ethics? The possibly surprising answer, however, is "usually not." The personal moral compasses of people are established long before they become professional or even enter college. Psychologist Lawrence Kohlberg suggested that this "morality largely already in place" date arrives between the ages of 7 and 10.[9]

Despite this pessimistic take, extreme value is still associated with learning more about the long-term persuasive power that accrue to individuals who earn branded reputations for being ethical, fair, and honest. Then there is the fact that anyone can and should learn more about the negative long-term consequences associated with making unethical decisions. These consequences can prove nasty. Today's world is simultaneously too smart and too small for anything for truth. At the least, then, learn more about how to make ethical choices when branding yourself through spoken and unspoken behaviors in situations where the line between right and wrong is blurred. These situations, by the way, arise more frequently than many assume.

The adage that "your reputation precedes you" is grounded in truth. Because their glistening reputations stride ahead of them, new doors are opened to well-branded professionals. Moreover, and as importantly, old doors will likely remain open even when negative incidents arise that might ruin less ethically grounded relationships. As inevitably will happen. Mistakes, missteps, and/or misunderstandings occur in every relationship. That is, if relationships last long enough for "bad stuff "to happen.

Never Exploit

Professionals sometimes occupy powerful positions from which they can exploit others, if they elect to do so. There are many reasons why you might enjoy this opportunity. But these reasons always wrap around a single fact: you possess, because you have earned, the more powerful brand. Yet you should never act unethically by taking advantage of clients or other audience members, even if you can. That is, unless you never plan to do business with that client again, or aren't concerned about the negative messages the ill-treated client will likely convey to other potential or actual clients. Never risk being branded, perhaps permanently, as a rape, ruin and run professional. As one who exploitatively rips out the last dribs of ore from weaker clients or other easily manipulated/exploited and typically weaker constituencies. Of course, currently powerful professionals who rapaciously exploit power advantages just because they *now* can also ignore the fact that great oaks emerge from little acorns. Our point being: Today's small-time clients may grow powerful brands of their own across time. Then the newly powerful branded actor will be in a position to reciprocate in kind.

Respect the long term. Respect, as in honor the value of long-term, mutually beneficial relationships in which you and your clients each come to realize that you are each better off together than you would be apart. Script out ethical behaviors and responses, perform based on your professional script, and manage for the future. You know, the place where we all plan to live, play, work, and succeed—presumably with each other.

Ethics, as it relates to professional brand management, is not about being clever in moral crises or encounters. Ethics instead is about developing, over time, the sort of professional character that does not realize it has experienced an ethical challenge until challenge has the ended. Highly desirable branded identities will follow as a logical consequence of the behaviors that this sort of character will produce.

Do you see how relationships in which good and bad—or fair and unfair—exchanges of value occur remain continuously relevant? Choose wisely, as you first cultivate and thereafter manage those relationships. Wisely, in this context, actually means "choose ethically." While they aren't the only element that ensures branding success, ethical reputations provide a foundational basis for almost all brands that are successful over the long term.

Who Owes What to Whom?

Every client and audience member with whom you interact enjoys various rights. As do you, a performing professional. This condition is natural, must be expected, and should be respected by anyone who plans to develop a winning brand. These rights exist as part of a "getting and giving" of value—the previously referenced "exchange process"—that unifies you with your clients. Indeed, exchange processes make professional–client relationships possible. Nothing more and nothing less.

Client Rights

Consumerism is a consumer protection, or here, a client protection movement. Consumerism exists to improve or protect the rights and power of audience members in relation to the rights and powers of professionals. Consumerism's Western roots extend back more than one century. But the father of modern consumerism is Ralph Nader. The erstwhile U.S. Presidential candidate wrote a paradigm-shifting book called *Unsafe at Any Speed* in 1965. *Unsafe at Any Speed* accused the American automotive industry of resisting the introduction of various safety features, such as seatbelts, simply because doing so would have raised prices.

The historical evidence is clear: Automotive leaders of the era consistently came down the side of saving money rather than lives or the environment. Sometimes it appears this remains true today. Remember General Motors,

Toyota, and Volkswagen? Nader's book is often mistakenly identified as the book about the Corvair, a rear-engine car whose branded design was ahead of its time. But the Corvair's safety standards were emphatically behind the curve.

Largely because of the ever-evolving consumerism movement, clients enjoy the rights to:

- Not buy something they don't want to buy.
- Expect any products or services (i.e., solutions) they receive to be safe.
- Expect whatever products or services (solutions) they acquire or consume to perform as the professional promised.

Professionals' Rights

Exchanges always feature two participants. Participants might include a professional performer and client. Exchanges always feature "a get and give"; as in a getting and giving of value. Consequently, ethically branded professionals enjoy rights, as well. You enjoy the right to:

- Create any value so long as the value delivered does not injure anyone or anything.
- Change any fair price for the value you produce, so long as no client or group of clients is discriminated against.
- Employ legal and moral incentive schemes to motivate or influence clients.
- Promote the values you create while employing of any amount of resources you choose to support the promotion
- Use any message you choose, so long as the message is neither misleading nor dishonest but instead accurate or so outrageous that no reasonable client would believe your assertion was accurate and true.

The final clause in the preceding sentence describes a marketing and advertising concept known as "puffery." Puffery is both legal and ethical. Puffery was introduced earlier.

How Can You Become More Ethical?

The task of becoming and remaining more ethical is probably harder than many previously supposed. Philosopher Immanuel Kant, probably a closeted atheist (he never publicly renounced religion, preferring survival over principle), probably offered the best–worst reason why. He famously wrote: "Out of the crooked tree of humanity no straight thing can ever be built."[10]

Hope exists, however. Writing in *Improvisation: The Drama of Christian Ethics*, Samuel Ellis argued that ethics is not about being clever in a moral crisis. Instead, the ethical path is about forming a character that does not realize it has been in a crisis until the "crisis" is resolved.[11] One way to ensure you are tracking toward a more ethical sort of brand-able moral character entails never viewing others simply as means to your selfish ends.

But it is not our job to improve your character. Your authors experience enough difficulty keeping their flaws in check themselves. Most humans inhabit similarly leaky boats, vessels built from "crooked timber." And for better or worse, people are fully formed, comparatively moral or immoral beings long before earning their professional stripes. Still, you might consider:

- How valuable is your reputation to you?
- Will the quality of your brand influence the type and quality of relationships you are able to develop or sustain?
- How long did it take you to develop the brand identity you now enjoy, assuming you have earned an admirably branded reputation?
- How quickly, however, could the value and power of your exemplary branded reputation be blown to hell?
- Do you understand that the points just made about your reputation apply equally to the reputation of any organization you own, manage and/or represent?
- Or that while the occasional professional or firm seemingly gets away with underhanded or abusive dealings, over the longer run, most don't?

If your now more enlightened answers are all correct, then you similarly understand how important ethical and socially responsible choices are to professionals as they burnish new brands or replenish old brand value.

Four practical methods exist through which you can learn how to routinely make more ethical branding decisions. Which is all that we "curved-in-on-themselves" professionals, being only human, can aspire to. Each approach is useful. Some more so than others.

The Deontological Method

The daunting word "deontology" means, simply, rules. Deontology is an ethical philosophy that evaluates the morality of a decision or action based on the decision's or action's adherence to a particular rule.[12] The Hammurabi Code featured 216 Babylonian, think modern day Iraq and Iran, Laws. Each was written by a great ruler named Hammurabi around 1763 BC. The Code is the first known set of law-like do's and don'ts. The Ten Commandants, written around 1100 BC, are similar to the original code. Notably, Judaism eventually developed 613 laws, or rules, in an ultimately futile attempt to have discrete guidelines available to discriminate right from wrong choices in all possible contexts featuring ethical content.

Today, marketing, accounting, financial, human resource, informational technology, legal, medical, architectural and for all we know plumbing professionals each have Codes of Ethics. Each code is intended to address most ethical dilemmas that might arise in the particular sector with which it is associated. Which is surely a worthy end to pursue.

But several flies taint the deontological ointment. For starters: Technology, in particular, as well as other dynamic social, cultural, economic, and global forces, are creating newfangled opportunities for branding professionals to cheat, chip, chide, or con others faster than presumably governing professional bodies can institute and disseminate new rules. Another problem: No one can remember all the laws. Finally, yet another more pressing shortfall is associated with any rule-based approach to moral branding: Largely due to our intrinsically selfish nature, having these rules in place simply does not work.

Genuine question, offered to enlighten not shock: How many of the Ten Commandants did you break last month? Okay, likely no reader killed anyone during the last 30 days. But did you fail to act or think in ways that would bring all honor due to your parents? Have you recently coveted something that someone else had, or born false witness about anything or anyone? Be careful, mere gossip qualifies as "false witness," by the way. Used the name of God, if you believe in a higher being, in vain? Or, failed to honor the Sabbath by writing these very words on a Sunday? No need to cower in shame or engage in covet cover-up if your answer is "more than one." As noted, we sail in that same creaking, crooked timbered boat with you.

Having the right rules in place is a great first step toward an ethical brand. But rules are often not enough when the subject to ensure ethical performance that would always bring only honor and prestige to your brand. We've already seen how easily the most basic Judeo-Christian rules are broken. Still, having some standards in place is better than having nothing at all.

The Utilitarian Method—or Consequentialism

Most readers are familiar with *Star Trek*. Knowing *Star Trek*, they are also acquainted with Mr. Spock. Mr. Spock, as originally played by Leonard Nimoy, dies during the second, original TV cast *Star Trek* move, 1982's *Wrath of Khan*. More to our point, Mr. Spock willingly sacrifices his life to save the starship Enterprise's entire crew. His dying words: "Remember, the needs of the many outweigh the needs of the few."[13]

These words capture the essence of utilitarianism as the philosophy applies to ethical and socially responsible branding choices. Utility is a synonym for value. What Mr. Spock inferred, then, was that the decision that yields the most value for the most people on any stage is always the most ethical choice. This premise remains valid even if an individual or even groups are unavoidably hurt as a consequence of the decision.

Whenever you make professional decisions, behaviors result. Behaviors, in turn, always generate consequences. These consequences may spawn favorable outcomes for some and undesirable outcomes for others. But as long as more people benefit than are harmed as they experience the consequences of your decision, you have made an ethical choice. And your branding identity, over the longer term, should benefit.

Utilitarianism is imperfect. Utilitarianism clearly challenges whatever minority group gets the short stick. But the utilitarian decision-making criterion is typically deemed more suitable than the deontological approach as a means to discriminate right from wrong choices. And in situations where you cannot employ the rule-based method because no rule exists to resolve moral dilemmas that have arisen, utilitarianism is always viable.

The Facebook and Your Mother Method

The "Facebook and Your Mother" approach is practical and easy to use. The method also works well. What's not to like? Consequently, the approach comes highly recommended.

Suppose you're in charge. All decisions, as well as the consequences your choices produce, are yours to make and bear. Further suppose that an ethical quandary arises. With good cause, you're worried the wrong choice could damage clients' perceptions about the integrity and trustworthiness of your brand. You're genuinely struggling to discriminate right from wrong in the choice you make. Black and white distinctions have faded to oblivion. Instead, multiple shades of gray hold sway. Situations like these actually arise in various settings or professional stages. Finally, assume you seek, at the least, to make the least worst unethical choice.

Now imagine that the decision you are about to make and the outcomes it will generate will be posted on your Facebook page. Post post, Mom, your Facebook friends, associates, prospective and actual customers, and potentially the entire wired world will be able to examine the "facts." Now how do you feel about the choice you are about to make?

If you're sensing that you'll experience shame when Mom and the world sees the report of your decision and the consequences it generated, you're probably holding hands too tightly with an immoral choice. And your brand may suffer negative consequences, too. But if you're comfortable with what Mom will soon see, you're likely walking as close to ethical as you can get given the prevailing circumstances.

The Truth-Telling Method

The "truth," as we best understand it, and ethical branding decisions and behaviors walk in lockstep as close allies. But ironically, you do not always have to be wholly truthful in order to remain entirely ethical. Clients, peers, reports, or superiors always require and therefore deserve accurate branding information to make the best possible decisions themselves. Audience members do not, however, inevitably require all possible available information in order to make every choice. Philosopher J. Brooke Hamilton and marketer David Strutton, writing in the *Journal of Business Ethics*, contend:

- Truth-telling means giving clients and other audience members full and accurate disclosure of branding information to the extent that the information is necessary for, say, clients or superiors to make well-informed, well-grounded, and safe decisions.[14] Different types of branding professionals consequently face different truth-telling standards.

Pharmaceutical professionals and their firms, for example, face far higher truth-telling branding standards than professionals or firms who peddle smartphones, everyday underwear, or chewing gum. Because when customers consume pharmaceuticals, what they don't know could kill them, or more likely, make them ill. This is why when they encounter 30-second pharmaceutical advertisements on television, audiences inevitably experience the following chronological sequence. First, 5–6 seconds of imagery and verbiage that describes the problem purportedly solved by the drug being promoted. Next, another 5–6 seconds of content is provided to explain how the product will solve the product. Third, another 10–12 seconds explaining the potential side effects, which are often nasty. Finally, the problem and the solution are quickly re-encapsulated. More branding attention is necessarily allocated toward explaining what could go wrong than right, because the truth-telling branding standards are so high. When promoting sneakers or hairstyles, branders' truth-telling standards are not nearly as high.

This divergence in truth-telling standards across different contexts makes perfect moral and branding sense. Because, at your professional core, you are a problem solver. But when you're ethical you can never make decisions entailing immoral commission or moral omission that would transform you into a problem creator.

Develop Sustainable Values

Branding professionals guided by situational ethical values would generally do whatever situations permit them to get away with. They would usually selfishly engage in questionable or worse behaviors absent much or any longer-term and forward-looking regard for the best interests of their firm or clients. Or significantly, absent regard for the longer-term value of their brand.

Professionals guided by sustainable ethical values would do the opposite. They make decisions affecting their brands as if they realize that their reputations will always exist for better or worse. Individuals guided by sustainable ethical values are concerned about the future. These future-oriented professionals will more likely behave in ways that support and lift up clients, their professional sector, and those around them. They are also more likely to perform in ways that support the current and future versions of the brand they aspire to create and communicate.

Always employ sustainable ethical values as guides to your branding initiatives. Few people, however, become more ethical simply because they've been exposed to and perhaps now understand some cherry-picked Sports Center Highlight-like religious beliefs. Or as a result of their good intentions. Indeed, "the road to hell is paved with good intentions," right? The force of your sincerely motivated iron-like will won't permanently lock you into an ethical place, either. For the all-too-human you to become more ethical, and enhance the power and prestige of your brand, exploit your intelligence. Use your intelligence and do only those things that you think and know is in your "ethical brand's" best self-interests to do. Surely professionals, among most human categories, should be able to invoke reason.

So there is hope. To grow more ethical, learn how best to stop acting in ways that belie reason. No longer act in ways that negate what is best for you. Particularly over the long run. The long run, where we all intend to live one day, as we play out our professional lives. When you confront any decision featuring moral content, you should make decisions today as if you were looking back from the future at the consequences that emerged as a result of your decision. A variation of Suzy Welch's 10-10-10 rule should prove useful in this context:

- When you are about to make a decision that involves some sort of moral deliberation, ask how you will feel about your choice and the consequences it generates 10 minutes ..., 10 months ..., and 10 years ... from now.

Notes

1 Bhattacharjee, Judhijit (2015). The First Year. *National Geographic.* Retrieved October 13, 2015. http://ngm.nationalgeographic.com/2015/01/baby-brains/bhattachajee-text.

2 Bainton, Roland (1995). *Here I Stand: A Life of Martin Luther.* New York, NY: Penguin Books.

3 Levitt, Steven and Stephen J. Dubner (2005). *Freakonomics: A Rogue Economist Explores the Hidden Side of Everything.* New York, NY: William Morrow.

4 Hitchens, Christopher (1995). *The Missionary Position: Mother Teresa in Theory and Practice.* London: Verso Publishing.

5 Swanson, Judith (1992). *The Public and the Private in Aristotle's Political Philosophy.* Ithaca, NY: Cornel University Press.

6 Panera Bread: Pay What You Can Afford (2010). *St. Louis Business Journal.* Bizjournals.com. May 18, 2010. Retrieved October 7, 2015. http://www.bizjournals.com/StLouis.stories.

7 *AMC Entertainment and the Autism Society of America Announce Partnership* (2009). Business Wire: A Berkshire Hathaway Company. Retrieved April 1, 2016. http://files.sharholder.com.downloads.AEN.

8 Jargon, Julie and Jesse Newman (2016). Fresh Ingredients Came Back to Haunt Chipotle. *The Wall Street Journal.* February 2, 2016.
9 Walsh, Catherine (2000). "The Life and Legacy of Lawrence Kohlberg." *Society,* 37(2): 38–41.
10 Ultman, Jennifer (2010). *An Introduction to Kant's Moral Philosophy.* Cambridge, UK: Cambridge University Press.
11 Ellis, Samuel (2004). *Improvisation: The Drama of Christian Ethics.* Ada, MI: Baker Books.
12 Kant, Immanuel (1964). *Groundwork of the Metaphysics of Morals.* New York, NY: Harper and Rowe Publishers.
13 Shatner, William and Chris Kreski (2005). *Star Trek Movie Memories.* New York, NY: Harper Collins.
14 Hamilton, J. Brooke and David Strutton (1994). "Two Practical Guidelines for Resolving Truth-Telling Problems." *Journal of Business Ethics,* 13(11): 899-912.

PART II
Essential Recipes

CHAPTER 5

Managing Brands, Professional and Otherwise

"Two components are key to business success: brands and brand delivery. The problem associated with brand building and delivery is getting complex firms to execute based on such simple ideas"

—Marty Neuemier (1947–?).

Cyrus Curtis began his professional life as a young, unlettered man from backwoods Maine. When Mr. Curtis launched a career destined to earn him fortune and fame as founder of the Saturday Evening Post and Ladies Home Journal he knew he could not match the advances paid by competing publications to engage with prestigious authors. Mr. Curtis also recognized that his personal prospects for publishing success during his time and place - 1820s America - demanded the sort of "brand equity" that the presence of already renowned authors would confer to his fledgling enterprises. In response, Mr. Curtis initiated a subtly powerful branding strategy. By executing the strategy flawlessly, he influenced celebrated writers to contribute their work to his publications. Mr. Curtis, for example, convinced Louisa May Alcott, author of Little Women, to write for him at the pinnacle of her celebrity. Mr. Curtis secured Ms. Alcott's consent through the simple gesture of offering $100.00, paid not to her but directly to her favorite charity. What Mr. Curtis did to achieve his goal was manage Ms. Alcott's initial impressions of his brand. He branded himself, in her eyes, as a charitable man of and for the people. Similarly luminous contributors soon followed as the power and persuasiveness of young Mr. Curtis grew.[1] And the branding power of his fledgling publication grew in lockstep.

Contemporary professional "marketers" seeking to create more powerful professional brands would do well to remember a lesson Mr. Curtis apparently learned early in life. Here, "marketers" is an honorific label apropos to most professionals, since every professional sells something, especially their solutions. Mr. Curtis inherently understood that what gets done conversationally and symbolically during professional-client or professional-professional interactions involves more than what gets said, although spoken or written words still matter. He also understood that professionals should be concerned about the image and identity they project personally and in service of their organizations. Like everyone, you are routinely judged by people with whom you interact based as much on what you don't do or say as by what you may do or say. Sustainable success or avoidable failure, in fact, often hinges on how effectively you manage your brand.

Mr. Curtis's subtle but masterful use of ingratiation to sell the idea to Ms. Alcott that she "ought" to contribute her venerated ideas to an unknown "start-up" exemplifies a fundamental branding principle. No matter their field, professionals will more than occasionally find themselves in situations where they must be willing and prepared to do whatever is reasonable and necessary to project desirable brand images to specifically-targeted others. In other words, you will need to successfully manage the perceptions – the imagined realities – that others develop about your brand in order to succeed. Branded impressions matter in every professional encounter. Branded impressions matter first, last, and in-between.

Consider what happened to the relationship between two prominent (at the time) firms and brands whose identities and images were managed far less gracefully. About 15 years ago, footwear giant Nike announced it expected a quarterly earnings shortfall. Nike then proceeded to attribute the disappointing results, in large part, to the failure of I2 Technologies, a partnering firm. And bashed I2 unmercifully. Nike had selected the then giant software vendor to implement a supply chain software system. The programing had gone awry. What sort of impression do you believe Nike's decision to bash I2's brand on potential or actual partners of Nike? No one can know for sure. But, in a result that underscored the power of Nike's brand, I2 Technology's previously untarnished reputation took a huge and public hit. The burgeoning software empire that had been I2 soon crumbled.

Performing on Stages

A revealing parallel links these positive and negative examples to a statement Erving Goffman made in 1959.[2] The sociologist wrote: "… thus, when an individual appears in the presence of others, there will usually be some reason for him to mobilize his activity so that it will convey a desirable impression [brand image] to which it is in his best interests to convey." Drill down to the essence of what each actor in our opening vignette sought to accomplish, and you'll see how Mr. Curtis and Nike engaged in the same general activity in pursuit of similar outcomes driven by differing tactical means. The man and the firm were each also doing things we do regularly in our working lives. Mr. Curtis and Nike each attempted to manage perceptions that important others developed about their professional and corporate brands, respectively.

Mr. Curtis nimbly used ingratiation and self-promotion to brand his magazine as a viable outlet for Ms. Alcott's ideas. He did so as part of a branding strategy. Nike, by contrast, was decidedly less subtle in its blatant attempt first to intimidate and later to divert attention away from its own strategic decisions, which were what actually triggered Nike's temporary struggles, and toward a vendor's shortfalls. Nike simultaneously torpedoed all prospects for any long-term relational success that might have been earned had it retained I2. As written, what sorts of branding impressions do you think Nike's ruthless behaviors made on other current or potential supply chain partners?

Whether the act is recognized or labeled as such, brand management is pervasive across professional fields. Brand management is and should be practiced at individual and organizational levels. This book, of course, focuses on brand management as it should be executed by individual professionals. Most professionals generally understand they should manage impressions that their behavior, appearance, words, and surroundings create and convey to others. Whether they execute their performances effectively often is an altogether different story.

Brand Management Is Theater

Goffman's original insights about the human tendency, need and desire to "manage others' impressions"—to engage in "impression management"—eventually were integrated into a discipline called dramaturgy. Dramaturgy explains how the major elements of drama are featured in and played out through staged life performances. We describe this process simply:

- Professional brand management is theater. Whether you realize it, you live out, perform, your professional life on a stage. The sooner you accept this and learn to manage this fact, the better off you, and your brand, will be.

With his timeless declaration that "all the world's a stage," William Shakespeare underscored that much about working as well as personal life corresponds to a dramatic performance.[3] Myriad performances unfold in settings featuring actors, an audience, props and a stage for each performance, plus the reviews that follow. More than occasionally, then, you should behave mindfully in ways that have been specifically scripted to create more favorable brand impressions.

Alternatively described, you should routinely create specific impressions that best promote your interests when performing on your stages. You might recognize, for example, how times arise when your goals or initiatives are best served by purposefully coming across as either confrontational or conciliatory, aggressive or passive, or angry or calm. Deciding to do one thing often comes at the expense of a missed opportunity to pursue another, often more suitable or impactful, thing. An opportunity you should rarely ignore. Deciding to brand more strategically is one of the best career moves you could ever choose to pursue.

Shakespearean

Shakespeare's comparison of the world to a stage—and what happens on those stages—aptly captures and encapsulates what happens during many interpersonal professional encounters. These experiences might range from casual banter emanating from "chance" encounters involving peers, superiors, or clients at a Rotary luncheon to well-rehearsed ad libs or presentation styles used to deliver proposals pitched toward potential partners. Five core dramaturgical elements ALWAYS exist that can be managed in ways that support your brand management efforts. The elements are:

- *Actors—In professional settings, everyone performs.* Some present, act out, and manage their branding impressions better, some do these things worse. Others strut onto stages absent branding plans and often suffer dreadful consequences, particularly over time.

Professionals, being human, intrinsically feature certain core traits. Core traits that either cannot be changed or only change slowly over time as a consequence of great, focused effort. This is because these traits are close to absolutes. Gender, age, race, or body type (tall/short; thick/thin), for example, are absolutes. The near constant human tendency to want to fervently fight, fornicate, and feed ourselves, often to be point of excess, are likewise nearly absolutes. Which unquestionably makes sense given the homo sapiens species, all of us, is always competing over what in our minds are too few desirable resources or high perches to occupy.

Human beings naturally also feature other, more pliable personal characteristics. These personal characteristics are relative and comparative in nature. Comparative characteristics include acquired and adaptable proficiencies. Acquired proficiencies could include your physical fitness, demonstrated propensity for listening patiently, adroit speaking ability, or proven technological prowess. Adaptable proficiencies are subject to purposeful or evolutionary change over time.

We are concerned with your ability to purposefully change them in this book. Each proficiency—along with others—can be managed to influence the perceptions or impressions—the "imagined realities"—that "audience members" develop about your brand. The proficiencies that you already possess or could develop should influence the brand images and impressions, or identities, that you seek to pursue and the identities you are most likely to generate and retain.

Your staged professional performances might similarly display predetermined levels of certain psychological characteristics or traits. These performances will also influence audience perceptions of your brand. Psychological traits include publically displayed attitudes, beliefs, and personality traits. These public displays, in turn, influence the extent to which you can successfully stake claims to certain branded roles. Staged professional branding roles that you might decide to consciously act out include "wise elder," "up-and-comer," "great-in-a-crisis" (*Godfather*-like wartime consigliere), "steady-hand," "creative-problem-solver," "enforcer," "never-suffers-fools-gladly," "closer," "expert," "trusted confident," or "funny guy/gal."

- *An Audience—Various targets of brand management initiatives.*

  The prevailing attributes of the audiences that you target through your professional branding efforts should decisively influence how you package, position, and present yourself. These attributes might include the power, status, or attractiveness of audience members as potential or actual clients, mentors or protégés, reports, superiors, partners or champions, donors, and so on. Let's assume, we hope realistically, that we're all reasonably self-aware; that we routinely monitor the effects our behaviors stimulate among others; and that we are, at most, only moderately narcissistic. Then let's further assume that we've all conducted this sort of internal calculus throughout our lives. We might have, for example, changed our look by managing attire, hairstyles, or cosmetics; what we've said or refrained from saying; or even where we sat during important meetings. We did or did not do all these things based on the roles we were performing out for different audiences across different settings. There, your prior behaviors suggest you already understand the concept of an audience.

But if you are not doing these sorts of things, you should begin. Never assume, however, that in the doing you're somehow "selling out". You're not. Instead, assume that you are "trading up." Trading up in terms of consciously deciding to elevate the value, power and persuasiveness of your brand.

You must understand the characteristics of the core audience groups you are targeting. Otherwise, you will not know which aspects of your branded-self to project and perform.

- *The Stage—The situations, contexts, or settings in which professionally initiated and/ or managed interactions with audience members occur.*

  Certain exchanges should elicit far different branding performances than others. An initial presentation, given at her office to a potential investor, features well-defined norms that govern your expected branding behaviors. By contrast, the nature of behaviors expected during informal conversations playing out during a medical convention in an exotic locale might prove more ambiguous. Professional encounters are always, at some level, "staged" performances. Insightful professionals who plan their brand work and work their brand plans can often arrange stage settings in ways that complement their specific branding goals. Various ways to arrange your stage are discussed during Chapter 10.

- *Your Performance Itself—During all interpersonal exchanges, professionals constantly perform and concurrently earn more or less favorable reviews from audiences or critics.*

  Professional performances feature various behaviors. These behaviors may be tightly scripted or spontaneous. The nature of scripted or unscripted performances might include the "verbal," that is, speech patterns or vocabulary content; the "nonverbal," that is, body position or tone of voice; and the "artifactual," that is, our attire, office décor or even out body type.

The play "The Homecoming" offers profound insights about life, language and the art of storytelling. Author Harold Pinter has written extensively about "nonverbal" communications that unfold on stages inside actual theaters. He said: "Before the play but after writing my script, I thought theater was about the spoken. After the play, I understood the eloquence and power of the unspoken." Pinter's revelation led him to a lifetime of listening carefully to "hear" what others left unsaid.[4] Presumably, you should similarly listen carefully to what was not said before, after, and during your staged professional branding performances.

Actor Al Pacino tried to explain why Mike Nichols, director of *The Graduate, Carnal Knowledge, Whose Afraid of Virginia Wolfe*, and other renowned films, was the greatest director with whom he ever worked. Pacino: "[Nichols] doesn't say anything, and yet he does."[5] However, just before his death in 2015 Mr. Nichols shared some thoughts about the stage and staged performances. He offered an insight that you definitely should tuck into your branding toolbox before, as, and after you perform with and for audiences. In a documentary titled, *Making Mike Nichols*, Nichols himself said: "Only three types of scenes are played out on stage: seductions, negotiations, and fights. That's it, there is nothing more." Your learned ability to effectively or ineffectively perform out "seductions", "negotiations," and "fights" on professional stages that you should learn to command will contribute materially to branding success or failure.

When you perform, you seduce. When encouraging "audiences" to accept your ideas, recommendations or do your bidding, you seduce.

When you perform, you negotiate. Much of professional and personal life entails ongoing negotiations.

When you perform, you sometimes may engage in feigned or genuine fights. Particularly when your seduction or negotiating performance failed to command the stage.

Plan, develop, and learn how to perform it out effectively, and the power of your brand will grow. That growth will enhance your effectiveness as a seducer or seductress, negotiator, and fighter. That effectiveness will elevate your persuasiveness.

In the process never discount the value of artifice. Your branding performance may pivot based on how well you "say it"; how you look while saying it; your stagecraft; and how well you manage, manipulate, and sell your solution in accordance with the key values that are coveted and/or honored on the specific stage on which you perform. This is no small thing: branding performance is a primary driver of your branding success.

The nature of your performance should likewise turn based on your branding motivations and goals. Staged brand performances may be motivated by a simple desire to appear more congenial or competent. Brand performances might be driven by the goal of being deemed a serious-minded player with whom others would not to cross swords.

- *A Review (Audience Reactions)-Successful brand management occurs on stages when actors cultivate scripted images, perform them out, and obtain desired outcomes from targeted audiences.*

A desired outcome might be as straightforward as securing a second meeting. By and large, brand management performances that generate favorable reviews facilitate desirable professional branding outcomes. Hopefully exactly the brand identities you planned to achieve.

Acceptance …

If you're a professional seeking to succeed and sustain success in contemporary America, you had better like crowds. You should embrace the notion that you perform on stages, and all that acceptance of this notion implies. You should likewise perform knowing your performance will be subjected to continuous assessment—or reviews. Those reviews will often be harsh.

Accept, and plan to act based on your acceptance of the fact that:

- As a professional you probably work in the crowd-creation and satisfaction-provision business. Which entails, in the end, being in the problem-solving business. Structure and perform out your branded and brand-able solutions accordingly.

The City States of ancient Greece competed vigorously against each other. They often competed to the point where active warfare against each other broke-out. But Athens, Sparta, and Corinth, for example, competed even in terms of the amount of conspicuous wealth that they developed and accumulated, but also publicly displayed on one crucial stage. The stage? The exterior and thus highly conspicuous walls of Delphi's Treasury building, where the bulk of Greece's wealth was once stored. Delphi, now an archaeological site and modern town located high on Mount Parnassus, was the spiritual and cultural center of ancient Greece. (You may have heard of the Delphi Oracle.)

Many professionals pry their trades and perform out their solutions on stages as competitive, conspicuous, and critical to their eventual branding success or failure as were the National Treasury walls in ancient Delphi. Are you among these ranks? We thought so.

Successful Branding: Grounded in Marketing Principles

Facts are stubborn things. The material nature of facts never changes across context or time. Nor, typically, does their relevance. This premise, this baseline, is important to understand. Opinions, recommendations, or planned acts should usually not be formulated until after one understands and has evaluated all possible relevant facts.

Facts, after all, tend to stick around. All the while, their presence determines and limits professional branding options.

Consider two relevant facts about professionals performing on contemporary stages—and the consequences emanating from each. The first fact:

- The earned attention, trust and/or respect or fear of your audience is among the most precious resources that you could ever secure and exploit on the typically crowded, competitive and noisy stages where you compete. Secure and exploit, that is, for purposes of favorably and ethically differentiating your brand.

The attention, trust, and respect or fear of others—typically, your clients—are scarce, finite, and valuable resources. In these respects, these earned assets are similar to money. Or, less directly, to time—insofar as life is finite and time is irreplaceable. One more thing to know or remember. On contemporary professional stages you cannot count on "owning" client attention, trust, or fear/respect. Instead, you typically can only aspire to rent these assets. "Renting" them, generally as a consequence of the power and persuasiveness of your professional brand. Get strong, yes; then you must stay strong, brand-wise, in order to retain the attention of others.

Don't waste time, money, or audience members' attention, trust or respect or fear by not branding, branding for unethical purposes, or failing to brand properly. Meanwhile, audience members engaged with professionals constantly make resource-allocative choices of their own. Generally about their own money and time. Resource-allocation decisions clients make about the brands with whom they elect, or decline, to interact can make or break careers.

Do you suppose client impressions and the decisions they make turn based on the degree to which they attend to, trust, respect, or fear you, and sense that you confer all "honor" due to their finite stores of time and money? We do.

The second fact:

- Audiences seek more than functional utility or solutions from many of the professionals with whom they voluntarily choose to engage. Clients also seek meaning from you. And your brand.

When brand meanings exist, they frequently foster emotional connection between professionals and their audiences. These meanings and the emotional consequences they generate often contribute materially to or profoundly detract from your ability to create, retain and/or strengthen relationships with prospective or actual clients.

Professionals are Products

Successful brands exist as living narratives. Function as the story behind you and your power. A story that bolsters your value, as a product. Brand "stories" confer meaning to the distinct sets of benefits, values and solutions that any well-branded product promises to deliver.

Any entity that solves problems by delivering satisfying benefits and values is a "product." The professional version of you, therefore, is a product. So are we, as professors and authors. So too is this book. Well-branded professionals exist and perform as *differentiated products* that deliver *value* by creating *exchange* relationships with targeted audiences. If you aspire to become well-branded, you should understand all that the preceding sentence implies. The highlighted concepts known as *product, differentiation, position or positioning, exchange, value* and *relationships* are foundational to successful professional branding initiatives. Each concept takes flight—or crashes—in the context of exchange relationships you create with your clients.

Any product can be branded. Thus any product can be differentiated. This has been true for even seemingly undifferentiable products at least since 1911. The year when Morton's Salt Co., marketing the most homogenous and plentiful mineral on earth, established a uniquely differentiated brand based on a little girl, a yellow umbrella and rain slicker, a blue cylindrical container, and a simple branding identity statement: "When it rains it pours." Based on this singular story, Morton's Salt has sustained the power of its brand ever since. Like Morton's Salt, your brand should honestly embody and embellish the story behind the meaning that generates your *differentiation,* establishes your *position,* and underscores your *value.*

Products, defined specifically, are "bundles of attributes" that deliver benefits and values satisfy people's wants or needs and solve their problems. For you these people would generally be clients. This definition of product is purposefully broad. Products are not limited to physical, or tangible, goods. Services, accounting or medical; ideas, liberalism or conservativism; places, The Big Easy or The Big Apple; organizations, such as the Dodgers or Yankees baseball teams; causes, Black Lives Matter or Global Warning; and especially humans—politicians, celebrities or athletes, clergy and all manner of professionals—all can, are, and should be marketed as products. Because these "things" each deliver value. And any value that is deliverable is also differentiable.

Successfully branded products, for example, can persuade actual or prospective clients to like or trust them more than less effectively branded alternatives. Successfully branded professional products induce clients to think of them, first, when problems of the sort that performers from your specific professional field who perform on stages similar to yours are uniquely qualified to resolve arise. This brand-induced is called "top-of-mind awareness."

The practical value of having clients like or trust you more, or think first about your problem-solving proficiency when troubles arise, is difficult to overstate. Particularly insofar as modern clients typically enjoy many other options or alternatives that they could choose to solve their problems.

Well-branded professional products may amass power that makes audiences respect and acquiesce to their requests, sans any need to actually exercise visible power. You, as a well-branded product, may accrue the sort of persuasive power that inspires peers or other audiences to understand their best interests will be served by associating more closely with you or, at least, never pissing you off. In other words, a reputation suggesting that you'd be a great friend, but a worse enemy. Similar to the branding power the U.S. Marine Corps has earned and leveraged so well since "The Corps'" 1770s origin.

This sort of sideways but overpowering benefit— "yea, good guy but don't screw with him/her"—routinely migrates to certain well-branded power players. Each outcome would reflect a huge win for attorney, Certified Public Accountant, physician, professorial, consultancy, political, clergy, business, or social leaders performing in various public and private sectors. Any and all of these professional types would benefit from honing Teddy Roosevelt-like "soft voice, big stick" personae.

Value and Differentiation

Value is best understood as the "problem-solving benefits" you are able to deliver to others, generally clients. If audience members perceive that the values you deliver are "different from" and "better than" comparable values delivered by professionals against whom you compete, you have successfully differentiated your brand. In brief, you are then more likely to win. The ability to achieve and retain favorable differentiation is a key to sustainable branding success.[6] The fundamental outcome sought when you develop and execute personal branding strategies is differentiation. The reason why the well-branded you is more likely to succeed is because you earned favorable differentiation that elevates your value the minds of clients. Your brand would then rise-up toward the top of clients' minds.

Three Ways to Differentiate

Three broad methods exist through which you might earn and sustain a well-differentiated professional brand. First, you can differentiate by creating a branding reputation as a technological leader on your stage. In the decades prior to his death, Steve Jobs wielded this differentiation approach to brand himself as the world's most prodigious and prestigious entrepreneur. Nike, on a corporate branding stage, leverages perceived technological advantages, and has successfully done this for decades. Consequently, the brand name Nike concurrently commands consistently high prices and market shares. High market shares and high prices rarely walk hand in hand. Never happens unless the firm, product or individual in question also "owns" a powerfully persuasive brand.

Second, you can differentiate your branding power by earning a reputation as a low-cost provider who still delivers acceptable levels of quality on your professional stage. Richard Branson leveraged this differentiation strategy when he launched Virgin Airlines in America. Walmart, another corporate brand, has successfully differentiated the benefits and values—the solutions—it delivers based on a low-cost provider strategy.

Third, you can earn sustainable differentiation by creating greater customer intimacy. That is, by establishing stronger, long-term, mutually beneficial and loyal relationships with targeted audience members with whom you share your stage. Close relationships where audiences "understand" that the performer, hopefully you, cares about them and others like them. The sorts of relationships where clients sense, correctly, that you empathically understand the broad nature and exact causes and consequences of their problems. Relationships where clients trust confidently that you will quickly set things even if things temporarily break bad.

By operating on a one-on-one stage this chapter's opening character, Cyrus Curtis, exercised the customer intimacy differentiation method to earn branding advantage in Ms. Alcott's eyes. Yet the behemoth that Steve built, Apple, also illustrates how greater customer intimacy, as a differentiating device, can be wielded to earn tremendous branding advantage on a genuinely global stage. Few other brands can charge customers far more than what the products being marketed are actually worth. Fewer brands still can motivate legions of loyal clients to congregate at midnight anxiously aching to be first to acquire its parent firm's, that would be Apple, latest overpriced item. But other brands exist that clearly have leveraged the power of customer intimacy as a branding and differentiating device. Think *Star Wars* and its span-the-galaxy movie and merchandising franchises. George Lucas's and now Disney's empire earned its branding prowess through the same combination of technological prowess and intimate customer relationships that Apple has exploited so adroitly. By the way: In writing "exploited" we are not castigating but rather elevating and congratulating Mr. Jobs and Mr. Lucas for how well they developed and managed powerful professional brands. And for that matter, Mr. Walt Disney himself.

Other ways exist to earn differentiation. Each differentiation approach, however, exists only as a variation on these three foundational strategies. Which basic approach to achieving differentiation best suits your particular skill sets, personal preferences and biases, and performance stage? Only you know for sure. But when you earn differentiation based on any one of the three bases, you will lay claim to a successful brand. Earn differentiation based on any two of the three differentiation bases, and you'll rock a mega-powerful brand. The simultaneous pursuit of differentiation based on a combination of technological leadership and customer intimacy is logical. As is the concurrent pursuit of low-cost leadership and customer intimacy. Skillfully strategic professional branders may pull off either dynamically differentiating duo.

Few if any professionals, however, could ever achieve technological leadership and low-cost leadership in parallel. The costs in treasure and time required to attain technological advantage are so high that it would neither be possible nor logical to sustain or justify discounted pricing strategies. Once you establish technologically based reputational advantage, for example, you should never "sell-your-ass cheap." Why give away the performance of solutions so powerful that they still "sell" despite their higher costs and concomitantly higher prices?

Positions and Positioning

A position is the mental image audience members develop and hold about specific brands. Your primary positioning goal should be to differentiate your brand by associating it with unique bundles of benefits that will attract and retain key audiences. Those specific benefits first should be developed and then combined such that the resulting bundle of value appeals favorably to substantial portions of your targeted audience. These bundles of professional benefits appeal because they collectively or individually appeal to your core audience. Do these two things, and you will never have to fight a fair fight. By the way, professional branders never want to fight a fair fight, against their competition, that is. The fight won't be fair because yours' will be the far superior brand. And your current and their old clients will realize, respect and react favorably to your differentiating value.

The benefits can be genuine or merely perceptual in nature. To illustrate, think pizza, and the consumer problems that pizza delivery could solve. Dominos wants you to think of its brand first, and to think of it as the best, whenever and wherever problems arise in your life for which the best solution is "professionally delivered" pizza.

Well-conceived brand-based positions can help you secure substantial customer followings, insulate you from competition, and promote your profitability by permitting you to raise prices. When you position, you are creating a personality for your brand. Your branding personality offers a statement that describes clients what you stand for with respect to the most important benefits or solutions you provide. Or perhaps, what you stand against. Politicians and other leaders, for example, frequently make their "branding bones" based as much on what they stand against as what they stand for.

Your branded position exists as a platform from which, you pronounce your "main thing" to audiences; the thing—that is, value or problem-solving acumen—that differentiates you from other professionals:

- Emphasize the thing that merits the best rather than the rest of your time, abilities, and attention.

Consider doing one more thing, please, when positioning your brand. Make sure the "main thing" you emphasize through your branded positioning efforts is important to clients as they make decisions about service providers with whom to engage or remain loyal. If you can achieve this outcome, you may develop the aforementioned "determinant" branding advantages over competitors.

Determinant branding differences are important and meaningful to targeted audiences as they "determine" whether to respect, fear, endure, ignore, or forget you. The presence or absence of determinant differences can make or break the persuasive power of your brand.

Brand positions should never be cast in concrete. Wise people have known forever that when the facts change their opinions should change as well—the words of eminent economist John Maynard Keynes comes to mind first. Need we remind you, there's that top-of-the-mind brand awareness thing, again. So your original position can and should change, particularly if it is not working to differentiate your value. And it frequently should transform across time as market conditions, the appeal of your current brand position, or as the comparative branding images of key competitive brands improve or deteriorate.

Change is inevitable in your, and our, lives. Our progress is not. Change does not always represent progress. But change will always prove necessary for progress to occur. In this case, positioning progress of the sort that eventually gifts you with an increasingly more powerful brand.

Clients Do Positioning Themselves

Clients will position products in their own minds regardless of whether professionals do it for them. But you, as a professional, should attempt to control or manage the process by "doing positioning to clients" before clients "do positioning to you." Many people reading this book are young or youngish. Given this, the Mercedes or Jaguar or even the BMW or Lexus brand likely occupies far more desirable places in your minds than the place the Cadillac brand occupies. This is because the Cadillac brand is generally positioned in the U.S. car-buying "market's mind" as an older person's ride. Which has proven an ongoing problem, now decades in duration, for General Motors. The problem is worsened by the fact that most people don't want to think of themselves as old, even if they are, and surely don't want to be perceived by others as old. Being perceived by others as "too-old, too-fast" is incompatible with most people's ideal view of themselves.

Not surprisingly, most domestic consumers who could afford to don't aspire to roll in a Cadillac, either. Humans generally prefer the new. We love shiny, fresh, and exciting new brands and products. So long, that is, as the new does frighten us too much, which can happen. General Motors' marketing team knows this. The auto marketer has attempted to change Cadillac's positioning station for literally decades. Sans much if any sustainable success. For years General Motors employed the "Not your father's …" repositioning statement for purposes of reinvigorating the Buick brand. The giant might have been better served had it reserved the repositioning phrase for its Cadillac brand.

Exchange

You engage and connect with clients through exchange. Exchange, as a concept, can be defined simply as "a get and a give." What is typically "gotten" through professional exchanges? The value of—the solution provided by—a product. In a professional context, you are this product. A product uniquely equipped to deliver differentiating benefits, values and solutions to your exchange partner—typically is a client.

What is typically "given up" in an exchange? Usually, client money. Meanwhile, superiors, peers, reports or other important publics such as voters or investors with whom you also engage likewise give up other forms of value. Money has great value to most people. But other forms of value might displace money. Clients' or key others' time; trust; attention; endorsement; their compliance or deference; their ideas, advice, and counsel; and so forth come to mind. Depending on the stage and the nature of the professional–client exchange relationship each client "give" might have great value to a branding professional. Regardless, some sort of value must be received by each partner who willingly enters any exchange. *Quid pro quo*. Value for value, always.

The world of marketing is peculiar. Unusual, one might say, insofar as the marketing world freely offers the "feeling of being right" to both buyers and sellers. Simultaneously. Which of course is physically impossible.

"Feeling right" in this context, and more importantly on your professional stage, means that each participant in any buyer–seller exchange must believe [it] gets more value from the relationship than [it] puts in. Each exchange participant must feel it is winning. Most of the time, in fact, "if it did not feel right" to each buying and selling participant, neither would participate.

The same principles apply to your professional stage and to all exchanges in which you engage. Every professional exchange relationship has a buyer, generally your client, and a seller, you. Each participant to an any exchange must generally "feel" like he or she is winning. Otherwise, at least when given the first even reasonably attractive opportunity, neither party will continue to play with the other. Yet on most stages either the buyer or the seller actually is right and the other is wrong to feel right about the just concluded exchange. Why? Because the value taken away from you by the client was less than the amount of value the client gave up to obtain the object of transaction—the solution—you provided. Or because the value you delivered exceeded the value the client gave up to obtain the solution being exchanged. To grow and sustain your brand's power and persuasiveness, take reasonable measures to ensure clients walk away feeling they have "won." This simple tact will always prove a winning brand hand.

Exchange is the core concept of marketing. Exchange is also the core relational building block for all relationships. Absent exchange, no professionals, business dealings or economy, government, technology or life on earth would exist. Think exchange—of an egg and sperm cell—and grasp the implications of the last phrase in the preceding sentence.

Everything you do to manage your brand on your professional stage should be done mindful of the need to create exchange relationships with prospects or other key audience members if an exchange relationship did not previously exist. Or, when a professional relationship already existed, everything done related to your professional brand should be motivated by your need to strengthen and sustain that exchange relationship. The long-term success of your brand is predicated on nothing less and nothing more. Your ability to generate, administer, and sustain relationships in ways that suit (satisfy) clients' and your own ends is foundational to branding success.

Value

Value should always be defined through the perspective of actual or prospective clients. Value is the ratio between the benefits clients get (receive) from you and the costs clients must give up in order to obtain those benefits. Products deliver benefits. The benefits you deliver satisfy client wants or needs and provide solutions. The solutions you provide generate perceived value in clients' eyes because these solutions solve client problems.

View yourself as a need satisfier and problem solver. Position your brand and its value that way, too. That's all you are, anyway, if you are a successful professional. Your ability to satisfy needs and solve problems better than your competitors or counterparts is absolutely enough to ensure your success. (That is, assuming you are not a total ass.) Usually, you should brand yourself in a similar fashion. Truth be told:

- In the views of even loyal clients you are little more or less than a problem solver. Stop satisfying client needs? Fail to solve their pressing problems better than other professional providers? How long will your erstwhile loyal clients stick around?

Conduct your professional life in constant accord with the embedded values prescribed by this perspective, and you can develop a powerfully persuasive brand. Ignore its simple counsel? Your struggle to be, become or remain powerfully persuasive will likely prove quite a struggle. Perhaps one that proves insurmountable.

Ceterus paribus means "if everything remains else equal." Ceterus paribus, targeted audiences always choose the professional that they perceive delivers the most value to them. And clients will remain loyal to you only as long as they perceive you still deliver the most value. And why not? These are professional relationships, not marriages. But isn't most of what we have written about branding advantages that effective "value-delivery" inspire also true of the health and sustainability of marriages?

Speaking of Relationships

Relationships play out for better or worse on any stage where you engage in any form of value exchange with one or more actual or potential clients. Sometimes the relationships play out well. At other times, poorly. These relationships are inseparable from the stages on which you as a professional perform and exchanges with your clients occur. Professional performances occur inside churches, synagogues, mosques, or temples. Performances unfold inside and outside classrooms, courtrooms, or examination rooms. Professionals perform inside corporate, health care, or governmental settings. Performances are delivered in the context of one-on-one exchanges. They might unfurl as one brand interacting with, say, 110 million sets of eyeballs. Carefully staged Katy Perry; Janet Jackson, she of the "wardrobe malfunction,"; or U2 Super Bowl performances, anyone?

Back to Brands ...

When successful, traditional brands help customers. The presence of trusted, reliable, and/or high-performing brands simplifies customer decision making in a world inundated with too many choices.

Successful brands help you. Again, primarily because the presence of successful brands simplify client decision making in a now globally accessible world inundated with choices. A primary task, when branding, is to manage your brand in ways that simplify client decision making on crowded and noisy stages full of other shiny objects purposefully designed or positioned to lure client attention away from you. No, we did not just repeat ourselves. Simplify client decision making by making them preemptively choose your brand, remain loyal to your brand and your problem-solving value.

Successful professional brands—yours'?—help clients. Brands help clients identify specific professional products as being distinct from and better than other professional products. Again, yours? When you execute the branding process successfully, the act, your branding performance, induces audiences to associate certain preplanned positive, intriguing or perhaps even threatening sets of expectations about you, your performance; and the type, nature and scope of the values (solutions) you will develop and deliver.

Absent branding, clients cannot easily compare one professional alternative against other options. Absent branding, then, the decision-making processes of your audience members become more time-consuming, difficult, and costlier. If you brand yourself and your value proposition successfully you improve (add value) the lives of prospective or actual clients by simplifying their decision making. Over time, your brand's amplified power and persuasiveness metaphorically says: "Choose me, right now, every time. And then you can relax."

Loyalty to your brand hopefully develops over time. The presence of loyalty again simplifies customers' lives. Loyalty frees up clients' time. No need to waste time evaluating alternative professional providers. Loyalty lowers nonfinancial costs that clients incur. As noted no need exists to worry or stress over those specific decisions or problems anymore. Instead; clients can find something else new to worry about. All the while, as clients feel like they are winning, you'll be winning as well.

Traditional brands affixed on products (or labels or packaging; or storefronts, parking lots, songs or jingles; or taglines, signs, words, etc.) tell prospective and actual customers what to expect from branded products. Traditional brands evoke meanings and associations. A well-branded professional "product," you, could be positioned as more efficient, proficient, effective, dependable, resolute, brilliant, creative, prestigious, technologically advanced, appropriately priced, lovable, sexy, funny, cute, and so on, than other professionals. Literally, your call to make. These evoked meanings and associations assist clients when they evaluate alternative professional product's value. Established and/or trusted professional brands function as "insurance" policies. Insurance that lowers customers' sense of risk or fear. Risks and fears that otherwise might burden and inhibit audiences as they consider interacting with professionals and purchasing their products. Burden and inhibit prospective clients to the point where sometimes they choose to choose nothing at all.

Brands ought to benefit professionals every bit as much as well-managed and well-positioned brands benefit marketers. Well-managed traditional or professional brands permit firms or professionals to develop client loyalty and raise or sustain higher prices. Don't just "Think Different," riffing Apple's memorable late 1990s branding overture. You should actually be different. Different in ways that first benefit your clients, then your brand, and ultimately yourself.

But let's "Think Apple," for a moment. Specifically, about Apple's influential "Think Different" branding campaign. The campaign featured images of Mahatma Gandhi, Martin Luther King, Jr., Albert Einstein, and John Lennon. All four men had been "1960s-era" icons. Each "hero-brand" well-earned reputations for integrity, even on stages where their integrity exposed them to great risk and turmoil. Adding to their and Apple's branding pathos, three of them had been martyred by assassin bullets.[7]

The manipulative power of "Think Different," as a branding message, was stunning. Apple's branding power initially took flight at this time. Since that time, the momentum of this branding power alone has enabled Steve Job's entrepreneurial love child to develop unparalleled loyalty and sustain extremely high customer prices.

Successful brands make it easier for marketers to introduce new products. Successful professional brands make it easier for you to introduce yourself. This is especially true when potential clients already vicariously know, trust and like you as a result of their or others' prior positive experience with your brand.

Well-managed brands provide formidable barriers against successful imitation. Powerful brands make it difficult for rivals to copy or dissipate the stronger brand's competitive advantage.

End Like We Began

Yes, we already said this. But the point is so important to you that we say it again. Two primary ingredients are essential for success in most business arenas:

- First, brands. And, second, effectively delivering the problem-solving promises made by to carefully targeted audiences. The central problem associated with building determinant brands and delivering them effectively to audiences is getting complicated business organizations to execute based on such a simple idea.

Does anyone believe that the two key success prerequisites for individual professionals—assuming they have acquired the knowledge, proficiencies and skill sets required to succeed on their respective stages—would materially differ? Cyrus Vance clearly did not believe this. We don't either. The problem, however, remains the same as the quandary presented in this chapter's introductory quote. Namely: Getting highly intelligent people like you to execute based on such a simple idea. Ready to learn more about how to do this?

Notes

1 Gladwell, Malcolm (2008). *Outliers.* New York: Brown, Little.
2 Goffman, Erving (1959). *The Presentation of Self in Everyday Life.* New York, NY: Anchor Books.
3 Shanahan, John M. (1999). *The Most Brilliant Thoughts of All Time (In Two Lines or Less).* New York, NY: HarperCollins Press.
4 Pinter, Harold (2011). Harold Pinter's Poetry: The Known and Unknown. *The Economist.* August 20, 2011.
5 Grobel, Lawrence (2006). *Al Pacino: The Authorized Biography.* New York, NY: Simon and Schuster.
6 Strutton, David and Kenneth Thompson (2015). *Marketing from Scratch: The Principles you really Need to Know.* Dubuque, IA: Kendall-Hunt Publishing Company.
7 Altstiel, Tom and Jean Grow (2005). *Advertising Strategy: Creative Tactics from the Outside/In.* London: Sage Publishing, Inc.

CHAPTER 6
Planning to Develop a Powerful Brand

"Strategy entails getting more out of a situation that the starting balance of power would suggest. Strategy encompasses the art of creating power"

—Sir Lawrence Freedman (1948–?).

Emu and kangaroos are both native to Australia. The emu is a large flightless bird. Imagine a less attractive ostrich with a larger tail. There you've got it. The better known, or is it better-branded, kangaroo is a large marsupial that boasts powerful oversized hind legs. Females "roos" feature a pouch for their young. The latter beast has long been identified as lovable and cute. The more obscure Emu is hardly identifiable at all. Yet each is featured on Australia's Coat of Arms, which functions as the nation's formal branding symbol.

The reason why each animal is prominently displayed as part of the proud Australia's brand is important, relevant to this Chapter's theme, and driven by one brand-worthy trait each seemingly disparate animal shares. The trait in question: neither creature can take a single step backward. Each animal is straight-ahead, all-forward, all-the-time. Just like the worldview, beliefs, values and national strategies that pervade throughout these animals' native country. Australia is absolutely resolute in its strategic commitment to economic growth, self-improvement, cultural-preservation, and national progress. While Australia pays all respect due to its iconic past (the country really was settled by British prisoners and their guards), the nation similarly remains utterly committed to moving forward. Hence, Australia's strategic branding homage to two animals that can only move forward makes perfect sense.

Branding strategies similarly should outline where nations, organizations or individual professionals are going, how they will get there, and what will be accomplished after arrival. Strategies, of any sort, are all about growth, moving forward, laying out and executing a road map to get there. The sort of scripts, if you will, that would permit professionals to achieve their goals. Here, naturally, branding goals.

The Value of Planning

World War II Supreme Allied Commander and former U.S. President Dwight D. Eisenhower wrote: "Plans are nothing, but planning is everything." "Ike's" (his humanizing branded identity) statement implies that plans rarely work out how they're supposed to on paper. As a well-known military axiom reveals, "No plan survives the first smoke of battle."[1] Or, as former heavyweight boxing champion Mike Tyson bluntly said: "Everybody's got a plan until he gets punched in the nose." All three quotes are germane on your stage insofar as circumstances, opportunities or threats change constantly; mistakes are frequently made; and enemies, competitors, clients, reports, superiors, and peers often fail to respond the way you anticipated. And then suddenly or slowly you find yourself having to seduce, negotiate with, or fight your audience members all over again. When this happens, may the branding force be with you.

But these naturally arising conditions do not undermine the inherent value of brand planning. One major reason is because deciding to plan your brand forces consideration of alternate brand identities or other recovery contingencies to pursue if your script doesn't work out as planned. The true value of brand planning is not that enviable results somehow automatically or seamlessly arrive just because you've done it. This outcome would be unusual. Instead the brand-planning act is valuable because the resulting script generates actionable knowledge. First, greater insights about your core strengths, weaknesses, and competencies. Strengths you should ethically exploit. Weaknesses you should work-around or strengthen. Competencies you should build upon. Second, actionable insights are developed about opportunities and threats that loom or already exist on your relevant stage, among key audiences or audience members, or within the larger professional marketplace in which you perform.

These actionable insights often prove your ultimate asset, weapon of choice, and source of truly sustainable advantage on contemporary professional stages. Or, your "secret sauce," if you happen to be a fast food professional. These insights should materially contribute to your brand-based power and persuasion, regardless of what happens as your branding script is executed.

The act of brand planning requires you to take a look around-inside your head. Engaging in the sort of honest and likely critical self-assessments that always challenges and occasionally hurts. As in, hurts your feelings or sense of self-worth. But this sort of pain is temporary. By contrast the cost of your "brand sucks" or, more likely, being less valuable than it could be if you don't conduct this self-assessment, is forever. Brand planning also demands that you look outward, externally, toward the various stages on which they perform. And then to look outward further away from those stages to factors that reside beyond them. Environmental factors that will influence for better or worse what happens on your stage.

This sort of inside-out planning effort is generally necessary for branding scripts to succeed. That's because the branding strengths or weaknesses you are seeking to "identify and then exploit or work-around" exist inside you. Meanwhile, the branding opportunities and threats you seek to "identify and then exploit or work-around" exist on your stage, within your professional sector, among your audience, perhaps throughout the world.

These environmental opportunities and threats would be present even if the professional you did not exist. You cannot create or change such opportunities or threats. But this fact does not detract from the branding advantage you can gain and presumably maintain if you identify and react to newly found opportunities and threats before your competitors or clients even know they exist. And then make prescience – a forward-looking visage – your habit.

Speaking of habits, William James, the philosopher, wrote:

- "The intelligence of humans is inseparable from our reliance on habit. Habits allow us to reserve brain power for things that cannot be predicted in advance, situations without relevant cues. Those are the circumstances we actually need to think about. Habits cover everything else."[2]

If you substitute the words "planning" for "habits" and "brand power" for "brain power" in James' quote, we quickly see that "habits" are worth discussing. Adopting the convention of planning your branding efforts is a good habit for you to develop. And once you begin to brand, planning and then re-planning your brand hopefully becomes a hard habit to break.

Two Mistakes to Avoid

While "performing" out their brand identities on stages, even stages they designed, professionals routinely make two mistakes. First:

- We often struggle and fail because we attempt to control the uncontrollable.

Second, and ironically:

- We often fail to control the things we could control.

One action item you can always control is whether you elect to create branding strategies designed to help you manage the progression of your career. Or, related to this book's context, whether develop you the sort of script-a plan-that will enhance your prospects for generating a powerful brand, and thereafter actually performing in accordance with your script.

Developing business, marketing or professional-branding strategies inevitably proves useful. Again, regardless of whether the plan completely succeeds or fails. The reason why is that a decision to plan, to script out, your anticipated branding performance:

- Encourages you to engage in systematic and forward-looking thinking related to how you currently are and one day could be branded.
- Forces you to create, clarify, and prioritize branding goals.
- Leads to more efficient coordination of your branding efforts. You may struggle to determine how best to allocate your finite stores of time-based, talent-based, and treasure-based resources. But new knowledge and actionable insights emerge from such struggles.
- Increases the probability that you identify the "right things to perform," perform "those right things right," and build your brand based on "those right things.
- Provides a safe harbor for you to engage in "possibility thinking." What sort of branding possibilities should you ponder? For starters: What "unusual" but potentially "determinant" new brand values could I possibly pursue?

Counsel from the Hardwood

The legendary University of California, Los Angeles basketball coach John Wooden wrote: "Failing to plan is like planning to fail."[3] The implication:

- Do you want to ensure branding failure? Then don't plan your brand.

The lesson is clear. View your brand-management plans, once you have created them, as an indispensable professional and personal resource. An asset that every self-respecting and self-interested professional should mindfully create.

Coach Wooden was known for sweating the details. So much so that the first thing he taught players during their first practice each season was how to put on their socks: Three pair, cotton inside and out, and nylon in-between. The second lesson demonstrated how to execute a simple chest pass. When planning your brand, you should similarly sweat the details.

Coach Wooden taught players to "move fast, but with patience." His admonition should likewise apply to your branding strategies and behaviors. Particularly when unique and likely ethereal opportunities are identified that you can exploit through your strengths. Situations where you must act now or say goodbye to that "ship" forever, because it won't return. Wooden's advice similarly would apply to threats you should preemptively seek to avoid. Hazards that left unattended might damage your branding reputation, or worse. All because one or more hazards aligned with comparative weaknesses you have yet to correct.

Coach Wooden is closely associated with another historical quote that actually originated with Mr. Wilson Mizner. The quote: "Be nice to the people you are passing on the way up because you are likely to see them on your way back down." We don't exactly know how to integrate the insight into this discussion. But wise, which also implies forward-looking, professionals clearly should honor its premise.

Brand Strategy Is ...

We view the worlds plan and strategy as synonymous. The word "strategy," however, is derived from the ancient Greek *strategos,* which meant military commander. The military reference still fits because successful branding strategies share much in common with successful military campaigns. Effective military or professional-branding campaigns require judicious utilization of inevitably scarce resources; the presence of an opponent, competitor, or enemy as well as actual and potential partners; and a relentless commitment to do what is necessary or appropriate to seize or defend terrain. Yes, terrain, described earlier as desirable "positions" or "places" inside the collective or individual minds of audiences.

Effective strategies permit planning units to secure more value from contested situations than the original balance of power suggested was possible. The strategic unit could be the U.S. Marine Corps. It could be Australia, a huge nation with a small population; only about 23 million human souls. But the Aussie brand clearly punches above its weight on global stages. Or the strategic unit could be you planning to create a favorably differentiated brand.

Strategy entails the art and act of creating power. Brand strategies are where your vision for a well-branded branded future and the actions you plan to initiate to eventually arrive in this desirable place intersect. No one can fully predict their futures. However, you enjoy an opportunity and have the means available to create a future more to your liking. But only if you effectively script and execute your plan. In today's professional world if you are not moving forward as a consequence of your new or renewed branding strategy, you're actually falling behind. The confluence of negative environment events described earlier will punish most professionals who fail to build their actual or perceived branding value on an ongoing basis.

Branding strategies, as noted, should outline where you intend to go with your brand, the specific tactics you intend to use to get there, and what will be accomplished after you arrive. Strategies, in all forms, focus on growth, moving forward, and laying out a roadmap or, on your stage, a script that permits planning entities to achieve their goals. Focusing effectively is important to many practical endeavors. The ability to focus is, well, a skill set upon which you should focus. And learn, if you haven't already done so. We describe "focus" as the ability to pay attention to the few things that matter most while paying zero or little attention to things don't matter, or matter less.

Professional of Action; Professional of Thought

The acid test for the success or failure of any branding strategy:

- If you knew then what you understand now would you still pursue the same branding approach?

That's nice, but you may be thinking: so what?. The "so what" is that you should plan now, in the present, as if you were looking back from the future toward what happened and did not happen in your past. Are you ready and willing to think forward while planning deliberately in the present as you develop and then execute your brand?

Seek balance and deliberation while developing and executing your branding strategies. A Coach Wooden-like "move quickly, but with patience," right? But never so patiently that it takes 2 hours for you to watch *60 Minutes.* Professional brand-management games are generally performed on stages that reward patience and a balance between action and thought. As you develop and manage a more desirable brand identity you should think like a person of action but act like a person of thought. Stated bluntly: When planning to develop your version of an ideal brand identity seek a balanced identity. Perhaps your branded identity could split the difference between brains, or thoughtfulness, and balls, or audacity. Or stated more delicately: Be cautious about the passions you portray through your brand.

But stay passionate. Passion, best branded-out as directional consistency. Passion, as reflected in your willingness to stick resolutely to an overarching goal-here, growing the power and persuasiveness of your brand-across the years. Your passions matter. Embed and display them as you perform out your brand identity.

Winston Churchill, a man branded as the British Lion, is by anyone's measure one of the twentieth century's two or three most persuasive leaders. Throughout a publically professional life spanning 50+ years, Sir Winston constantly displayed effectively equal measures of brains and balls. Or was Churchill displaying thoughtfulness and passion? Surprised his branding power redounds to this day?

As does the brand of the still youthful Taylor Swift, at essentially an infinitely less consequential level. Her contemporary musical brand continues to dominate like no other save Adele and Beyonce due to the risky but still logical branding choices Ms. Swift and her handlers have instituted. Truth be said, however, the ballsy but brilliant branding moves that Beyonce has recently shaken out merit a discussion all their own.

Confucius, writing around 500 BC, recognized the need to achieve an equilibrium between pursuing measured risks and acting with appropriate caution. In a classic teaching moment the Chinese sage sarcastically called out a contemporary: "Chi Wen Tzu always thought three times before taking action. Twice would have been quite enough."[4]

One thing is clear about whatever branding strategy you develop and pursue. Or even the strategy that you elect to never develop or pursue. If you insist on understanding with perfect clarity before deciding to do either, you will never decide to pursue anything at all.

The Professional Brand-Planning Process

The professional brand-planning process is deceptively simple. Presumably because the process features just three basic steps. They are:

- *Analyzing branding opportunities*: Opportunity analysis entails identifying where the best prospects for you to differentially brand your values reside. As the analytical step begins you should realize and accept that you cannot be all things to all people. No branded product has ever existed whose values could satisfy everyone's wants or needs and also be affordable—again, to everyone. Sure, all clients would prefer Ferrari-level legal or managerial consultative advice. But how many can afford or are willing to pay $375,000 to $800,000 to attain either? Some clients actually can, of course, but most cannot. Consequently, you must construct and thereafter carefully target you branding identities and values.
- *Selecting target audiences:* The targeting process entails identifying various audiences you are best equipped to target, pursue and serve effectively. Your actual ability to deliver on the promises inherent in your brand to satisfy a particular audience member's unmet needs or unresolved problems should be kept foremost in your mind as you specifically identify who will be targeted with your messages. Every branding promise you make represents a pledge. Your brand promise is a guarantee, issued to every relevant stakeholder, about the value or values you will always deliver.
- *Developing and executing branding initiatives*: This step requires that you decide how best to manage your actions, words, behaviors, and artefactual evidence in order to create and deliver the most appealing sorts of value to the audiences you target.

Creating Desirable Brand Identities

Before drawing brand-planning lessons from Goffman's dramaturgical framework, let's specify more precisely what desirable branding impressions might entail. Should you develop brand identifiers that project selfless and virtuous brand imagery? Position as one who is never emotionally reactive but instead is always thoughtfully responsive to clients' and other audience members' wants, needs, and problems? Should your brand identifiers primarily project competence and proficiency? Should the brand identifiers you pursue speak directly to your conscientious, flexible or accommodating nature? Or should they project you as a persistently ruthless jerk? Given that 10%–20% of the population are jerks, anyway,[5] the last branding identifier is not farfetched. In some professions it might take a jerk to counter, defend against, or destroy a jerk. Beyond even those extremes, times, stages and circumstances exist where the reputation as a "jerk" might serve your interests.

No one best answer exists to these questions. Each character "trait" referenced above is worthy, or could prove worthy, in its own right on the right stage. Meaning: The potential branding attractiveness of each branding identity will vary depending on the stage on which you perform.

When possible, your brand should be positioned based on your natural or acquired core traits and strengths. But only if those strengths "play well" on stages germane to your success. Any professional's branding reputation is reflected in how important audience members would predict, explain and generally accept or reject their judgment, knowledge and behaviors as valuable and genuine across different contexts. Stated more simply, your value is created only through your perceived usefulness to clients. Your branding reputation signifies exactly the type of value that clients can expect to receive from you, the provider.

Other branding "identities" exist that you should likely avoid. Name, claim, and then ban them. Recall the Old Testament story describing how Samson killed 10,000 Philistines with the jawbone of an ass? Who knows how many potential deals or client relationships have been slaughtered using the same device? Few clients have the time or desire to endure overly long, meandering or weak-kneed presentations. On the other hand, performances that are relevant and resolutely on-point contribute would universally contribute to more powerfully persuasive brand identities.

Keep Promises

Professional promises are made all the time. And sometimes broken. Professionals perform in staged roles that frequently span organizational, client, or bureaucratic boundaries. They thus routinely encounter temptations to speak or behave in ways that convey or display less than whole truths. When that happens, avoidably damaging branding images may result.

On the other hand, the task of developing and managing desirable branding identities, regardless of how many boundaries are spanned, can prove straightforward. As may the task of identifying the desirable stories your brand should "tell." But only when you properly script and then perform out your brand, based on that script.

"Under-promising" and "over-delivering" in relation to the values or solutions that you create and deliver is a broadly accepted path to desirable branding outcomes. The opportunity to develop a more persuasively powerful brand identify resides among these desirable outcomes. The pursuit of an "I'll try harder" branding identity similarly makes sense, especially when the means through which you "perform" the "I'll try" statement is authentic. Again, when you are keeping your promise. Such authenticity directly implies you would initiate vigorous efforts to do or make things right for your clients should something go wrong. This branding identity clearly could prove determinant. For as every client knows, something eventually will go wrong.

The degree to which you are or feel connected to your firm may make your branding identity indistinguishable from the identity projected by your firm. Should you be more concerned about the images you project as an individual, or those you project on behalf of your firm? The question can never be answered definitively. But you surely should avoid placing yourself in or remain noncommittal in brand—able situations where you speak for your organization knowing the possibility eixsts that it will not back up your brand commitments. That is, unless you are also your firm, which is possible. Promising anyone anything and delivering it late or never is worse than not having made the commitment in the first place. "Anything" could include a call, an appointment, a document, a solution, confidentially, or wise counsel. Be more concerned about the brand images you cultivate and project for yourself rather than as a member of organizations. Your ultimate loyalty should be to your family and brand rather than to any organization, even if you own the organization.

Address Cultural Differences

When developing your brand identity, address and accommodate overt and subtle cultural differences that might separate you from your audience if you failed to consider and prepare for them. The challenges associated with formulating and managing desirable branding images varies across cultural stages. Branding impressions that would be highly valued in some cultures may be *verboten* in others.

Not ironically, because its existence is historically and culturally logical, an entire branding industry exists in China whose sole purpose is to "save face." Namely the "face" of its clients, by issuing apologies on behalf of those third parties. The notion of saving face is critical to relational and business success across Chinese-dominated Asian cultures.[6] The act of "saving face" can be motivated by a desire to avoid humiliation or embarrassment or to maintain the dignity or preserve the reputation of one's client.

Or consider that in some nations, Germany, for instance, when you request something be done, it happens. No follow-up required. Sounds good to us.

Other cultural differences may off-putting. Such as, for example, how different cultures interpret time. If you invite associates to a 5:00 PM meeting, your guests will consider it polite to arrive on the dot in Germany, 5 minutes early in Wisconsin, 30 minutes early in Japan, up to 1 hour late in Italy, and some time that evening in Greece.

Strategic branding minds, however, should knowingly avoid "don't care about your saving your face" or "too early/too late" emotional responses. Because nothing untoward is happening on either stage. What happened, instead, is a logical response to broadly accepted convention in either culture. When you commit to managing your branding identity, no reasonable option exists other than conforming yourself, your expectations, and your brand image management activities for purposes of accommodating the culturally driven behaviors, beliefs, norms and values that other-cultured clients bring to the relationship. That is, unless you happen to own and consequently dominate the stage. But even then branding professionals should tread cautiously. After all, a stage you currently dominate may soon be dominated by the client you are now offending.

Another cultural issue should be considered: Once you remove or lower ethnocentric, subcultural, or regional blinders by "growing your understanding" as opposed to "building the resentment of others," various attractive opportunities to create more vibrant brands may emerge. You then might pursue those opportunities. New knowledge is new power, after all.

No Longer Globalizing

As explained, the professional world is no longer globalizing. Globalization has arrived. The professions are evolving at genuinely unprecedented rates. Myriad stages are now experiencing inexorable changes.

These two "conclusions" collectively speak directly to the need that you will likely encounter to adapt and change continuously. The changes that you encounter in your profession or its relevant environment will not always represent progress. But your acceptance, understanding and eventual mastery of those changes will always prove necessary for your progress to occur. As you brand accept your profession's or environment's as manageable challenges and renewable opportunities to create or re-create thriving brands, if you make good choices. Think otherwise, or ignore changes, and you may view "extinction" from where you are standing.

You will constantly encounter opportunities in which you may need to make substantial sacrifice or shoulder ample risks in order to successfully manage the branding impressions that others form about you. Channeling an old Ringo Starr song, successful brands "Don't Come Easy." Were the branding process otherwise, more professionals would distinguish the value of their service offerings successfully through branding initiatives. But because something is difficult does mean it is impossible or not worth doing. The returns in value that you can recoup from judiciously expending strategic branding efforts can prove career-altering. Situations routinely arise in which commoditized professionals are segregated into winner or loser categories simply through their commitment and ability to pay whatever price is necessary. But never commit to prices that require you to expense your soul or psychological well-being.

Monitor Impressions Created by Your Branding Initiatives

Your branding initiatives never exist or unfold in vacuums. You must keep all promises made while also accounting for cross cultural differences, as you have read. But the success or failure of your branding efforts will also pivot based on the effectiveness with which you discern signals emitted by your audience as they respond implicitly or explicitly to your branding performance. Brand impression monitoring will permit you to remain cognizant of and responsive to how your verbal, nonverbal and/or symbolic expressions are influencing how audience members' perceive you.[7]

Two basic steps are involved in impression monitoring. First, closely listen to and observe targets to discern how well your branding impression initiatives are being received in both the immediate and much longer term. Second, audience members you target may be engaging in brand-management activities of their own. Account for that possibility, as well.

Brand impression monitoring activities are similar in intent to the environmental scanning activities that ideally precede and sustain successful strategic planning efforts executed at corporate levels. The general goal of corporate environmental scanning is to identify external factors, such as unmet customer wants/needs, or trends moving in favor of or against a firm's best interests. This same basic premise applies to you and your branding efforts. When you monitor the branding impressions your performance is eliciting among audiences, you hopefully will quickly ascertain which brand images audience members are enjoying, and which they are merely enduring. If they're enjoying the image, keep going. If audiences are enduring, stop digging. At that point you should find it easier to add to, subtract from, edit, or renew your branding script in ways that reinforce positive or mitigate negative audience impressions.

One substantive strategic branding question remains: How best to manage the brand images and impressions that important others develop about you?

Account for the Other Side of Your Brand-Impression-Management Efforts

When you seek to "lead" targeted audiences toward any specific response to your branding initiatives, a predictable dynamic begins. This iterative process changes the nature and course of the interactions between you and targeted audience members. First, the attributions that targeted audience members ascribe to your performance behaviors are affected by how you frame your persuasion attempt. Attributions are best understood as perceptual interpretations that are not necessarily accurate or factual but are treated as if they were by the person making the attributions.

Then, based on the attributions they form, audience members decide whether to lean-in-toward or away from you and your brand. Ultimately, targeted audience members chose whether to comply with the response you are seeking. Or reject your persuasive attempt.

A specific client's rejection may be more implicit rather than explicit in nature. The longer-term consequences of a client's implicit rejection may be more deleterious than the outcomes associated with an explicit rejection. Primarily, this is because you then might not sense that anything is the net of this non-outcome, of course, is that you would fail to pursue ameliorative actions.

If you fail to monitor the immediate or longer-term consequences of you influence attempts, you are only dealing with one side of the branding management equation. During impression-driven exchanges, be a discriminating listener and astute observer of the effects your branding efforts have on targets. Make "sense" of the branding impressions your audience is developing about your performance and value.

When you encounter others face to face on stages that you should control, the looks in their eyes, their facial expressions, the lean of their bodies, how closely they are willing to approach you, and the anxious or relaxed character of their gestures will be revealed. As is, more significantly on your stage, their level of receptivity to your impression-making overtures. Attend carefully to these readily apparent cues.

To sophisticated listeners, the tone and rate of a target's voice and speech can become unerring and is rather easily read. If your target's reactions signal they are not "happily" catching the values you are pitching, a change of pace, new branding tactics, may prove useful. Henry Ford would agree, saying: "If there is any secret to marketing success, it lies in the ability to get the other person's point of view and see things from his angle as well as your own."[8]

Always demonstrate respect toward targeted audience members by listening carefully to them. Do so, whenever possible and reasonable, sans interruption or criticism. This studied approach to listening represents a universally appropriate starting point in interactive one-on-one or one-on-small-group branding processes. Generally, the more you talk, the less likely it becomes that your subsequent personal branding impressions will prove favorable. If nothing else, the fact that humans feature two ears and only one mouth supports validates this advice.

You willingness to listen will not ensure that rapport is established between the performing you and your clients or other audience members. But beyond question your first key to establishing rapport with others is paying attention to them. When you listen acutely to others, others "feel felt"; they feel "valued," and are far more likely to attune to you because they "feel" you first "tuned-in" to them.

One of the most important questions the "branding you"-or for matter, any businessperson-can ask is: What is the other guy, my targeted audience, thinking? Whether your firm is Amazon, OPEC, Burger King, or you are simply you, so much pivots on the answer. Setting prices, negotiating costs, determining supply levels, creating or altering core branding messages, strategies and tactics are but a few examples. To succeed in business, life, and branding initiatives professionals need to reckon, divine or simply listen deeply enough to determine what is happening in other people's minds. Especially when what is happening is other person's mind is critical to their success. Trust us, it is.

Listening more effectively simultaneously permits you to make more sense of the branding impressions the other person is managing or developing. And to adjust your professional presentation, performance, or provision of solutions accordingly. Listening ineffectively, or perhaps not at all, creates conversations in which people feel unheard; makes conversations louder; and renders them less productive. Absent good listening productivity, more specifically the opportunity to engage more productively with clients, is lost. At that point, your diminished brand would be just one unnecessary victim.

No one has ever criticized anyone for being a great listener. Instead once you are branded reputation-ally as a "good listener," presumably because you cultivated the willingness and skill sets to listen effectively, people will eventually share information, insights and perhaps even feelings with you. Their sharing "gifts" you with actionable knowledge. The cliché that knowledge is power is more than cliche. It is fact. Consequently, the more you listen better the more your brand will become powerfully persuasive.

To build branding power, say less than necessary, when possible. The ancient Chinese philosopher Lao Tzu underscored this principle when he wrote: Those who know do not speak; those who speak do not know. Other notables have risen to the top by saying less and listening more. 1920s-era President Calvin Coolidge, for example, famously opined: "Nothing I never said ever did me any harm." Were today's politicians more reserved they just might be more persuasive.

Professional-Branding Strategies: Basic Rules

Everyone must master specific profession-related principals or fundamentals before they can achieve sustainable excellence in their chosen endeavor. Principles or fundamentals tell us what works in specific professional domains.

Rules, by contrast, tell us what to do or not to do. Rules keep our behaviors, if not our thoughts, inbounds. Rules operate similar to how child bumpers function to keep kids' balls out of bowling alley gutters. Rules also permit us to more easily discriminate right from wrong decisions. Once you understand profession-or situation-specific rules, you are prepared to choose right more readily than wrong. Nothing but upside could ever follow from that outcome.

Ten professional-branding rules to follow:

- *Rule 1: "Be" Your Brand Rather Than "Seem" Your Brand*-This first rule may conjure images of Chevy Chase's character Ty Webb putting, "be the ball," on the 1980s movie *Caddyshack's* golf course greens. But "to be" rather than "to seem," in all things branding, is among our strongest counsel. This rule underscores that any brand identity that you choose to create should be firmly grounded in reality. Whatever you "say" about your brand should be real rather as opposed to merely appearing authentic. No jokes about faking it until you are making it, here. Never position yourself as a supposed expert in any arena when the truth is you have seen the movie but never read the book. Actually be the expert you purport to be through your branded messaging. Be the one who understands the related history, texts and contexts, and sources of information that provide or carry more information, more texture, facts, and subtly. You should even aspire to understand points of view that diverge from those that diverge from how you think. When brand building, never freelance. Instead you should build a strategically bundled branding identity that is as coherent and complete as possible.
- *Rule 2: Craft, Portray, and Polish Your Brand for Posterity*-Whatever branding identity you pursue should be carefully crafted, publically portrayed, and polished for posterity. Any branding identity you pursue should directly or indirectly answer one question: What solution or satisfaction would my clients lack if the values I create and deliver did not exist? All the while, never forget that the most dangerous position for any brand to occupy is "stuck in the middle." To be stuck in the middle is to brand absent any obvious or perceived cost, relational or technological advantage. No wonder Texans claim the only things found in the middle of the road are yellow lines and dead armadillos. Yes, we could have substituted "professionals" for "armadillos."
- *Rule 3: Choose Love or Hate*-Top-flight, hard-nosed professionals-you?-sometimes must decide whether they would rather be loved for what they are *not* or hated, feared, or respected for what they are? Would you rather be respected for what you are not, because you elected to create a fictional brand? Or respected for what you are, because you established a factual brand? These are not false choices. Rather, they are decisions that you inevitably must make. Why not decide early? Choose carefully, because your choices define who you are and what you will become, brand identity-wise.
- *Rule 4: Play Chess; Exercising Patience While Achieving Balance*-When playing chess, experts always think two or three steps ahead. When playing branding games, experts always think two or three promotions up. Professional branding strategies are far more chess than checkers. Well-branded professional lives play out as staged performances that reward patience and balance. Your actions, particularly seemingly ad-libbed behaviors, should underscore the degree to which you think like a person of action but act like a person of thought. Act

out your brand based on this general premise. Soon enough, favorable audience perceptions should coalesce around your brand.

- *Rule 5: Branding Success Requires Repeating, Repetition, and Redundancy*-Sounds boring. But it is not. There is a critical difference between repeating, repetition, and redundancy. Turn over, essentially rotating, key dimensions of your core branding identity through what you do, say or display. Or by what you don't do, say or display. Across time multiple facets of your brand's meaning will be revealed repetitively but not redundantly to even tangentially attentive audience members. Your branding mission is to compose a beautifully appealing lifelong symphony, as opposed to a five verse, 3-minute long pop song. And fortunately, as an accomplished but perhaps not widely acclaimed professional you have far more than seven notes of music to aggregate. And, then, once aggregated, to repetitively but not redundantly and then mix, match and manage as you build a long-lived brand. A brand long-lived enough that you will actually confront the need to remix, rematch, and reaggregate it.
- *Rule 6: Take Measured Risks*-You can take chances when creating your brand, so long as no outlie lies or misrepresentations arise as you message. Sometimes, the only difference between branding truth and fiction is that the branded fiction must appear believable. During New England's colonial days the currently extremely well-branded lobster was denigrated as the "poor man's chicken." Lobsters were fed to hogs! Fact! Today, customers, pay up to $100 for a lobster. The same frankly unattractive crustacean. The only difference is that contemporary lobsters *enjoy* a far more powerful branding presence. Lobsters are hardly a one-off example. Nor are they only bottom crawlers to fall prey to professionals who successfully took measured risks. True story. About 100 years ago, along the Florida gulf coast, stone crabs, if they registered at all, did so as junk catch, pests that snagged nets and had to be laboriously cut loose. Then an oceanic Steve Jobs type had a clever idea. Don't toss them, position stone crabs as a delicacy appreciated by sophisticated people. Then price them not at the bottom but near the top of the seafood market. In this way, a nasty nuisance was transformed into a luxurious delicacy. What started with fishermen bitching ended with Disney-like lines at Joe's Crab Shack. Two nearly universal branding principles are revealed. First, if you want to attract a crowd, charge a ridiculous price. And second, in the end, most people value brands they cannot afford. Often, an effective branding strategy entail setting high prices for your services, and convincing audiences your professional services' high value makes you worth the higher price. Do you dare exploit these stranger than fiction branding facts?
- *Rule 7: There Are Problems, Problems and Then There Are PROBLEMS*-A profound difference exists between the professional you having problems, the professional you causing problems, and the professional you blessedly being able to solve problems. When creating your brand never unintentionally bring

attention to the initial two. Instead, work diligently and publically toward earning an ossified, an absolutely locked-in reputation for the third.

- *Rule 8: Brand Yourself Forward with Patience and Balance*-See to develop and to maintain forward momentum throughout your working lives and relationships. Otherwise, each will shrivel up and die. Sharks must swim forward continuously or drown. To avoid becoming dead sharks emulate their constantly forward natures. When you stop making valued contributions, you begin to die. But the value of your brand will have long predeceased your physical demise.
- *Rule 9: "Sense-Make" While You "Brand-Make"*-Strategic branding success ends and begins with the ability to make good decisions. There are four steps in most decisions. First, branding strategists should accurately perceive and "make sense of" the relevant stage. All relevant situations in which branding power players find themselves represent either opportunities or threats. You can become great, mediocre, or worse as a result of the momentary decisions you make during your career. Second, branding strategists should conceptualize (imagine) all possible courses of action in response to the opportunity or threat that is embedded in any decision. Third, branding strategists should calculate which action is in their best moral power-play interests. Fourth, branding strategists must decide which actions to pursue. Experts have long assumed step three is the most important decision-making step. This assumption is based on the premise that most strategists engage in rational economic-like calculations and attempt to maximize their own self-interests. But recently, events increasingly suggest that your first step, your sense-making step, is most important. At first blush, it appears that perceiving your stage situation correctly should prove rather easy. Look around, determine what is happening, move on from there. But the activity that appears most simple is actually the most complicated. This is because most of our sense-making activity occurs below the level of conscious thought. Making sense of your world is an active, perpetual process of "meaning creation" that shapes, influences, and actively biases the other three steps of this decision-making chain. You must become aware of your own biases before you can make good decisions about your brand.
- *Rule 10: Respect Your Brand So Others Respect You*-Merely competent professionals can emerge as eminent or diminished brands as a result of momentary decisions they make throughout their careers. Becoming an esteemed attorney is strikingly similar to becoming an esteemed mechanic. Big-time success at either professional activity is more a matter of preemptive, think preventative, maintenance than an ability to pick up or clean up after crises. Rule 10 addresses "failure avoidance." This last rule also features three additional lessons:
  - Lesson 1: As you develop or solidify branding power never permit the perceived need to address the *urgent* overwhelm your genuine need to address the *important*.

- Lesson 2: Discipline, or more specifically its presence as part of your dominant personae, will always reward you.
- Lesson 3: If you cannot govern your own appetites or impulses, straying off course on stages of your own design, soon enough you will not be able govern anyone. Your lack of self-governance-ability would swiftly be reflected in the failure of your brand to influence anything or anyone at all.

Notes

1 D'Este, Carlo (2003). *Eisenhower: A Soldier's Life*. New York, NY: Macmillan.
2 Wiseman, Richard (2012). *Rip It Up: the Radically New Approach to Changing Your Life*. London, UK: Macmillan.
3 Mack, Karen (2003). Courtly Tribute to the Woodens. *UCLA Today*. Retrieved, January 13, 2016. http://newroom.ucla.edu/stories/campus/woodens.
4 ThinkExist.com. Finding Quotations Was Never This Easy. Retrieved February 24, 2016. http://en.thinkexist.com.
5 Roberts, David and Javier Zrracina (2015). Rich People Are Jerks, Explained. *Vox Social Policy*. Retrieved October 31, 2016. http://www.vox.com/2015.richpeople are jerks.
6 The International Herald Tribune (2010). Saving Face in China. *The New York Times*, December 13, 2010. Retrieved March 30.
7 Strutton, David and Terrence L. Holmes (2002). "Managing Buyer-Seller Relationships One Impression at a Time." *Business Horizons*, 45: 67-78.
8 Watts, Steven (2005). *The People's Tycoon: Henry Ford and the American Century*. Detroit, MI: Wayne State Press.

CHAPTER 7

Building Your Brand One Impression at a Time

"It is well, when one is judging a friend, to remember that he is judging you with the same godlike and superior impartiality"

—Arnold Bennet (1867–1931).

Consider another fictitious but effectual historical illustration - "A Few Good Men" was the first. James Michener's book, Centennial,[1] features a story about an elderly Indian chief named Lame Beaver. The account describes how prior to a battle with the Pawnee, his tribe's ancient foe, Lame Beaver walked out alone onto the barren plain. After identifying it, he assumed a position where the enemy's attack would be most severe. The old warrior was isolated and exposed, far in front of his tribe's primary battle line.

Once in position, the chief hammered a stake into the ground. He then tied his leg to it, stood up to his full height, and waited, rifle in hand. Lame Beaver was messaging to friend and foe alike that he would not be backing down. For him, compromise was simply out of the question. Death was possible. But failure was not an option.

Attempting to draw his fire, the first wave of Pawnee charged and then swerved to avoid Lame Beaver. He merely stood up to his full height and glared. A second the attacked from the rear, leaving a spear in his armpit and an arrow in his calf. Lame Beaver jerked each out, and thrust each weapon into the ground beside him.

Finally, Rude Water, the Pawnee chief, led a third charge. Assuming Lame Beaver was badly wounded, Rude Water rode straight at his bloody, tethered foe. Lame Beaver took careful aim and shot a single bullet through his enemy's eye. Absent their leader, the Pawnee were crushed in the ensuing battle.

So What … Is the Point of This Story?

Two dimensions of Lame Beaver's tale should resonate with professionals seeking to manage the impressions that the audiences develop about their brand. The first dimension, the nature of the brand that Lame Beaver purposefully established and subsequently managed, is highly relevant. By actually staking himself to a position, he forcefully communicated one determinant message to two audiences. The first audience was his enemy. The second, the tribe he led. His message: "I am one determined man, utterly committed to my people and my cause. I may die … nothing lives forever … but I will go down fighting." The second, equally relevant dimension is this: As he stood alone, Lame Beaver conveyed and strategically signaled a false impression of vulnerability. His strategically cultivated "brand" identity allowed him to lure in and destroy his opponent.

You could be excused for thinking, cool story. But does it have anything to do with my branding efforts? Could I ever have such high stakes riding on how well I manage the impressions others develop about me? The answers to these two questions are yes, and yes. The outcomes of even fierce conflicts can be influenced by the effectiveness with which you have managed and continue to manage the impressions others develop about your brand.

The "Impressions" You Create Matter Greatly

You will continuously face situations in which you should be willing and able to do whatever is ethical and necessary in order to project desirable images to key audiences. Client perceptions of your branded image—and relatedly, your problem-solving value—are substantially derived from the messages you implicitly and explicitly communicate through impressions. You should effectively manage the impressions that others develop about you and your brand. This is hardly the only way to succeed, obviously. But the ability to manage key others' impressions about you and your brand offers another proven path along which you can achieve branding success. Auspicious brand impressions will also help you sustain any success that you do garner. As you now know, favorable impressions permit relationships to survive failures or missteps that would destroy less well-positioned relationships. Potential or current clients may likewise be pre-sold or re-sold on engaging in relationships with you due to your favorable brand identities. Finally, professional actors who "own" more favorable brand images can often avoid overt conflicts with clients or manage such conflicts more effectively when they do arise.[2]

When you have the right brand impressions in place, they function similar to shock absorbers on automobiles work. Like shock absorbers, good brand impressions will not eliminate potholes from your road. But favorable brand impressions will make your ride much smoother when potholes appear. A huge win, clearly, for any professional. Because potholes pop up or down on every stage.

Everybody and everything is eventually "broken by life. But afterward some people become stronger at the broken places." Earnest Hemingway was not referencing professionals when he wrote this words.[3] He could have been, however. Because professionals who became stronger after having had client relationships broken, or almost shattered, probably already enjoyed strong branding images. Why? Again, because they had previously effectively managed the impressions that others formed about them.

Why Else Are Impressions Important?

At one important level, professional–client relationships are social interactions. Two or more people needing each other and coming together through exchange relationships because each party perceives he or she is better off together than either would be apart. Although, truth be told, often one, or both parties to such relationships fail to acknowledge or act as if they recognize this basic fact about their shared relationship exists. But not you, we presume. The fact that your and everyone else's relationships are social interactions is another reason why you can secure tremendous value from preexisting or newly formed favorable branding impressions.

The ability to create desirable branding impressions can generate huge benefits for successful "impressers." This ability may enable them, at times, to solve otherwise insoluble client problems. Professionals who strategically create more favorable images or impressions about their brands will win more than their fair share of client attention, "liking," and loyalty. Greater client mind-share and wallet-share generally follow these three outcomes. After all, more favorably impressive brands generally win positioning wars inside actual or prospective clients' minds. As a professional you are currently developing whatever solutions you deliver during a relationship era and on a stage where you must continuously act out the values and promises associated with your branding story to clients. As a contemporary professional, you likely perform stages where client, customer, or partner relationships that took years to establish erode or end quickly. Today's audiences are more cynical. Cynicism doesn't just make things bad. Its presence can create a new species of worse, allowing audiences to display unearned bitterness. Tougher crowds, in other words, enough to make professionals yearn for the good old days. Meanwhile, audiences today are better informed. Audiences today generally understand that far more solutions are available for them to choose from than at any point in history.

Some professions recognize this and are already responding logically. Medical schools, for example, are increasingly teaching "bedside manners" to burgeoning physicians whose prior training was driven exclusively by just-the-facts all-the-time professional–client interactions. The medical profession is responding strategically to its realization that the impressions emanating from health care providers are simultaneously impacting client satisfaction and loyalty.

Technology often receives blame or earns credit in discussions such as this. With good cause, we would add.

Yet Technology Does Not Care

But, deliberations regarding whether technology is a hero or villain on many modern professional stages not really matter. Technology, you see, has evolved into a force of nature that is always moving forward. And has already moved on. Technology always has its say; increasingly, "the last word." Technology, after all, always bats last and hits 1.000. Technology has taken up permanent residence as the primary agent causing underlying structural problems across various professions. Problems such as the ones described in the Preface. Problems that already are impacting or will soon afflict your field, and how clients interact with you and your profession.

Like Mother Nature, technology is just an amalgam of chemical, biological and physical factors. Technology is nothing more or less. That's all.

Technology consequently cannot be spun. You cannot manage technology by managing the impressions that the develops about you. Nor can you reason with or impress "the grand machine." You cannot ask, hey, we're having other challenges right now, can you please stand down for just 1 year from wreaking on my profession and work life. Instead you had best plan to adapt to these realities if you have not done so already. A logical place to start begins with the impressions you cultivate, refine, manage, and eventually broadcast or narrowcast to your human audiences. Do this, and learn how to do it well. Because technology won't adapt to accommodate your or your profession's needs.

Signs of the Times

Many professionals are plying hard-earned skills and competencies during an age where symbolism often triumphs over substance or narrative prevails over facts more often than many would prefer. Many professionals also perform during an age where the power of the argument that truth matters only to the extent that certain people want it to matter is demonstrated time and again. This, despite what was discussed during Chapter 4. One regrettable consequence is that you, if you are ambitious, have little choice but to perform out a more carefully choreographed career yourself. You should determine how best to choreograph certain events, behaviors and stages. That is, if you intend to develop a powerfully persuasive brand as a necessary precursor to your big-time success.

Decide whether you want to enter this brand new power game wholeheartedly or play a branding game you've already been playing, only better. Presumably your decision is yes in either case. Because it is good, right, and logical for you to play impression-management branding games as long as you play them using the right methods for purposes of benefitting the right people.

What are the practical ways, hows, whens, and whats associated with successfully executing the impression-management behaviors that you should engage in? This chapter answers each question within this question.

Managing Brand Impression Behaviors

When you intentionally perform in socially, functionally, technically, or politically desirable ways on any stage you engage in *brand impression management.* There is more than that to brand impression management, however. Brand impression-management behaviors are often directed toward objectives not made explicit by professional actors who are attempting to develop particular brand identities. Because the individual and collective impressions that you attempt to communicate to various audiences influence how they the respective audience members perceive, evaluate, and treat or "review" you, you already consciously behave in ways intended to create certain brand impressions in, say, the clients' eyes. Or perhaps, likely to your detriment, you are not doing this.

When attempting to manage client impressions of you and your brand, "observe" the impact of your words and actions. Do this to gauge the branding impressions that targeted clients are forming in response to your impression-management efforts. Brand impression management can also be acted out absent any strategic efforts to create specific new impressions. You also might manage impressions simply to ensure that currently favorable branding impressions remain intact.

Brand impression-management performances involve two discrete processes. The first process is called *brand impression motivation*.[4] When performing on your stage or stages, you should be highly motivated to manage or influence how others see you. Here, your impression-motivation efforts would be driven by the desire to create specific types of branded impressions in the minds of important others. Choose your poison, or your most spellbinding potion. Do you want to position yourself and your problem-solving acumen as the most powerful, caring, or coolest option available on your particular block? As the most prestigious and consequently most expensive option around? Or, more likely, as combinations of the two brand positions?

There is nothing wrong with ascribing high prices to the services and values you deliver, and then impressing upon audience members the fact that your branded solutions are worth the price. This practice and your ability to pull it off should be celebrated. A branding identity to which you might aspire. As noted, one thing is certain: Create this brand identity, and your brand and bank account will be grateful. All the while, however, remain vigilant about the need to exercise discretion. The fact that you feel motivated to engage in brand impression management need not necessarily result in actual behaviors. Times and stages exist where impression-management behaviors would be so transparent that your "branding identity" would be damaged if you engaged in them.

The second process is called *brand impression construction*.[5] Once motivated to create a particular brand identity, professionals may strategically alter their behaviors to elicit the necessary impressions. This second process entails not just deciding upon the sorts of brand impressions you will create. Tactical choices about exactly how to create desired impressions also must be made. Various effective ways—let's call them tools—exist in most professional settings that permit you to alter audience perceptions. When you change or influence audience perceptions—the genuine or imagined realities audience members attribute to you—you can manage the impressions they formulate about your brand identity.

The Gilded Age financier Baron de Rothschild apparently understood the array of branding impression-management tactics that were available to him or to others that the Baron allowed to enter his orbit. The powerful banker was asked for a loan by a casual acquaintance at the height of his fame and fortune. De Rothschild reputedly replied, "I won't give you a loan myself. But I will walk arm-in-arm with you across the floor of the stock exchange. You will soon have willing lenders to spare." The professional "banker" was wise in more than financial affairs. He understood an intriguing fact about a basic brand impression-management principle:

- How one is perceived by others can be influenced by managing information about people and objects to which we perhaps are only loosely connected.

The proverb "You can't judge a book by its cover" has long endured as part of the US cultural lexicon. The statement has endured for the best of reasons. It is true. People actually do continuously judge books, people, and other entities by their covers! An analogous impression expression was featured in a legendary series of 1970s/1980s-era Head & Shoulders shampoo advertisements. The shampoo's branding message constantly reminded American consumers that you "never get a second chance to make a good first impression."

Each saying assumes a special significance on professional stages. Because there, performing professionals are often judged based on the first impressions that audience members formulate about them. Sometimes, those initial client impressions will redound to your advantage and at times, to your detriment. On these stages, the possibility of placing oneself at an early or later stage disadvantage in an interpersonal encounter, due to "the other guy's" inappropriate or appropriate first judgment, is real. The importance of managing the branding impressions that your behaviors intentionally or unintentionally create is again underscored.

Professional Relationships Are Increasingly Irrational

Or, perhaps professional relationships are increasingly becoming *Predictably Irrational*,[6] as behavioral economist Dan Ariely titled his renowned book. Rational criteria are far from being the only considerations that influence the decisions made by consumer or corporate audiences. Emotions also always have their say. Emotions wheedle themselves into places from which they influence audience's decision-making processes. Our presumption is that you often manage others' impressions on stages where you ability to manage those relationships effectively may pivot as much on understanding Shakespeare and the emotions, frailties, and scheming that the Bard routinely portrayed as it will on your acumen with basic communication principles. We write this assuming you have already mastered your profession's principles.

The fact that emotions play prominent roles and make clients more susceptible to effective impression-management attempts should surprise no one. Especially not in a 24/7/365 Internet-mediated, perpetually socially networked, and incessantly texting world. A global stage has already emerged on which shallow, low-information thinking and decision making increasingly prevails among clients and consumers alike. A global stage on which T.S. Eliot's prescient words, authored in his 1920 essay *The Perfect Critic*, has found fertile soil. The poet wrote: "When we do not know, or do not know enough, we tend always to substitute emotions for thoughts."[7] Not that young Americans texting a median 75 times a day would substitute emotions for thoughts, or engage in shallow information processing. We apologize, perhaps, for our sarcasm.

Reading Client Emotions

Emotions and the possibility of establishing meaning-laden emotional connections between you and the various audiences you target is a significant matter. This possibility is a prospect that you should not ignore. This description also applies to the opportunity to leverage those emotions for your profit and your client's gain. When clients perceive that your values or interests are similar to theirs, the likelihood that your persuasive attempt will succeed or the client relationship itself will strengthen. All the while greater power should gravitate toward your brand. Your willingness to develop greater insight about clients' preferred communication styles, lifestyles, and interests, as you read and discern their often transparent emotional states, may prove essential to your impression-management-based power and persuasive success.

You might learn, for instance, when clients experience:[8]

- Anger, they become more optimistic, more prone to taking risks, and more susceptible to your branding impression attempts.
- Fear, they become more pessimistic and risk averse, less likely to make any decisions, and less prone to being persuaded.
- Sadness, they become more prone to poor decision making, and thus more susceptible to your persuasive efforts.
- Disgust, they become less likely to do anything at all; don't bother trying to persuade them.
- Decision information overload, they, again, are less likely to make any decision and therefore less susceptible to anyone's persuasive efforts.

Impressions Can Break Good or Bad for Brands

The ability to create and sustain favorable branding impressions will usually elevate your prospects for professional power. On any stage, but especially upon professional stages that are experiencing the consequences of Schumpeteriian-like creative destruction effects. Most contemporary professional stages, in brief. The favorable impressions that others attribute to you may permit you to avoid or mitigate undesirable associations, or overturn undesirable associations by facilitating better images. Your proficiency at establishing and sustaining relationships with clients generally follows from an ability to communicate reassurance, deliver signals that inspire trust, and signal commitment to fulfill client needs. These three outcomes would routinely emerge as a consequence of your ability to manage client impressions successfully.

The already powerful brand image and dominant market share of Johnson & Johnson's Tylenol brand, for example, bounced back stronger than ever in early 1986. What's unique and highly revealing about the preceding statement is that this "bounce back" occurred about three months after six people died after taking Tylenol in 1985. The "bounce back was possible because Johnson & Johnson managed impressions in ways that assured core audience members it was not to blame for the product tampering tragedy that led to several deaths. Post-crisis, Johnson & Johnson muscularly managed rebranding impressions.[9] The firm "bowed up," rebranding itself more through deeds than words.

In response to this 1985 terrorist act, Johnson & Johnson immediately removed all Tylenol products from all store shelves. Then the firm immediately and publicly took complete responsibility—even though the murderer's cyanide poisoning activities obviously were not the fault of Johnson & Johnson. Finally, when Tylenol was reintroduced to the market, the brand and all other Johnson & Johnson pharmaceutical products arrived with then new tamper-proof packaging. Actual branding impression-management behaviors spoke far more persuasively than mere branding impression-management words.

Unfortunately for the value of respective brands, some 15 years later behemoths Ford Motor and Firestone Tire & Rubber Company relied more on words than deeds as each firm attempted to manage market, customer and investor impressions being formulated about their respective brands. Each soon-to-be diminished brand obfuscated and skirted responsibility for a shared Firestone tire and Ford Explorer vehicle debacle that triggered customers' and general mayhem. Rather than shouldering mutual or individual responsibility, each firm resolutely pointed the finger of blame at the other. Each firm's representatives would have benefitted by remembering when waving at people or partners it is best to use all five fingers. Each partner opted for legalistic assault and public denunciation rather than orchestrated acts of impression management and restoration of their brand identity. Ford and Firestone each acted as if it believed bullyboy tactics designed to denigrate the other's brand could elevate their own. The results were predictable. After months of negative customer responses, a nearly 100-year-old relationship ended with acrimonious fanfare in 2001.

Neither Ford nor Firestone ever accepted responsibility for their mutual failure.[10] For years, the marketing impressions created by Ford's brand mismanagement suffered. Firestone tire is now a subsidiary of Japan's Bridgestone Tires. Ouch! Does anyone think the loss of this former American branding icon is a coincidence?

The sometimes perverse and often convoluted family of impression-management behaviors that you could exercise to enhance your brand identity inside relationships include assertive and defensive branding initiatives. Assertive brand-management behaviors can be employed to create desirable or appealing impressions in the minds of current or prospective clients, partners, reports, peers, or superiors—audience members all. Defensive behaviors focus on the repair, rehabilitation, or protection of desirable brand images that are suffering injury or experiencing threats. Assertive and defensive behaviors can be verbal, nonverbal, or artifact based in nature.

Assertive Impression-Management Behaviors

Impression-management behaviors are not always "nice." "Not-being-nice," however, does not discount the value and potential effectiveness of brand impression management. But it does underscore how important it is to understand the most opportune time to utilize either assertive or defensive impression-management behaviors. Particularly on stages that are not universally nice themselves but instead are populated by clients, partners, competitors, and other audience members who are generally resourceful, guileful, and cunning themselves.

Ingratiation

Ingratiatory brand impression-management behaviors might include complementing clients on tasks well-done or choices well-made or strategically agreeing with targeted superiors or key peers on major issues while disagreeing with them on minor ones. You might even knowingly nudge neutral third parties to reveal your favorable opinion of a superior or key partner. Skillful branding actors often ingratiate only to enhance significant others' images of them, even while they behave as if the issue at hand was their only concern. Yes, this tactic is cold and calculating. But it works.

There is a catch, however. The audiences that are typically targeted by ingratiatory tactics often hold sway over significant rewards or present or future value. And the typical target is well-aware of this situation. This is why ingratiatory branding scripts usually should be directed toward objectives not discussed or made apparent by you. Ingratiation works best when used subtly. Ingratiatory impression-management activities rarely succeed long-term unless you are able to employ them subtly.[11]

Ingratiatory behaviors should only be executed with the long run in mind. Are you "wise and forward-looking enough" to plant trees today knowing the shade may not benefit you for years and patient enough to play the long game? You've probably heard the nutritional cliché: "You are what you eat." Actually not a cliché at all. In other words whether you'll need knee or hip replacements, heart surgery, or diabetes treatments at some future point is based, in part, on dietary choices you make today. Consequently, as you engage in ingratiation, self-promotion, and other assertive impression-management behaviors for purposes of enhancing your brand's attractiveness—and persuasive power—keep the long game in mind.

But still, you should ingratiate, and for that matter, self-promote—as explained below. After all, if you don't, who will? In man"-bites-dog" inversions of conventional wisdom, however, you should also seek opportunities to praise current or potential partners for *their* activities or accomplishments. Ingratiating behaviors include searching for ways to provide favors for prospective or actual clients. Professionals who provide comped or highly favored services for preferred clients and also deliver them themselves are purposefully or inadvertently practicing ingratiation. The need to engage in such flattery or "other-promotional" behaviors underscores the importance of doing "one's own homework" to understand the erogenous, or "turn on," zones of targeted clients. Doing your homework also helps you to identify decisive factors that might strengthen or weaken exchange relationships before engaging in pricing or contract renegotiations with key clients.

Well-staged acts wherein some targeted audience member's vanity, pride, or efficacy is strategically massaged while, all along, you are mindfully elevating your current branding identity, have ancient roots. Sculptors as renowned as Michelangelo, Bernini or Rodin all inevitably idealized the appearance of the human model they were sculpting—and who was paying them. This happened persistently across cultures in order to flatter the beneficiary and benefactor by creating superior versions of the actual subjects. Mere coincidence? Or strategic impression management, arriving in the tactical form known as ingratiation?

No one should be surprised or "put off" in a world where the most powerful contemporary professional routinely engages in similar ingratiatory tactics. Laypersons have surely pondered: Why don't American Presidents simply exercise their supposedly great power to make others behave? Perhaps those "critics" fail to consider the fact that even successful presidents essentially are glorified public relations operatives. Show us an American president, and we will show you a well-branded professional. After all, these executives go to work most days in their own houses as the most powerful person in the world! Walking downstairs every morning as one holding sway over the literal and metaphorical wherewithal to kick anyone's butt in order to get them to do the President's bidding, for 4 years, at least.

But what actually happens? As branding actors, American Presidents spend more time kissing-up to targeted audiences than pounding on them. This kissing-up involves acts of flattery targeted toward or outright dispensation of favors to key voting blocs, congressional members, other world leaders, and special interest groups. Presidents do all this for the purpose of persuading audiences to do something. Why the suck-up? For the same reason anyone engages in any voluntary behavior. Because the behavior, in this case ingratiatory sucking-up, actually works. Well-executed ingratiatory behaviors can work wonders for your brand.

Dangers Dead Ahead

An ongoing quandary that most of us face in our social life is how to persuade others about "how wonderful" we are without letting our audience know we want them to know. The use of ingratiatory and other self-promoting branding behaviors is similarly suffused with danger. That's because the sorts of staged relational encounters on which you might be most tempted to ingratiate are also the ones on which ingratiatory efforts are most obvious to targeted audiences. On such stages, your motives may be so apparent that audience members easily discern the falsity of your performance. The phrase [don't] "telegraph your punches" comes to mind. Small wonder why poorly executed ingratiation efforts often backfire.[12]

Ingratiation is not a "suitable-for-daily-use" brand impression-management tool. But ingratiation should remain available and present when needed, inside the toolkit of strategically minded branding actors. Avoid overly obvious agreement with important audience members in situations where you genuinely don't agree. Never ingratiate on stages where blatant favor giving or excessive praise for marginal achievements may strike the targets of your impression-management efforts as a "praise carried too far."

Self-Promotion

Professionals often worry that key audience members have not adequately recognized their talents or accomplishments. This, of course, is true of most humans. Been there, felt this, right? After all, no human brand wants to get left behind, recognition-wise, because this painful condition means their prospects for getting ahead just diminished. You might initiate self-promotion campaigns to enhance your prospects and to receive credit for a successful outcome you engendered. You might simply want to more effectively promote and publicize your strengths.[13]

Four basic self-promotion brand impression tactics exist. Skillful professionals can routinely employ all or a combination of them, depending on contextual staging factors, to generate positive branding outcomes when interacting with important audience members. The tactics entail the use of entitlements, enhancements, obstacle disclosure, and the initiation of association.

Entitlements

Entitlements are typically summoned when branding actors believe they have not received sufficient credit for positive outcomes they created. Essentially, branding professionals seek to claim responsibility for some or all of something good that happened. Brand-enhancing entitlements can be performed through formal communication channels or informal conversation. For example, you might causally mention how pleased you are that the solution you recommended to resolve a previously vexing problem worked out so well.

Some conservative critics argue that the U.S. entitlement state "succeeds" by giving away free stuff. Not so with professionals. You must earn your success. Stand up and take credit when it is due. Never let anyone push you away from the reputation-enhancing prize.

Peers or subordinates should not be permitted to cut you off when you are speaking. To ensure this rarely happens while also enhancing your brand's power and persuasiveness, you generally should concentrate on saying less than is necessary. If the person in charge of you or who reports to you wants or needs more information, they will ask for it. Then you, as a smart, long-game-playing, up-and-coming, or "holding-strong-to-my-earned status" professional can provide it. Be the one who gets the point quickly. Soon enough, your brand may evolve into the one whom others listen to more carefully as you speak.

The use of entitlements is not limited to individual professionals. Professional firms can highlight their positive outcomes to develop more powerfully persuasive branding positions among actual or potential clients. Corporate providers of consultative services might instruct their professional employees to strategically and publically offer certain values gratis or at discounted rates to clients who cannot afford to pay full freight. Seeds planted today may grow into fruitful relationships sooner than one thinks. Such gestures underscore to other already powerful audiences that your munificent firm is trustworthy, fair-minded, and socially responsible. Each branding identity—or impression—benefits.

As is true of most assertive brand impression-management tactics, the use of entitlements is fraught with risk. But only when the forays are self-evidently transparent. Like ingratiation, entitlements should be used, but not overused. Regardless of your stage, your brand will likely grow stronger faster when you take a bit less credit and assume a little more responsibility. This appears particularly true over the long run. Despite your occasional use of entitlement, if you're discerning you'll also display a "window-and-mirror" maturity. Such displays, which undeniably can be in nature, offer a more certain path to successful brand impression management.

"Window-and-mirror" maturity works like this. Over time, when things go right, if you're wise, you'll point out of the window and give credit to people or factors other than yourself. You consciously shine a light on others who contributed. Yet when things go awry, "window and mirror" professionals never blame circumstances or other people. Instead look into the mirror and tell others: "I'm responsible." Imagine how earning a reputation for such behaviors, simply because you engaged in them, would influence your branding identity. Especially if you engage in additional "other-oriented" behaviors consistently across time. Talk about doing well by doing good, for others. This particular branding identity would surely serve you well in an increasingly narcissistic domestic marketplace.[14] Selfie-fatigue, anyone?

Enhancements

At times, skillful professional branders might pursue enhancement. You might offer statements or evidence suggesting the positive outcomes that you generated are only part of the picture. An adroit consultant, Evelyn, might purposefully point toward other favorable results beyond the known good things she generated that are equally or more important *and* also associated with the first outcome. And Evelyn happened to have her finger in that pie as well. Evelyn might strategically revisit the fact that a particular product recommendation she made was critical in solving a client's quality control problem while also elevating the client firm's employee morale *and* profitability. Evelyn is enhancing others' impressions of the contributions she made.

Corporations also can invoke enhancements. Walmart first used enhancements effectively on a national stage to gain leverage with vendors or impress vital public and private constituencies about 30 years ago. The retailing giant first grew into national prominence on the backs of a widely publicized "Buy American" branding strategy. The strategy was enacted and promoted to expand the favorable impressions cast off by Walmart's brand.

Specifically, Walmart publicized how many American jobs were "saved" because, at the time, it mostly purchased domestically produced products. These jobs-saved assertions were diffused so widely throughout a huge domestic economy that no expert could accurately validate or invalidate them. In brief, their accuracy could not be vetted.[15]

More recently, in response to criticisms about Walmart's purported propensity to exploit workers, the retailer rebranded based on the fact that all its hourly workers would soon receive wages that significantly exceeded minimum Federal levels. This change was almost certainly initiated to enhance Walmart's brand impressions among strategic audience sectors. Or, as marketers would describe them, among key publics and targeted consumer markets.

Obstacle Disclosure and the Initiation of Association

"Obstacle disclosure" and "association" are two additional assertive tools through which audience impressions can be managed. A resourceful Evelyn, for example, might seek to further enhance her branding identity by casually noting obstacles she encountered and overcame in route to eventual triumph. She could quietly "confess" how wonderful it feels to have "pushed" the partnership she represents through a previously inaccessible but highly lucrative client door. And don't forget that she succeeded despite the fact that a colleague—or is it rival—was absent due to maternity leave. Hold the applause, please.

We've already wrote these impression-management tactics are far from uniformly "nice." Scary, risky, sometimes nasty work, this self-promotion business. But obstacle disclosure can prove effective when wielded subtly.

You can and should think relationships. You can and should constantly think about your brand identity. You should remain constantly cognizant of long-run consequences and goals as you manage your relationships and brand. This book consistently emphasizes the value of each factor. But, as Evelyn understood, the ultimate success metric for most professionals inevitably dances close to revenue or profit lines. Favorably branded impressions, and correspondingly more powerfully persuasive reputations gravitate toward individual performers who excel at tasks that contribute directly to their organizations' profit lines. Remember the Tom Cruise film *Jerry Maguire*, and its famous tagline. Then *Show [Them] the Money*.

Bold branders might try to associate themselves with positive outcomes or highly respected colleagues or outsiders while also elevating their role in the relationship. Self-promoting one's brand through association with influential or well-known others even has a name: "basking in reflected glory." The use of associations as a brand impression tactic is related to the authority and persuasiveness that even an indirect connection to other prominent people or events can confer power to actors who manage the "link-in" well. The opportunity to cultivate or exercise power through the right branding associations provides a logical rationale for corporate sponsorship of charity tournaments, fundraising events, or other socially worthy causes.

You might be seen repeatedly chatting up more powerful others at Rotary meetings or during quarterly conventions where powerful clients, prospects, or partners are also present. Soon enough, you might may be tagged "an up and comer" or as that young man who "knows the right people." Of course, you also might become brand-identified a "shameless suck-up." Your branding outcome, the set of branding impressions you generate, depends on how well you explicitly or delicately manage the "basking in reflected glory" process.

The conversation may have been about the latest National Collegiate Athletic Association tournament results or where the Fed is headed with interest rates. Genuine branding impressions, generated in the eyes of key audiences with whom you share a stage, may follow just the same. Unfortunately for people who work hard but keep their heads down, style sometimes does triumph over substance. And, it follows, self-promoting professionals sometimes do manage to gain unfounded, unfair, or inappropriate branding advantages.

We're Sorry But ...

If you've been disgusted, disturbed, discouraged, or otherwise put off by our discussion about how the effective use of ingratiation and the four self-promotion tactics unfairly elevates the power and persuasiveness of adroit and sophisticated impression managers, we're sorry. But the world is neither full of love nor characterized by legions of nice or naïve "guys" who finish first. Professional stages are often pitilessly competitive places where you're better off learning how to do these things to others before those others do them to you. Or at the least learning about these tactics so you will not fall prey to other's skillful or misuse of them.

You still may gain solace, however, from knowing that despite the potential utility of impression management, self-promoting and ingratiating actors each face the same clear and present danger. Indeed, anyone playing impression-based branding games encounters the same paradox. It is that:

- The stages on which the potential value of ingratiation or self-promotion is greatest are the same stages where use of the tactics and potential exposure of the branding actor's underlying motives are most apparent to audiences.

You should be aware that this paradox exists. If you're seeking to manage the impressions you convey to others you must manage this paradox effectively. To succeed as an impression manager, you must be or become skillful and careful enough to not arouse suspicions about your supposed assets or accomplishments. Fail to do this, and your brand identity claims may be investigated and rejected by audiences. And there's no doubt about what would be rejected next, is there?

Intimidation

Situations may arise in which you seek to signal to others that they would be better off having you as their friend rather than their foe. To cultivate such impressions, you might behave gruffly or brusquely during certain relational encounters. Such encounters might include presentations, negotiations, interviews, staff meetings, etc. Intimidation creates an impression of danger by inducing fear or the prospect of threat. Fear, as an impression-management tactic, would convey the message to presumably precisely targeted audience members that they had best not mess up or there will be hell to pay. Perhaps they had best just line-up behind your plan, now.

Intimidation, as an impression-management tactic, should be used sparingly. Yet the ability and demonstrated willingness to intimidate may strengthen the power and persuasiveness of your brand. Intimidation makes more sense when the relationship is nonvoluntary in nature, or when the intimidating brander has the capacity to inflict serious harm on the targeted audience members. But still, fear works. Fear also motivates, presumably because it is one of the two most powerful human emotions. In fact, there are only two primary emotions: Love and fear. All other emotions arise from one or the other source. Happiness, joy, contentment are love-based emotions. Hate, anger, depression are derivatives of fear.[16]

As noted, few people have ever woken up in the middle of the night due to their happiness. Most everyone, however, has lain awake because they experienced fear or concern about something. Fear grabs attention; it is persuasive, influential and sticky. If circumstances were otherwise, discerning marketers would not ground so many promotional efforts in descriptions of how problems that message recipients fear most can be prevented or resolved if audience member are wise enough to choose correctly.

Take a preacher, priest, rabbi, mullah, or Buddhism master. (No, no joke to follow.) Note how each individual holds membership the same discrete and frankly exclusive professional class. Religion, their shared profession, thrives on the development and promulgation of fear as well as the promotion and distribution of hope to their clients and prospects. That hope, of course, arrives in the form of a presumed and promised solution being advocated by each professional. Absent the fear of sanction, loss, or even pain—bad behavior carries no sanction, the clergy person's authority would then win scant attention.

People often don't see life as it is. Instead we experience versions of life distorted or influenced by our hopes, fears, and attachments to things we love. Your ability to invoke fear in others through branding impressions is a powerful asset. Never reject, out of hand, the value of fear or the prospect that you might selectively use it when pursuing ethical and socially beneficial ends.

But obviously, the ends for which fear is employed are not always ethical. A professional stage might arise on which a larger franchisor requires a smaller and less powerful franchisee to order a minimum amount of product or lose its franchising rights. Franchisors, defined, are parent firms, often nationally branded [such as the KFC corporation, which is actually part of Yum Brands]. Franchisees, defined, are "offspring firms, operating as part of a franchising chain (each local KFC store)." Suppose a local KFC store owner (the franchisee) refuses to make these required purchases. KFC the parent franchisor, then terminates the relationship and publicly communicates the termination to crucial audience members across all franchising family firms. The fear of losing their franchising rights may induce other franchisees not directly involved to accept even more restrictive purchasing demands.[17]

You might similarly wield intimidating branding behaviors to successfully imprint negative impressions on specific targets. Negative impressions might contemporaneously convey the message to important audience members that you are credible, serious in purpose, not to be trifled with, and highly motivated in intent. These audience perceptions would generally represent a win for your brand. A win, which in turn, would amplify your power and persuasiveness on a stage you now are likely dominating.

Intimidation, in our view, is how KFC, the parent franchisor brand, was able to bully local KFC store owners into accepting global branding powerhouse Oprah Winfrey's plan to give out coupons for a free chicken to all of America during 2016. Or perhaps the more powerful Oprah brand coerced KFC's head-shed into thinking that somehow giving away free chicken to everyone was a good idea. Okay, clearly, the most likely scenario was that Oprah's powerful brand identity intimidated the less powerful KFC franchisor who in turn bullied their franchisees. Why? Because the franchisees had the weakest brand.

The KFC meals indeed were free. Except for the local franchisors, who paid for the free meals themselves. Riots; sit-ins, until furious coupon holders were served; general furor; and specific and likely lasting enmity emanating from KFC franchisees targeted toward the parent franchisor that each shared ensued in quick order.[18]

So yes, of course, downsides are associated with the use of intimidation. Because with one exception, there is always potential downsides when one brand-builds through assertive impression-management tactics. Many clients and other professionals may respond poorly or unpredictably to fear-based incentives. Professionals who mindfully or thoughtlessly use intimidation without carefully considering the potential repercussions may do more harm than good for their brands. Intimidate only when you are willing to waive the prospect of ever being liked again by the targeted audience member. Powerless, easily intimidated puppies of today may grow into big dogs in the future—revisiting a theme discussed earlier. The use of intimidation also depresses the prospects that cooperative relationships might be developed in the future.

Exemplification

We gladly report, however, that the use of assertive brand impression-management activities does not feature universally negative connotations. Nor does such tactics necessarily involve efforts to mislead or fool an audience. You always should manage branding impressions when presenting your core values—the best and most genuine version of yourself—to others. Sometimes you should even use words. Implying, that you also can mightily impress others and grow your brand's attractiveness by utilizing example. For starters, by demonstrating integrity or other praiseworthy behaviors in all your activities. Or, paraphrasing what Mahatma Gandhi wrote: "[By being] the change you want to see [in the world]."[19]

Powerfully persuasive branding identities can be created and managed through the use of exemplification. For starters, work harder, smarter, and generate more positive effects than your counterparts. Or, you could exemplify moral *bona fides* by contrasting your socially responsible behaviors with behaviors initiated by less "green" but unnamed competitors. In supply chain settings, senior managers at a retail clothing manufacturer engaged in negotiations with a textile supplier could present themselves through stated intentions and pursuant actions as the marketer in the domestic apparel sector who cares most about the survival of American textile manufacturers. A few such firms still operate in North Carolina, South Carolina and Georgia. Dearborn, Michigan-based Carhartt has favorably distinguished its brand identity through its willingness to partner with domestic textile mills. The exemplification of such behaviors might ease the way toward reasonable concessions from other suppliers being targeted by Carhartt.

Demonstrating value is always more powerful than merely talking about your value. As comedian, actor, writer, and banjo player extraordinaire Steve Martin once said: "Be so good they can't ignore you." Martin, however, was actually quoting Cal Newport's wisdom.[20] As long as substance does at least occasionally defeat style, which we assume most agree is hopefully always true, your ability to exemplify the right values and outcomes will be your brand's best friend.

Some use of brand impression management is necessary simply to get along better. As we have previously stated, particularly in the increasingly globalized and commoditized worlds in which most contemporary professionals operate. Properly managed brands already represent more than mere nice-to-haves on such stages. After all, experienced professionals understand that while they should compete ethically they are under no obligation to "fight fairly". (Remember, we have already explained why branding professionals should never fight a "fair" fight. With more discussion to follow.) Your properly burnished branded identity might provide sustainable, resource-based, and determinant advantages that permit you to set yourself apart meaningfully as being different from and better than your professional counterparts. Or is it professional "competitors?"

Properly managed brands, in other words, can make otherwise fairly matched professional "fights" unfair. The Biblical book of Proverbs says it best: "A good name is to be chosen rather than great riches."[21] On stages your good name, as manifested through your brand identity reputation, would often presage great wealth. Entirely because your good name enhances your powers of persuasion.

You can employ exemplification to create favorable attributions, among important audiences, to show that you are moral and worthy of their consideration or loyalty. Exemplify, demonstrate, the appropriate evidence and this branding victory will be yours to claim. As noted earlier:

- "The best sermon I ever *heard* was the one I *saw?*"
  We further recommend:

- Exemplify whoever and whatever you aspire to be, branding wise, in every decision you make, every action you take, every word you say, and often as importantly, don't say.

Defensive Impression-Management Behaviors

Defensive brand impression tactics try to mend or maintain intended desirable brand identities that are currently or potentially experiencing assault due to an undesirable outcome. Defensive tactics usually should be employed when brand-threatening predicaments arise in your professional life. Crises might result, for example, from an attorney's inexperience with and resultant mismanagement of an important legal client, or any professional's demonstrable incompetence. The repeated use of defensive brand impression tactics on any stage in any relationship is never appropriate. If you frequently use defensive brand impression-management tactics, you're not effectively managing some core aspect of a relationship you once may have but are now just enduring with clients. In brief, something else is wrong.

Times will arise, however, when defensive impression-management behaviors are more than just necessary. Their use is absolutely appropriate. Three defensive impression-management tactics that are often used and usually prove effective are discussed below.

Accounts (Excuses and Justifications)

Branding accounts involve attempts to excuse or justify some aspect of your behavior based on the anticipation or arrival of some negative feedback. Essentially, actors who initiate accounts attempt to explain the potentially or actually damaging behaviors in ways that protect their brand identity and reputation.

Excuses generally entail some denial of responsibility. When excuses are employed, you provide information to targeted audience members that are intended to lessen attributed responsibility for poor performance. You might, for example, blame a third-party provider for deficit service. Use "excuses" prudently. Too many excuses create the impression of ineptitude or deceit. After all, you or your firm presumably engaged with the deficit third-party provider only after having done due diligence.

Still, excuses, as means to restore or sustain branded reputations, are frequently trundled out on national stages. "Everybody does it" represents an excuse you might expect from naughty teenagers but not from a putatively polished and carefully crafted brand. Yet "everyone does it" was the exact excuse offered by then Presidential candidate Hillary Clinton during 2016. That was Mrs. Clinton's, a professional politician, one-time defense, or excuse, for making closed door handsomely rewarded speeches to investment bankers and refusing to release her transcripts. "Handsome" is in $11,000,000 paid during 2014 and 2015's first quarter. This is according to a *New York Times* editorial. Worth mentioning, the newspaper's extremely well-branded pages have never been confused with a Right Wing attack dog.[22]

Justifications, by contrast, attempt to legitimize some undesirable outcome or alleviate negative consequences that otherwise might emerge from poor performance. Suppose a certified public accountant was contractually obligated to complete a project for another company by a date certain. But she failed to honor the contract. The certified public accountant might attempt to justify her tardiness by explaining how an unexpected emergency involving another client had arisen. The "justifying" branding actor had no option but to address the more pressing crisis first. Moreover, the CPA could emphasize that she would have performed similarly for your firm had the circumstances been reversed. This message might work, or at the least forestall more negative pushback.

A textile executive might justify huge domestic price increases as an unavoidable result of higher raw material costs. As indeed happened when global cotton prices rose overnight due to a "100-year" 2009 Bangladeshi floods.[23] In either case, one professional seeks to deflect blame away from himself or his firm. As reported, Nike employed this tactic during 2001 when blaming i2 Technologies for its earnings shortfall.

Apologies and Restitutions

Branding actors occasionally confront branding predicaments from which there is no escaping, denying, or obscuring damning facts, events, or outcomes that have transpired. Stuff happens, after all. The use of excuses or justifications is probably inappropriate on such stages. Your best course of action in such situations may entail appealing to the "better angels" of offended audience members' natures.

Do this, first, by "owning" the oversight, mistake, or misdeed. Second, apologize for the part that you have played. What is your audience going to do? Hit you, yell at you, dismiss you, or end the relationship? Perhaps. But a more likely outcome is that the "other" will confer grudging but genuine respect for your decision to act like a fully grown, responsible, ethical adult. And then opt to work with you for purposes of salvaging the relationship and recouping whatever values can be retained with you.

Abraham Lincoln referenced humanity's better angels during a Civil War era speech. He did so in a passionate appeal to the mercy and kindness of others that he offered to others. His appeal eventually worked. One probable reason: Forgiveness actually is part of most people's nature. American citizens have traditionally loved a great comeback story, particularly when they are the ultimate beneficiaries.

Worth noting: Forgiveness, particularly interpersonal variety, is something you do for yourself. When forgiving you are always the real long-term beneficiary. Not the person or firm being forgiven. But when apologies are properly issued, the forgiveness granted from audience members can prove a starting rather than ending point for a newly enhanced and revitalized brand. And consequently renewed or restored client relationships.

Promises Made, Promises Kept?

If you earn the honorific label of "effective-marketer," promises made must be promises kept. Otherwise, your branding value could never be nurtured, much less sustained, over the long run. So promises broken eventually should be restored. Presumably, as quickly as possible. There is no other ethical or logical choice. Because successful professionals are successful marketers.

You now know that your brand is your promise. And for many professionals operating in highly fluid fields as opposed to merely fluid fields, your branding promise and your restorative apology, when necessary, are essential bookends of effective long-term brand-management strategies. Because, obviously, mistakes will occur. As will genuinely unexpected "exigencies" that preclude you from "promise-keeping." Consequently, the long-run success or failure of branding strategies often pivots either on who makes the least mistakes or who manages mistakes best after they arise.

At a blue collar but still professional level consider a master mechanic. He works for a third-party fleet maintenance firm. The professional mechanic mistakenly installs the wrong fuel filter on a local diary's delivery truck. The result was a fouled engine and spoiled cargo. The maintenance firm organization is clearly culpable, even though no malice or ill-intent was in play. A reasonable response might entail maintenance firm's most senior person or owner writing a formal letter of apology in which he accepts responsibility for the incident. No emails, no texts, a real letter. Then deliver the letter in person, with the mechanic in tow. Then both men can apologize personally to the diary's management. To further ensure that things are made "right," a *restitution* in the form of compensation for all current losses, plus price discounts offered in return for future business, would be appropriate.

Apologies are delicate matters that should be handled with care. Sophisticated and strategic brand apologists understand the difference between "excuse me," "pardon me", "I'm sorry," and "forgive me." What difference is that? In the context of "forgive me", otherwise broken relationships may well be restored. And resurrecting our previous reference to Hemingway, be strengthened in formerly broken places. Things can get better. Good generally improves professional relationships every bit to the degree that bad generally makes those same relationships worse. But life, especially among career professionals, generally averages out. Especially when relationships can be sustained long enough for the long run to play out. However, your brand will appear weak or incompetent if too many apologizes are offered.

Distancing and Disclaimers

Occasions arise when branding actors who are not directly responsible for a negative event or outcome are nonetheless caught in their sticky web. Contemporary alliances routinely assume multifaceted forms, routinely professionals from three to four firms. Each aligned, or partnering, professional is expected to provide unique expertise, experience, practices, or, perhaps, reputational presence in one or more functional areas. Suppose an alliance partner firm botches a research and development project that badly undermines the strategic plans of another partner. Unfortunately, the partner was one you and your firm introduced to the cabal. And suppose further that the damaged partner is your best customer.

You could *distance* yourself from this predicament by subtly informing executives at the injured partner firm that you inveighed against the decision to include the "offending" party in the strategic alliance. Indeed, you may have offered to provide an alternative that others rejected. If successful, the tactic would permit you to distance yourself from the group and any attached accountability for failure. Though ethically questionable, at best, similar distancing performances are frequently staged. The expression "Success has many parents, but failure is an orphan" would not have persisted absent cause.

One adage implies, fundamentally:

- While many seek credit for success few accept responsibility for failure.

Truth be told, rather than distancing yourself or your role, you might decide to damn-"distancing" and lean into the truth. That is, if you're able and willing to play branding chess, thinking two or three steps ahead, rather than branding checkers. Do this, and you likely also take ownership of, responsibility for, and eventual control over the stage. Your ascension would be based on your recognition that earning a differentiated brand identity as one who "tells the truth," especially in scenes where truth-telling does not come easily or naturally, would add long-term luster to your brand.

Remember another relevant lesson provided earlier than also applies here, (again) from Proverbs:

- "A good name is to be treasured more than money"...

Disclaimers, by contrast, involve distancing tactics employed prior to possible negative outcomes. A research firm might find it useful to agree to certain report-delivery schedules but make delivery contingent upon the availability of certain secondary data produced by an third party. Then, if delivery is late due to the other party's belated performance, the research firm's professionals have insulated themselves against that possibility and cannot be held responsible.

More Than a Little Self Awareness ...

Whenever possible—always?—become more aware of your current impression-management behaviors, the images you currently project, and the specific branding identities you would like to create for your future. Your current impression-management behaviors may flow from situational scripts that have been reinforced by successful reviews on past stages. But your audiences, reviewers, and the stages on which you acted out those behaviors change continuously.

Examine your current to ensure it still captures sets of images and identities that are genuinely worth pursuing. A brand identity that worked well during one stage of your career might fade in value or appropriateness (one cannot be an "up-and-comer" forever) as your career progresses, client, or competitor mix evolves, or stages transform. Consequently you must regularly update the quality and content of your impression-management scripts to ensure that they remain relevant and helpful.

Monitor your audience and the stages on which you seek to manage impressions continuously. The characteristics of audiences you target should influence your performance. Audience characteristics will influence the reviews you receive. Audiences, particularly counterparts with whom you routinely interact, are usually aware that their status and power affects your self-branding initiatives. As such, many detect "performances" easily. In particular, those who possess power themselves generally expect ingratiation attempts by subordinates. Especially, if you, as a subordinate, depend on this powerful source for rewards or success. In such situations, your integrated use of subtlety and directness to manage branding impressions should generally yield higher rewards.

You should only select branding identities that are consistent with your goals, abilities and core traits. Then present yourself to others through patterns and tactics that are consistent with and contribute to that identity. Once you have determined your desired branding image, attend carefully to verbal and nonverbal feedback that clients or other targeted audiences provide. Recognize the dangers inherent in the branding impression tactic you are using to attain your desired impression. When necessary, account for those dangers. Apart from exemplification, each branding impression-management tactic features risks. The surest way to minimize these undesirable consequences is to first be aware that they exist.

We recommend that you manage the impressions that important others create you—and your brand. This recommendation, however, should not be viewed as a universal endorsement of the practice. Not that our "universal" qualifier really matters. Impression management will be used universally by serious, determined, and ambitious professionals regardless of what we write. What we endorse instead, is that if brand impression-management behaviors are destined to unfold on your stage anyway, learn how to execute and to parry them better.

Your Stage is always the Right Place to Build Brand Identities

Times may arise when your best branding tactic is simply: "Show up." Catch a plane, for example, and travel where you must to meet the right people at their convenience, on their stages. This impression management tactic would sometimes be dictated by protocol. At other times the tactic could be predicated by the gravity of the opportunity or other stakes involved. But remember, your office is your theater. It is your stage to control and command, and upon which you should "kill" as you present the best, most-appealing and ultimately determinant dimensions of yourself. Great teachers, presenters, or professional branders always take control of rooms when time, circumstance and opportunity dictate that they should take control. You should always endeavor to own your room, in compellingly persuasive, power-enhancing, and brand-friendly ways.

We purposefully used the evocative term "kill" in the preceding paragraph. There is a reason why, when we have done well as a presenter, we say we have "killed." Making people pay attention is, at its essence, an act of domination. Yet making people pay attention is likewise clearly a prerequisite for them to learn—and you to to persuade. Or to your ability to induce audiences to choose your professional solution and not another competitive alternative. Persuading people to pay attention, through whatever socially responsible, ethical, and moral means necessary, is a precursor to power. With greater power contributing to greater persuasiveness, of course, we hope, for you.

Still, even if all you can boast as your career begins is a power cubicle, you will find it best to meet on you own turf. You can exercise control over meetings with clients or prospects in your office that simply is not available elsewhere. And because these "territorial imperatives" abide, any interactions conducted there are accompanied by a sense of "invasion" by your counterpart. Tension will be present no matter how subtle or sublimated it may appear.

By managing your branding impressions in ways that make your office guest more comfortable, you can diffuse this tension. Office décor and accoutrements, including furniture, can infer what is acceptable or expected from clients or other audience members. Comfortable chairs, even in smallish spaces, or visible tissues implicitly suggests it is acceptable to relax, express emotions, or possibly even cry. Photos of you laughing in social settings or vivid/action oriented art or sculptures might brand you as a happy warrior. Prominent lists of rules and the consequences of breaking them might position you as a fearsome warrior. (Additional discussion of this exact topic follows in Chapter 10.)

The last two actions would draw audience members toward your brand. This outcome, in turn, permits you to integrate a certain unacknowledged but never subliminal confidence in and respect from your audience for your brand even before meetings begin.

Branding: The Ultimate Professional Competition

Professional actions, particularly those grounded in a desire to create influence and exercise power, always entail competitions. Those contests are won or lost in one place; inside the minds of clients, prospects, and other audience members. Competitions sometimes devolve to the point at which conflict arises between people reporting to you or the individual to whom you report. You have a responsibility to the integrity and future success of your branded self to diminish dissent or resolve conflict through legal and ethically acceptable means. Again we see how and why the weapon known as impression management should be featured in every professional's branding arsenal.

The impact of brand-based impression-management tactics on relationships and the positive or negative outcomes generated through those relationships is frequently overlooked. Perhaps, because the use of impression-management strategies is so commonplace. Even so, it is helpful to learn more about available strategies, as well as the motives promoting their use. Then, regardless of whether you manage your branding impressions or are targeted by other professionals' brand impression-management efforts, you should perform more effectively as an informed, discerning participant in what genuinely is an ongoing drama. Shakespeare, indeed. We all really are playing on a world stage. No wonder Shakespeare's theater was named "The Globe."[24]

After selecting your preferred brand identity, present yourself in a manner consistent with the image you seek. After and as you present this branded self, attend carefully to the verbal and nonverbal feedback that targeted audiences provide. If necessary, behaviors and artifacts can be changed as you matriculate toward your more successfully branded self.

You should likewise recognize the full extent of the reputational dangers associated with whatever impression-management tactic you choose to pursue on a particular stage. Each impression-management tactic, save exemplification, is associated with known disadvantages. To minimize these undesirable consequences, you had best remain aware of them.

A final guideline may trump all other suggestions for better impression management and a more sustainably compelling brand identity: When choosing and pursuing your desired brand image, never attempt to be something you are not. Others will see through the façade sooner or later. Work hard, always projecting the best version of yourself but never at the cost of your true identity or integrity. At day's end, the surest approach to making a great brand impression, first, last, or in-between, on any stage is:

- Work hard enough and with sufficient focused passion to become and remain a high-end performer. Bottom line, that means exemplification.

Even or perhaps especially the greatest of the artistic greats knew this. Take heed of Michelangelo's blunt but revealing observation:

- "If people knew how hard I had to work to obtain my mastery, it would not seem so wonderful at all."[25]

The Simplest Way to Make Great First Branding Impressions

Tibetan culture teaches young citizens to give a smile when they see a smile. Half their smile is for the other, because their receipt of a smile benefits the other. Half young Tibetan person's smile, they are taught, is for them, because they benefit. Who knew the act of smiling at someone else was at least halfway self-centered?

Were he alive, old school but well-branded to this day motivational speaker and author Dale Carnegie would surely agree. Mr. Carnegie once described a personal experience that provides an excellent way to end this discussion. The simple message contained within his story also provides a peaceful way to close a discussion that opened with violence spears. Speaking in the gender-biased parlance of his time, Mr. Carnegie once said:

- "I recently attend a dinner party in New York. One guest, a woman who had inherited money, was eager to make a pleasing impression on everyone. She had squandered a modest fortune on sables, diamonds, and pearls. But she hadn't done anything whatsoever about her face. It radiated sourness and selfishness. She didn't realize what every man knows. Namely, that the expression a woman wears on her face is far more important than the clothes she wears on her back."[26]

One of the best brand impression-management behaviors for you to execute is the easiest to execute. When meeting someone else who is, has been, or one day may be incredibly important to you, smile your biggest, best, and sincerest "happy to see you" smile. If your choppers don't flip an audience, at least they should tilt them toward your side of the stage you will now control.

Notes

1 Michener, James A. (1976). *Centennial.* New York, NY: Penguin Random House Publishing.
2 Strutton, David and Terrence Holmes (2002). "Managing Buyer-Seller Relationships One Impression at a Time." *Business Horizons*, 45: 67-78.
3 Epstein, Joseph (2006). *The Yale Book of Quotations.* New Haven, CT: Yale University Press.
4 Strutton and Holmes.
5 Ibid., 55.
6 Ariely, Dan. (2012). *Predictably Irrational: The Hidden Forces the Shape Our Decisions.* New York, NY: Harper Collins.
7 Southgate, Troy (2012). *Eliot: Thoughts & Perspectives.* Vol. 7. New York: Black Front Press.
8 Murray, Peter N. (2014). How Emotions Influence What We Buy. *Psychology Today.* Retrieved April 15, 2016. http://www.psychologytoday.com/blog/inside-the-consumer-mind.
9 Bell, Racheal. (2006). The Tylenol Terrorist. *Crime Library.* True TV.
10 James, Erika Hayes and Lynn Wooten (2010). *Leading Under Pressure.* London: Routledge Academic.
11 Cooper, Cecily D. (2005). "Just Joking Around? Employee Humor Expression as an Ingratiatory Behavior," *Academy of Management Review*, 30(4): 765-776.
12 Bohra, Kayyum A. and Janak Pandey, "Ingratiation toward Strangers, Friends and Bosses." *The Journal of Social Psychology*, 122: 217-222.
13 Hogg, Michael A. and Graham Vaughan (2008). *The Sage Handbook of Social Psychology.* Sage.
14 Naderi, Iman and David Strutton (2015). "I Support Sustainability But Only When Doing So Reflects Fabulously on Me: Can Green Narcissists Be Cultivated? *Journal of Macromarketing*, 35(1): 70-83.
15 Liechtenstein, Nelson (2009). *The Retail Revolution: How Wal-Mart Created a Brave New World of Business.* New York, NY: Metropolitan Books.
16 Bourke, Jessica (2005). *Fear: A Cultural History.* London: Virago Publishing.
17 Strutton, David, Lou E. Pelton, and James R. Lumpkin (1993). "The Influence of Psychological Climate on Conflict Resolution Strategies inside Franchising Relationships." *Journal of the Academy of Marketing Science*, 21(2): 201-217.
18 Goldman, Russell (2016). KFC to Honor Oprah's Fee Chicken. *ABC News*, Retrieved February 26, 2016, http://abcnews.go.com/Business/story?id=7527626
19 Bolander, Daniel (1969). *Instant Quotation Dictionary.* Munderlein, IL: Career Institute Publishing.
20 Newport, Cal (2012). *So Good They Cannot Ignore You: Why Skills Trump Passion in the Quest for Work You Love.* New York, NY: Hachette Book Group.

21 Holy Bible (1999). *Holy Bible: New Standard Revised Edition.* Nashville, TN: Thomas Nelson, Inc.
22 Editorial (2016). Mrs. Clinton's Speeches to Big Banks. *New York Times,* February 26, 2016: A22.
23 Hofer, Thomas and Bruno Messerli (2014). *Floods in Bangladesh: History, Dynamics and Rethinking the Role of the Himalayas.* Tokyo, Japan: United Nations University Press.
24 Nagler, Alios M. (1958). *Shakespeare's Stage.* New Haven, CT: Yale University Press.
25 Useem, Jerry (2016). "Is Grit Overrated?" *The Atlantic,* 317(4): 30-33.
26 Carnegie, Dale (1998). *How to Win Friends and Influence People.* New York: Gallery.

Chapter 8

Power Rules: Growing the Power and Persuasiveness of Your Brand

"To exaggerate is to weaken"

—Jean Francois de La Harpe (1739–1803).

For the best or is it the worst of reasons the reputation of CEOs has suffered for years. Say hello to the leaders of Volkswagen, General Motors, Enron, Hewlett Packard, World.com, Omnicom, Martha Stewart Living, British Petroleum, Computer Associates, or RadioShack. These firms topped-off a recent Time magazine list of most suspicious characters. And you know this list could have been substantially extended. Unremitting corporate scandals coupled with exorbitant pay scales and routinely empty assurances are partly to blame. Frequently moribund stock prices, domestic and international economies that seemingly slide sideways or worse year after year, and their own personal failings have also dinged the collective brand of many business leaders. CEOs have also been victimized by their often blatantly false rhetoric. Having sung off-tune off the promised-shareholder-returns sheet of music for so long many magpie-like CEOs have seemingly forgotten how to sing anything else. The power of their brand has clearly suffered on a national stage.

The magpie status of CEOs is closely mirrored by a now-professional political class. One major domestic political brand perpetually promises it will create a Santa Claus-like government to solve all your problems. The Democrat message, cut to the bone: "Give us power so we can do great things for you." The other major political brand message repeatedly promises to keep Big Government's hands off your guns or out of your bedrooms or churches. The core Republican message: "Give us power so we can give you the freedom to do great things for yourself." Two clearly persuasive yet demonstrably untrue branding messages, summarized in 11 and 16 words, respectively. And almost to a voter their respective audiences know politicians, regardless of the liberal or conservative side upon which the professional's teleprompter resides, are lying to them.

Consider, for example, the political stage on which the first three "key words" used by a large sample to describe the leading Democratic candidate during the 2016 Presidential nomination campaign were, in descending order, liar, dishonest and untrustworthy. Yet Mrs. Clinton was comfortably elected as the Democrat Presidential nominee. This "not-imagined reality", okay, this eligible voter perception, was borne out in fact by the fact that the candidate lied repeatedly for about 18 months about her home-brewed serve misuse and abuse. Until the Federal Bureau of Investigation inexplicably failed to indict Mrs. Clinton—and she no longer really had to discuss the topic. But perhaps the FBI's decision was explicable given that Director James Comey seemingly purposefully did great damage to Mrs. Clinton's political brand in his detailed public description of why the FBI did not recommend indictment. After all, Comey had his branding identity to worry about, as well.

No wonder the average political brand is less powerful, influential or respected than at any point in U.S. history. Trust that their core audiences once placed in them has largely evaporated. Meanwhile, cynicism and contempt first grew and has since solidified.

These are the reputations that contemporary political and executive professionals generally must endure. The branding reputations of CEOs and politicians are terrible because the reality of their branded identities is worse. Each professional cohort has ironically but not unexpectedly lost control over the reputations they created for themselves.

There is good news/bad news, however. Neither the CEOs nor politician class faces imminent extinction. Won't happen. Not in a capitalist democratic society in which the functions each cohort performs are indispensable. And fortunately, we are not here to bury CEOs or politicians, or even to critique their performance. Instead our purpose is to show political and business professionals how to lift their individual brands up from the morass that they and their fellows have created.

There is actual good news, however:

- *The same branding principles that apply to and would help CEOs or politicians apply similarly to all professionals seeking to elevate the power and influence of their brands.*

Seven Rules for Elevating the Power of Your Brand

Two principles drive chapter's discussion. First, the power of individuals performing on the CEO or political professions or for that matter business, engineering, legal, architectural, health care, software programing stages, and so forth, will wax or wane based on how effectively they manage their current and future branding reputations. Second, the branding power and persuasiveness of individual professionals will rise and fall together.

We'll assume you know what you are doing, functionally and therefore professionally. Let's further assume that you also deliver exemplary practical solutions on whatever professional stage you occupy. Given this, and the fact that most of your fellow professionals perform with similar effectiveness, your best hope for earning sustainable power and persuasion may lie in fundamentally changing or strengthening your core branding identities. More candor, more truth-based attention to your reputation, are good places to begin. Sure, this may well entail an upstream swim on stages populated by intrinsically self-centered beings. But as a logical starting point, you might break with standard practice on your stage and metaphorically pound your lance into the ground. Do this passionately, in a manner similar to how Lame Beaver performed. First stake and then tether your current and future reputations to what is proper and good and to fulfilled promises to fix what is improper and negative. And then do your absolute best to honor these commitments.

Do this, and the favorable consequences that would accrue to your branding reputation and subsequent power might be astounding. Michel de Montaigne understood this exact branding proposition, although he never referenced brands or branding. The 16th Century philosopher wrote: "Everything else is subject to trade; we let friends share our goods and our lives if necessary. But a case of sharing our name and fame or making someone else the gift of our reputation is hardly to be found."[1] Amen—a word that simply means, yes—to that! What good things would happen for you and your family if you ascribed higher value to the long-term persuasiveness that would be yours for the wielding if you developed a stronger, more powerful, branding reputation?

Seven "branding power rules" that could be applied to grow your branding power follow. Each power-enhancing rule is derived from traditional experiences. When discussing how best to accumulate power, historical knowledge and past precedent are logical sources to tap. After all, "there is no knowledge that is not also power," as 19th century poet and journalist Ralph Waldo Emerson wrote.[2] Simon Kierkegaard, a Danish philosopher and theologian who lived during the same century, reasoned similarly. Kierkegaard counseled:

- "Life must be lived forward. But life can only be understood looking back."[3]

Less portentously, but no less sincerely, we recommend:

- Get a leg up now your future branding success by immersing yourself in as much relevant history as possible, including your own historical wins and losses, as soon as possible.

Branding Power Rule 1: Make Your Reputation Unimpeachable

Reputation is the critical base from which all movement toward the ability to execute discretionary in professional sector will originate. (Discretionary power, in this context, can be described as persuasiveness or influence that does not directly emanate from whatever formal position you occupy.) Reputation is a critical foundation of branding power. Desirable reputations increase personal presence. Similar to how having the right or wrong sort of friends embedded in your sphere can help or hurt you in that domain, good reputations multiply your personal strengths. Bad reputations will divide them. Stated more directly:

- Show us your reputation and we will show you your future.

Nothing in history is permanent with the possible exception of a bad name. A fallen brand, if you will. Et tu, Brutus, for example; Pontius Pilate, who may have earned a bad name just for doing his job as Roman governor; or Benedict Arnold and Richard Nixon. We could have referenced Lee Harvey ... well, you know, everyone knows his last name. Their undesirable branding legacies echo hollowly across generations. Some obviously for reasons for worse or more impactful than others.

Remain on the right side of the reputational ratio. You might, for example, strive to earn a reputation for sharing with your fellow professionals (teammates), like National Basketball Association star LeBron James has done. Or you could pursue a reputation for selfishly seeking to shine brighter than your teammates, like the recently retired professional basketball star, Kobe Bryant. He is also branded as the "Black Mamba," a singular identity cultivated by Kobe himself.

Earn the right reputation and you become less vulnerable to attack. You'll generally enjoy more opportunity to intimidate gently or directly and to on potentially or actually contentious stages through either method. Few assets could ever supplant the value of an exemplary branding reputation. You hopefully recall: professional brands "encompass the set of beliefs, values, and *assets* associated with a particular professional."

Whether your branding reputation inspires admiration from, intimidation of, or desire to emulate you among key audiences, so long as your reputation inspires, much of your work is done before you "stride" upon any stage. To the extent that branding performances can be managed, those aspiring to achieve greater power and persuasiveness should similarly strive to create unassailable reputations for themselves. No other reasonable option exists but to plan, for purposes of achieving a more desirable reputation. As you brand plan, always distinguish between what is thought and what is known to be true about the sort of brand reputation you should desire or seek to avoid.

Professionals who plan, eventually master, and thereafter manage their reputations will exercise more control over their futures.[4] No one can ever fully predict their futures. Perhaps you've heard the joke: Want to make God laugh? Tell Him your plans. But professionals still enjoy the opportunity and means to create futures more to their liking. But typically, those futures appear only after you've planned and executed your branding-management scripts effectively.

Master, Then Manage, Your Branded Reputation

Professional stages are usually conspicuously transparent places.[5] Open- and closed-door opinions are freely registered about everything, every action, and every person of note, which presumably does or should include you. During this digital age these views travel at the speed with which tweets, texts, and e-mails are transmitted. Subjective "thoughts" are likely to be expressed about "rising stars" or about professionals who assertively seek to manage the impressions that audiences form about them in order to gain recognition and advancement. Nothing can be gained by those who choose to not manage their reputations. But much might be lost. Especially, in comparison to others who elect to strenuously and effectively manage their branding impressions and benefit from their resulting reputations. Another undesirable outcome might also arise if you ignore your reputation. By not managing impressions that core audiences form about you, you de facto encourage or permit others to create your reputation for you. A professional reputation is too valuable an asset to permit it to be managed secondhand by ambivalent or, worse, malevolent third parties.

In professional settings, your "appearance" provides easily discernible cues on which audience members may base their judgements of your reputation, or brand. Stage "appearance" could entail dimensions such as your:

- Physical presence, including apparel choices, physique, and general fitness level, posture, or gestures; actions, pursued or not pursued; and words, spoken or unspoken.

The musician Bob Seger's 1980s-era ballad, *Against the Wind,* effectively summarizes certain ongoing challenges that mindful branding professionals will confront when seeking to manage their actions and words. To create your best possible future branding reputation, as the song's lyrics suggest, you must strategically decide "what to leave in and what to leave out." *Against the Wind* also poignantly pronounces, "Wish I didn't know now what I didn't know then."[6] Lyrics that aptly summarize the understandable angst that experienced professionals feel about things they should/should not have done in their past. Anxieties that are perhaps even more understandable amongst younger professionals given that they don't yet know whether their scripted or unscripted lives will play out delightfully or dreadfully.

You may be young or seasoned in age or even in heart. But if you're reading this book you're probably old and experienced enough to have turned professional or see your future professional self from here. Believe it or not, however, one thing you need not overly worry about now is your future reputation. Not if you follow the branding power principles outlined below. Follow these principles, and lower the risk that you will end up a less than fully realized professional who looks back mournfully at the past from some future date bitterly lamenting ... wish I knew then what I know now.

Focus, Then Focus More

From the beginning to the end of your career focus on building a reputation based on one outstanding genuinely difference-making quality that will prove germane to success upon your professional stage. That is, you should work to establish a differentiated reputation based on one *determinant* distinction that is highly either by external or internal audiences.[7] Or hopefully, both audience types. Distinctively reputation-enhancing qualities, differences that should generate stronger and more favorable brand positions, might include:

- Purposefully demonstrating decisiveness when challenges arrive.
- Acting creatively when solving big-hairy-audacious problems.
- A demonstrated ability to focus, keeping the main thing the main thing, as you perform.
- Calmly and succinctly delivering evidence of experience-born wisdom, insights, and/or patience during crises.
- Exhibiting simple collegiality or equanimity on stages too often are characterized by neither.

Each quality entails a desirable personal and professional distinction that would deliver positive branding differences that key audiences should value. Your possession and routine demonstration of any one or all of these strategic brand qualities should differentiate you, as a brand bearer, in ways that prompt others to speak or think more favorably about you and your reputation.

Machiavelli might have suggested your next logical step is then to build awareness of your consciously branded quality among as many audience members as possible. But he didn't so we just did. Do this, and a foundational cohort of brand followers or "admirers" would emerge over time. Then, with the passage of time, you should add additional distinctive qualities. But add additional points of differentiation only after you've determined how these new qualities complement or add incremental value to your reputation and brand.

Branding Power Rule 2: Brand Yourself through Action Not Argument

Greater branding power generally should accrue to professionals who get others to agree with them through actions rather than words. Here, Machiavelli's succinct counsel was:

- "Demonstrate, don't explicate."[8]

On competitive, potentially contentious stages words are seldom neutral. When you argue with superiors, subordinates, peers, or clients, you risk implicitly impugning their intelligence or motivations and provoking indignation. Because competent people typically believe they are right, and because your superiors, peers, and indeed your subordinates or clients generally are competent, only rarely will mere words convince these audiences to alter their thinking.

Contentious remarks usually fall on deaf ears, create belligerent feelings, and often inspire overtly belligerent responses from listening audiences. When anyone is cast unnecessarily and essentially against their will into an argumentative scenario on any response, their most natural response is to argue back. While professional-on-professional or professional–client conflict sometimes generates favorable outcomes, it usually does not. The most likely outcome is that existing rifts would widen while your brand identity and reputation suffers.

Another branding problem associated with attempts to prove points to clients, peers, or superiors through arguments is that even victories can be Pyrrhic. Short term, ultimately hollow wins, in other words. Pyrrhic victories, so-labeled in honor of King Pryrrus of Epius, are tantamount to defeats due to the long-term tolls they extract from the "winning" performer's branding identity and reputation. One too many Pyrrhic victories, grounded in arguments they "won", has been the undoing of many contentious professionals.

Who knows for certain how arguments affect important audience members? They may agree publically with you while harboring private bitterness. You may have said something that unwittingly offended someone whom you prefer not to have as an adversary. Even seemingly harmless statements, seemingly to you at least, harbor an insidious capacity for misinterpretation. Who can predict how or when your client's endemic mood, personal insecurities, or in the moment disposition might lead them to misconstrue your true intent? The fact remains:

- Words truly are a dime of dozen. Everyone past the intellectual age of 12 understands that many people will say anything to win or avoid an argument. As always, of course, dependent upon the stage they occupy. Then days, but more likely hours or minutes later, such actors regress back to old beliefs.

When push comes to shove, as occasionally happens, your more informed professional behavior, or perhaps non-behavior, is to avoid counterarguments whenever possible. Do this, however, in ways that demonstrate your branding strength rather than signal any weakness. Many people somehow seemingly assume they alone have mastered the universe of logic and reason. We often do. You too, probably. Even when our presumed mastery is self-evidently is not the case.

The branding power associated with demonstrating rather than verbalizing your ideas will usually flow most directly from one indispensable benefit. The benefit: Audiences, including clients, generally become less defensive. And absent defensiveness, more receptive to your persuasive forays. Situations in which ideas that otherwise might be framed in an argument are presented in ways that permit clients, collaborators, or even competitors to see or experience their benefits create stage-managed opportunities for you to convert their hearts and minds. In brief, you'll become and remain more persuasive than if you merely verbalized your ideas. When fewer people are offended, you enjoy more opportunity to drive home fundamental points or strategic distinctions. Those key points or distinctions then will coalesce in ways that allow your brand's power to grow. You also always enjoy the opportunity to differentiate your branding persuasiveness through the skill with which you can indirectly demonstrate the virtue, value, and ultimately the power of your ideas. The process will prove difficult and subtle but never impossible.

Even Communists Understood This Rule

During a 1956 speech delivered to an important Union of Soviet Socialist Republics—today, primarily Russian—audience in which then Soviet Premier Nikita Khrushchev castigated Josef Stalin's crimes, an antagonist interrupted him by shouting, "You were with Stalin, why didn't you stop him?" Khrushchev could not see his critic. But the Premier paused, and shouted: "Who said that?" No hand went up. Following a pregnant silence, the Soviet Premier quietly stated, essentially using a stage whisper: "Now you know why." Rather than arguing publicly that anyone reporting to Stalin literally would have been scared to death to object to his crimes, Khrushchev acted in a way that demonstrated to this audience what it would have felt like to confront the malevolent leader. Such is the power of branding through demonstrable action rather than through argument.[9]

Or, as an only slightly more effusive Spanish Jesuit Baltasar Gracian wrote during the 1600s: "The truth is more often seen than heard."[10] Demonstrate, rather than explicate, the two or three best parts of you that one day soon will be recognized as the best parts of your branding identity.

Balls or Brains

Despite this *kumbayah* interlude, we would be remiss to not re-visit the interminable "balls versus brains" route to persuasion.

Intimidation, as introduced above, represents a viable impression-management tactic when it is strategically employed in certain scenes, on select stages. Former President Lyndon Baines Johnson understood the potential value of this branding tactic. The big man persistently employed intimidation, especially during his lengthy tenure as Senate Majority Leader. "Grab them by the balls and their hearts and minds will follow" was how L.B.J., in his south Texas vernacular, described his intimidating and power-enhancing tactic.[11] (The President was branded as "L.B.J.")

For reasons described earlier, L.B.J. experienced far more difficulty when attempting to exercise power for persuasive purposes after he had ascended into the Presidency. That is, he encountered problems after an initial burst of remarkable legislative accomplishments—motivated largely by the legislative branch's understandably emotional reaction to President John F. Kennedy's then-recent assassination. Had L.B.J. concentrated more on building a "kinder and gentler" basis for his branding power his administration, in the personage of a second term, may have survived the Vietnam War.

Branding Power Rule 3: Speak Less Than Necessary

Professional branding power is a game of appearance. When you say less than necessary, others around often view you as more powerful or knowledgeable than you actually are. This result redounds favorably to any professional brand. Restraint typically projects a confidently competent, "things are under control" branding image. A brand identity that similarly radiates power. When engaging on uncertain or ambiguous stages, audiences are instinctively motivated to seek interpretation and achieve understanding. If you prudently control what you reveal, contending, competitive, and even collaborative audience members cannot ascertain your entire meaning And thus can be more easily frustrated or weakened if and when those outcomes further your branding—or communication—goal.

On many stages, saying less than necessary makes you appear more profound, insightful and rational. Consider, for example, the fictional Chauncey Gardner from the 1979 movie *Being There*. The previously anonymous Mr. "Gardner"—who actually was a "gardener"—rapidly and implausibly ascends to powerful heights through the utterance of very few words and frequent silences that were hardly strategic.[12]

Then there was "Silent Cal" Calvin Coolidge, who against high odds but by all appearances—and contemporary photogenic accounts demonstrate he did *look* the branded part—rose to the Presidency. He gained the presidency largely by performing out informal branding script that prescribed: "Nothing I never said ever did me any harm."[13] "Silent Cal" honored his self-assigned prescript—his peculiarly powerful branding rule—as he campaigned and led and legislated as President. Our bet is that few contemporary politicians would campaign based on such a premise. Then again, contemporary political differ markedly from the stages that existed in the 1920s.

Or, finally, consider what Denzel Washington's lead character said in the 2007 movie *American Gangster*: "The loudest man in the room is the weakest man in the room."[14] Frank Lucas, Denzel's character, uttered this phrase right before shooting the room's loudest man in the head, before 30 or so witnesses. Mr. Lucas, a real life gangster, apparently calculated that the branding power he stood to earn by combining an opportunity to speak less than necessary with the opportunity to exercise intimidation on a stage shared by many witnesses would function as a singularly effective branding impression-management tactic. And it did, insofar as surviving witnesses surely spread the good or bad word about his "professional" gangster branding performance.

And the point in fact is that Mr. Lucas's bold plan did work in real life. Until, the FBI and New York Police (NYPD), two other well-branded organizations, infiltrated his crime syndicate and arrested the gangster. We are not recommending, however, that any reader "cap" anyone. Not even, if "they deserve it." We're joking, of course. But readers likewise may recall how in the movie *True Lies,* Arnold Schwarzenegger's character confessed to "wife" Jamie Lee Curtis: "Yes, I have killed people. But they were all bad guys [who deserved it]."[15]

One branding takeaway is clear:

- The less you say, particularly on stages where any utterance likely will not improve the silence, the less risk you run of saying something foolish or offensive to an important customer, critic, or friend.

This information is good to know. And fortunately, other ways exist for you to persuade or project power to others. Machiavelli labeled the human tongue "an unruly beast." He then noted how few are able to master it. The Renaissance-era courtier may have cribbed the Bible. The B.I.B.L.E., which some have cleverly acronymized and rebranded as Basic Instructions Before Leaving Earth, makes 17 references to the need that humans routinely encounter to bridle their tongues. The Gospel of Matthew (15:11), for example, offers useful branding power counsel: "Not that which goeth into the mouth defileth a man; but that which cometh out of the mouth, this defileth a man," and his or her brand. When they rumble untamed, tongues can run amuck and create great grief for their bearer's brands. Branding power rarely accumulates among those individuals who squander their treasure of words though overuse or carelessness.

Another lesson related to potential branding failure is simpler still: Once words spill out, they cannot be taken back. Words should be dispensed sparingly and thoughtfully on professional stages. Their fellows, superiors, reports, and clients rarely view verbose professionals as wise, polished, or powerful. Speak too much, or absent sufficient forethought, and descriptions like undisciplined, blowhard, or "know-it-all" will more likely to attach to your brand identity.

Still, Too Little Can Be Too Little

Some skepticism, however, is merited. The "say less than necessary" rule just offered is hardly universally desirable, suitable, or applicable. At times you would be foolish to intentionally withhold information. A routine reticence to disclose necessary information might arouse suspicion about your character, judgement, competence, or ability, especially among superiors or clients. Vague responses or commentary, issued on the wrong stages, would expose you to less than desirable audience interpretations of your brand.

Silence and brevity should be used strategically. But only on appropriate stages. When done right, people you work with, for, or manage leave meetings feeling slightly less than satisfied and consequently pondering and more easily recalling your past and future words. This outcome elevates your branding power. Extra attention paid to your brief comments, as or after they are issued, enhances the potential persuasiveness of the branding purveyor who uttered or did not utter them. Leonardo da Vinci, Renaissance-era Milan's great artist and inventor, wrote persuasively about this exact principle: "Oysters open completely when the moon is full. Then, when a crab sees one, it throws a piece of stone or seaweed into it, and the oyster cannot close again. Such is the fate of one who opens his mouth, and thereby places himself at the mercy of his enemy."[16]

Branding Power Rule 4: Master the Art of Timing

Time is an artificial construct. Time is an interpretable object created by humanity for its own purposes and exploitation. No one can reclaim lost time. Nor can anyone influence the extant quantity of time. Time's velocity and its value depend on perceptions. Consider, for example, how radically children's perceptions differ from adult perceptions of time. Of course, one year of a 10-year-old's life represents 10% of his life. Meanwhile, one year for a 50-year-old woman entails only 2% of her life. The facts that time is human-made and perceptual in nature intimate that professionals can manage certain "time" dimensions in order to develop certain desirable branding outcomes for themselves. But only if you learn enough, are strategic enough, and bold enough to initiate and complete the mission.

Philosophers have discussed the need to manage time and master the art of timing, since, the origins of recorded history—again, time! The Roman sage Plutarch wrote:

- "Time is good friend and ally to those who choose the right moment. But dangerous foe to those who rush in at the wrong moment."[17]

Plutarch and other ancient luminaries understood then that two time-related decisions were always in play. You should understand now that this remains true today. One choice is to control time in ways that make it your ally. The second choice is not to master time. Remember, when you choose to not act you have still made a choice. But here, however, you would be making a choice that effectively exposes your brand to high risks of victimization by the hands of time's unbending nature.

During ancient times leaders were taught to master three categories of time. Each time category featured unique constraints. In turn, each imposed certain threats. If you address time with the proper perspective, you can leverage these time embedded constraints into branding power opportunities. This makes sense, because Plutarch also wrote: "Time can be wisest of all counselors."[18]

The wise man wrote something else that would prove useful should you decide to steer the progression of your brand: "Perseverance is more effective than brute strength. Many [branding?] challenges cannot be overcome if you try to do everything at once. But these will yield if you master them little by little. Steady, continuous efforts followed by periodic but purposeful thrusts are irresistible, for this is how time captures the greatest powers on earth."[19]

Managing the Long Term

The first category of time that you should master is the *long term.* Despite economist John Maynard Keynes' quip for the ages that "in the long run we're all dead," successfully branded professionals must manage this drawn-out sort of time. Machiavelli suggested effective leaders should address long-term time defensively. He wrote about the art of *not* acting impulsively but instead *waiting* patiently the right branding opportunities to arise. Or, as the previously referenced John Wooden taught, "letting the game come to you" ... by being quick in mind, thought, and spirit but rarely hurried in one's actions.

Seeking a more powerfully persuasive brand? Slow down long-term time to the point where you can discern, capture, and respond in harmony with the "spirit of the times." Spirit of the times, also known as *Zeitgeist*. Success may require you to appropriate a studied, yes, "professional," detachment and a knowing distance that tamps down emotions and facilitates insight about the shape of things to come. Those results should subsequently point out your most promising branding identities. Or, say, whether you should primarily intimidate; engage in self-promotion, exemplification, or entitlement seeking; strategically but ethically withhold information while executing based on insights you enjoy that others don't possess; or enlist some combination of all these tactics.

Slowing down time while waiting "patiently" for opportune moments to act requires self-control. Control over your emotions, of course. But at times, also controlling to the extent possible the emotions of your clients, peers, or subordinates. In sum and in brief, audiences who, mistaking action for accomplishment, may expect rash decisions from you.

One practical implication for professions seeking long-term accumulation of brand-based power: Never make important decisions today that can reasonably be put off until tomorrow. That is, when you can assume more information will be known with greater certainty tomorrow. Because the passage of time, facilitated by your patience, allows more reflection to be injected in the decision-making context.

This branding tactic may require you to artfully engage in procrastination. Even "purposeful procrastination" will prove difficult when trying to get things off your desk or satisfy anxious clients as quickly as possible. Subordinates are particularly likely to press for quick decisions. Perhaps so you won't enjoy time to consult with others or fully deliberate longer term intended or unintended consequences of the decision you're being pushed to make. Hold fast, however, because acting rashly may damage your brand, especially over the long term.

On the other hand, Machiavelli admonished his Prince to promote the opposite behavior in one's rivals. Then, he advocated, multiple opportunities to step in and pick up the pieces might arise. Picking them up while concurrently elevating your brand identity, we hasten to add.

Managing the Short Term

The *short term* is a second category of time you should master, presumably to no one's surprise. Times may arise when your branding power can be enhanced by disrupting the others' timing. But only for ethical purposes, of course. Two time-tested approaches exist. The first method entails making the "other" wait. The second entails making audiences or audience members hurry up, often suddenly and thus unexpectedly.

People who lack time to think are more mistake-prone. So you can manage other's deadlines if such slippages serves a larger, and ethical, branding purpose.

Alternatively, giving people more time to linger and think—by making them wait—can make them feel anxious and create timely branding opportunities for you. Machiavelli admired the legendary Cesare Borgia. He was notorious in using the latter timing technique. During seemingly leisurely negotiations, Borgia would often abruptly and vigorously push for a decision. Borgia was purposefully upsetting his opponents' cum partners' timing and patience. The fact of how well this tactic worked soon became well-known. Or perhaps Borgia simply exploited the branding power that flowed naturally from his well-earned reputation for guile and opportunism in ways that kept others who shared his expansive stage off stride.

Managing Action Time

There then is action - "go" - time. On many stages, occasions arise when carefully constructed branding-related plans should be launched quickly. Professionals who master long-term time have presumably waited patiently and identified the right moment. Professionals who dominate the short term may have nudged others off their own power games by confounding their timing. Neither result, however, elevates your brand identity unless you're willing and able to then close forcefully the line by executing your branding plan with decisive focus and purpose.

The United States Marine Corps philosophy for eliminating threats is grounded in the mastery of timing. The Corps' *Tactical Handbook* explains[20]: "Tempo is created using speed and time. *Timing* is knowing when to *act*. *Timing* is an appreciation for the rhythm of combat and then exploiting it to our advantage. It is impossible to go 'peak tempo' all the time. The key is to know when to go full speed and to rest when the enemy cannot hurt us. *Timing* means knowing when to act and when *not* to act. Sometimes waiting is a better option. We may need to create a situation to create an opportunity. Decisive *action* at the proper time is the goal. A decision not to *act* can also save forces for later engagements."

Substitute the term "professional branding" for the word "timing" in the preceding passage. Then, insert "perform professionally" for act or action. Do this, and if you're perceptive you'll gain insight regarding how best to develop, execute, and manage your branding power for the greater good. The greater good includes not just the welfare of your clients but also that of your self, firm.

Branding Power Rule 5: Act Boldly

Faint hearts have won few fair ladies or gentlemen. Or so the adage suggests. Bold rather than timid branding performances similarly elicit strikingly different audience responses. Including, not least, lost or won client hearts. Hesitation may cultivate obstacles that impede your movement toward distinctive branding power and persuasion. Your *learned* daring can obliterate the same barriers. Once this professional branding power principle is understood and applied, you should more easily overcome any natural timidity that may currently characterize your performance.[21]

Professional power players should constantly gauge the strengths and weaknesses of others around them as soon they are encountered. When encountering a male who may prove friend or foe for the first time, most men instantly either implicitly or explicitly calibrate whether they can "take down" the other physically or intellectually. (Male is the only gender category your authors understand firsthand; we don't know whether this premise pays out among females.) During first encounters with vital clients or audience members, a demonstrated proclivity for backing down or uncertainty will subject you to higher risks of over-assertiveness from your actual or potential exchange partner. Even among audience members who are not naturally predisposed toward assertiveness.

Audience reviews emerging from seemingly purely social interactions are often substantially influenced by appearances. Appearances on stages are concurrently tantamount to "authentic" and "dramatized" branding impressions. If you earn a reputation, rightly or wrongly, as one who goes conciliatory quickly, others may try to push you around. Responding too slowly respond on combative stages can create branding cracks permitting others to defend their or attack your position.

Boldness, by contrast, can make you appear larger than life. 18th century author Johann Wolfgang Goethe wrote:

- "Be bold, and mighty forces will come to your aid."

Timid professionals fade into the background. Their audacious counterparts draw attention. And what attracts attention generates brandable power. Bold strategies lead to bold actions and performances that make you appear more skillful or powerful than you are. When bold moves seemingly arrive suddenly, they inspire respect and/or fear. Precedents can be created from which healthy branding reputations as leaders are established, maintained, even burnished.

When you come on strong during initial interactions with others, they may lurch more readily into defensive postures, respecting, and perhaps fearing your alpha professional brand's next moves, when interacting with you in the future. At times, even problems created through daring performances can be remedied through mere audacity.

Professionals who are not sociopathic or psychopathic generally prefer to avoid conflict and the companion stress, anxiety, and tension that conflict's arrival engenders. Many professionals might logically fear the consequences of acting boldly in pursuit of a powerful brand: What will others think? What problems might arise if my reach exceeds my grasp? Can I resolve them?

You might justify timidity as a manifestation of concern for others, a desire to neither hurt nor offend. Yet timidity, by definition, is self-absorbed. By contrast, strategically deciding to act boldly in your branding performance is other directed. Bolder branders are less repressed.

Great value can gleaned from consciously choosing not to be afraid of being afraid. One of your many professional branding objectives should be to discover where that powerful value—not being afraid of fear—can best be exploited. Then exploit the discovery by becoming sufficiently motivated to act boldly when the context is right.

The Few, the Proud, the Naturally Bold

Stepping out and stepping up are challenging. Human beings are hardwired to overvalue certainty and to hate losing more than they love winning. The default human condition, in other words, is to fear the pain that ensues from failure more than covet the thrill of victory. (Most people hate losing more than they love winning and consequently avoid situations where they might lose.) These propensities embedded so deeply across humanity that many professionals unconsciously fail to try to boldly elevate their brands. At net, because the prospect of failure weighs too heavily on them.[22] These professionals demonstrably sacrifice prospects for material future-branding success in exchange more certainty and less risk in their present-day work lives.

What about you? If you're ambitious you should improve your branding station by taking measured risks. Particularly the risk of having bold branding performances occasionally fall short. Why? Because bold branding initiatives, even those resulting in failure, often function as precursors to more powerful futures.

The desire for certainty is the primary reason why few people are naturally bold. (A brand-deflating embrace of "certainty" is simultaneously wrapped into and a consequence of your fear of failure.) Even reputedly bold Napoleon had to consciously cultivate aggressiveness in war because he instinctively understood that acting decisively in battle could convert defeat into victory and ensure the survival of loyal soldiers. The Russian Czar who become known as Ivan the Terrible rebranded himself instantaneously from an inoffensive royal youth to a powerful young leader by boldly pointing a finger at a critical moment. His timely assertiveness elicited a quick and powerful response from his courtly audience. Ivan's new reputation was instantly sealed, in a way redounding directly to his personal and "professional" interests.

Negotiating sessions are one of the best stages on which to perform boldly to further your brand. When negotiating final prices, terms under which contracts will be executed, or beginning salaries or raises, begin by ascribing a high value to what you're making, marketing, or promising. Only back off grudgingly, if at all, on this presentation and illumination of your presumed problem-solving value. That is, if you want to become a great branding strategist and true power player. Former Secretary of State Henry Kissinger understood that insinuating bold demands during negotiations worked better than seeking or granting piecemeal concessions aimed at meeting one's counterpart halfway. Dr. Kissinger was simultaneously a wonderful brand strategist and power player.

Obviously there is more to negotiating successfully than merely performing perfunctorily bold branding acts, however. Imagine what could happen when "opposing" professionals act in similar bold and assertive ways. But when this happens, try to discern whether your counterpart's aggression is merely a ploy. Meanwhile, determine how best to prevent your counterpart from learning what aspects of any bold branding incursion emanating from you might similarly be a ploy.

Bold brand performances work best when used periodically and with good timing. The fact that your branding plans would rarely unfold exactly as you desire should neither surprise nor shame. Plans seldom survive the first smoke of battle, as you have read. But your strategy, your branding-management script, and the branding outcomes you seek remain essential. Before initiating bold branding gambits, think ahead, script out intended actions or non-actions, and implement assertive moves that allow you to dominate the stage.

Boldness can be learned. Boldness is a personal asset that you can cultivate for yourself. Once cultivated, or if it was already present, you should leverage and deploy boldness on a discretionary basis in situations where your script, the stage, your audience, and relevant context congeal in ways that support and indeed probably call for bold action. When these circumstances combine, the motive, means and opportunity for you to brand boldly have cohered. Then, frankly, we believe you should learn to go for it.

What can be learned can also be controlled. And boldness should be controlled, by you. Many audience members would be routinely offended by professionals who never rein in excessive or overly audacious self-branding initiatives. Professionals who constantly brand boldly are often doomed to eventual failure. So be careful, and choose your spot carefully. Again, we reference the 16th century Jesuit Baltasar Graican. He wrote:

- "Fear of failure in a performer's mind is, for onlookers, already evidence of failure. Actions are dangerous. When there is doubt as to their wisdom, it would be safer to do nothing."

Doing nothing, however, is often not the best option, or an option at all. Written instructions provided by first Marine Division Commanding General J.N. Mattis to his troops admonished them to act boldly. General Mattis wrote and delivered these words just before his Marines blasted Saddam Hussein's Iranian occupiers from their Kuwaiti positions. The text exemplifies the need that often arises for you to act boldly. His words:

- "When I give the word, together we will cross the Line of Departure, close with forces that choose to fight, and destroy them. While we will move swiftly and aggressively against those who resist, we will treat all others with decency, demonstrated chivalry, and soldierly compassion for those who have lived a lifetime under Saddam's oppression. Be the hunter, not the hunted. Never let your unit be caught with its guard down. Use judgement. Demonstrate to the world that there is 'No Better Friend, No Worse Enemy' than a United States Marine."[23]

That is a by-God and frankly God-based a powerful brand identity. Beyond question The Corps boasts a persuasive brand. One grounded in a well-earned reputation that surely has won more than one fight before the actual battle began. Be bold when time, place, or prevailing circumstances demands boldness. Or pack up your brand and go home. Perhaps you could wrap it in your noodle-like reputation.

Branding Power Rule 6: Pursue Change Temperately

Two branding lessons related to how you should treat and manage the past are universal and unimpeachable. Each lesson features actionable value. The value revealed should provide to be useful regardless of your stage—or whether you seek to lead or manage change on your stage.

The first lesson is that the past is and will always remain powerful. Even when intelligent, open-minded audience members understand intellectually that a need for change exists, at "rubber meets the road" levels most remain chained to habit. Consequently audience members are inevitably disturbed by changes that upset their daily habits and routines. Or by changes that arise in your professional performance or how you present yourself. Our consul remains the same: When change you must, and indeed times arise when change you should, do so deliberately.

No significant revolution—American, French, Russian, or more recently, Egyptian, Syrian, or Sundanese—has ever ensued without a powerful reaction against it. Call the phenomenon revolution, evolution, transformation, or insurrection; the the branding label ascribed to this process does not matter. Nothing important or complicated ever changes in a straight line regardless of whether the ends you seek are ethical or unethical, reasonable or unreasonable, or mandatory or discretionary. The only globally meaningful revolution in which the same people who began the insurgency finished it alive was American's revolution against England. The Gandhi-led Indian revolution against the British rule might have fit this bill. But Mahatma Gandhi was assassinated by an internal Hindu insurgent shortly after India freed itself from British rule. As might have the Civil Rights revolution lead by Martin Luther King, who patterned his movement on the same passive resistance model pioneered by the Mahatma. That is, had Dr. King not been killed by infamous assassin James Earl Ray.

There's no need to view the presence of client habits and their commitment to them as good or bad. When you brand, audience habits should simply be treated as an "is." As discussed, habits emerge because human brains continuously seek to conserve effort. When habits solidify, human brains no longer fully participate in decision making. Habits are constructed from cues or triggers; routines, which may be physical, mental, or emotional; and rewards, which help human brains determine whether this routine is worth remembering.

The second branding lesson is that the past in most professional settings usually is dead. We offer this assertion notwithstanding Mississippi author William Faulkner's well-known view to the contrary: "The past is not dead; it is not even buried." But Faulkner wrote about racism, love, and human disappointment and failings. We'll merely opine about professional stages.

The actual factual demise of the past in many professional settings makes it subject to your positive or negative reinterpretation, in accord with your branding goals and what actually transpired during the relevant past. If what happened in the past, for example, was undesirable or destructive, you would be foolish to associate your branding reputation with it. Alternatively, if the contemporary stage on which you perform is troubling or appears poised for deterioration, your brand power and persuasiveness might be enhanced by strategic referencing to the successes, comfort, or traditions of a more celebrated past. "I was there when" … or … "remember when we worked together to defeat …"

Three Branding Mantras

Mantras are chants—intonations issued about revered figures or traditions. Mantras are generally repetitive but hopefully not overly redundant routines. The preceding discussion reveals three brand for power mantras.

The first mantra is by now old-school:

- Pay attention to the times and to time itself.

When the need for changing your current branding script or performance can be justified but change likely won't be greeted with universal acclaim, continue your branding initiatives if only to avoid the emergence of a vacuum. Nature is not the only force that hates a vacuum. If branding professionals do not brand themselves, someone else will often backfill your reputation through negative words or deeds. Remember the wall, the barrier you must ascend in route to establishing branding power? As an alternative to doing nothing, you might, for example, "preach" the need for change or enacted reforms by or among clients. In the meanwhile, frame your "threats" to their "habits" through the comforting veneer of traditional rituals and patterns.

The second mantra, definitely related to the first

- When branding, make public displays of support for the past.

When pondering about the past, even liberal thinkers typically display a natural conservatism. Thoughtful branding professionals should give at minimum lip service to this spirit. By managing impressions carefully and respecting existing protocol, even passionate rebranding performances can be positioned in ways that make them appear less zealous. Identify elements of your anticipated brand identities that honor to the past and emphasize the congruence over time. Do this, and even radical brand changes that follow will be received with less pushback. When branding or rebranding your identity exploit the past by conforming its best or most respected parts to your future brand. Except, of course, in rare instances where the past was truly irredeemably horrific.

Astronomer Galileo Galilei followed these tactics early during his paradigm-bending life. The scholar accumulated great power and prestige in short order. Later, Galileo became more confrontational with the Catholic Church, his superiors, by directly criticizing the past. He summarily paid a high reputational price.[24]

The third professional branding mantra:

- Attend to the spirit of your time.

If the brand identities you pursue genuinely are too far ahead of their times, anxiety, misunderstanding or even rejection from clients or essential others will arise naturally. On such stages, you might "position" rebranding initiatives as less innovative than is actually the case.

Machiavelli wrote extensively about this branding power principle, though obviously, he did so indirectly. The princely advisor counseled:

- "He who attempts to reform himself successfully must at a minimum retain the semblance of the old forms. Do this so that it may appear to the people that there has been no change in your or the institution, even though in fact each is entirely different from the old. For the great majority of mankind is satisfied with appearances, as though they were realities."[25]

Machiavelli was among the first intellectuals to codify the notion that for most people their perception is their reality - or, as we describe the perceptual process, their "imagined" reality.

Temperate (moderate) branding changes have also been executed successfully on international stages. Until recently (the last 30 or so years), few groups have ever clung more resolutely to the past than Chinese peasants. Almost all 700–800 million of them. While branding himself as a powerful leader at the outset of the Chinese communist revolution, Mao Tse-tung apparently understood this audience character trait better than his competitors. Throughout the 1940s and 1950s, Mao's personal branding strategy was simple: Rather than struggling against the past, he leveraged his insights about Chinese history and traditions to his advantage.

To develop and then execute his brand identity, Chairman Mao first paired core communist values with romanticized figures and images embedded in Chinese lore. Then Mao "cast" or branded himself as a leader in the mode of former cultural savior Emperor Chuko Liang. Next, Mao leveraged and elevated the importance of the "cultural savior" role, or brand identity. Finally, he inserted himself into that role on a global stage that featured an interminable struggle between communist China; the Soviet Union, advocate of a different brand of communism; and the United States, as an evil capitalist society. Mao's insightful interpretation of past and present allowed him to understand that his Chinese audience would not be satisfied unless a great "Father Figure" *brand* was available for them to admire.[26]

Mao's change management branding strategy worked royally for decades. That is, until he moved radically away from the revered past during his Great Leap Forward rebranding campaign. This initiative was Mao's one great branding failure. Mao erred by thrusting too far ahead of his time by proposing changes that traditional Chinese audiences could not reasonably or easily tolerate—in that most important branding place, their minds.

Branding Power Rule 7: Brand Plan through to the End

No one cares who wins a 90-yard dash or half-marathon. What matters greatly instead are people who run races through to their logical end and especially people who end up securing the win. Perhaps, that's because winners have demonstrated their ability to plan and execute their plan successfully on competitive stages.

Ends are important to everyone playing out their lives on any stage. Endings are perhaps even more crucial to those playing branding games on professional stages. How branding performances end influences and at times determines whether your brand earns or loses value. Endings determine whether relationships with clients are established and strengthened or weakened and eventually shut-down. Endings determine whether the tide of power "owned" by your brand ebbs or flows. Even among nonbusiness professionals nothing that is genuinely difference-making happens until somebody creates, sells, buys, or benefits from something. That's when, where, and how wins and losses are tallied.

Branding professionals, however, sometimes succumb to the error of not knowing when to stop. Hint: Never stop 90 yards into a hundred yard dash or run miles beyond a marathon's finish line. Instead, identify the points at which your interests are better served by declaring victory and heading home. Or, identify whether and when the time has arrived to strategically pursue now more relevant new branding identities.

One correctable reason why many professionals never learn when to say when is simple:

- Professionals fail to conceptualize the branding-end being sought in a concrete fashion.

One consequence: Often, even after an identifiable branding goal has been achieved, nonstrategic professionals continue to hunger for more of the same. More of the same even when a shift toward a new branding identify is clearly now more appropriate. Strive too much, too long, and too far in one particular (brand-identity) direction and you may run past an inflection point where the gains you have earned in important audience perceptions begin to degrade in those same eyes.

We've advocated action. Advocated patience. Even suggested you should seek a balance between brains and balls as you strive to identify and execute differentiating initiatives intended to grow the power and persuasiveness of your brand. But here, as and after you have achieved initial branding goals, we advocate moderation. Practically any positive human activity, engaged in to an extreme—can generate undesirable results. Moderation, in almost everything, is usually a good thing. Too much pleasure, after all, can prove painful.

Yet precedent suggests that among many professionals the willingness to engage "full stop" after targeting and reaching a desired branding identity would be nearly miraculous. Hopefully, however, no miracles will be required for you. Not if you purposefully decide to plan through to your logical end. What does "plan through to your logical end" mean? The phrase implies branding professionals should know or learn when to say when. Machiavelli taught that this type of mindful willingness to not act further on certain stages contributes crucially to the maintenance of previously earned power. People who stride too far in triumph—branding victory lap?—can stimulate audience reactions that inevitably degrade their brand and its power.

Don't Stop Thinking about Tomorrow

Yes, this subheader co-opts lyrics and a song title made famous by 1970s soft rockers *Fleetwood Mac.* But old-school professional Cardinal Richelieu spoke, albeit less directly, on the same subject:

- "Experience shows that, if one foresees from far away the designs to be undertaken, one can act with speed when the moment comes to execute them. And to then halt when the moment to stop arrives."[27]

One sure solution is to play the long game. That means exploiting *long-term* time. On stages that truly matter, your conclusion—the core brand identity endpoint that you seek—should be crystal clear and kept constantly in mind.

From the moment he rose to power, Otto von Bismarck operated with only one core goal in mind.[28] The goal was to form an independent German nation led by Prussia. Mindful of this goal, upon which he staked his "branded" reputation, the Iron Chancellor (one strong brand identity) first initiated war against Austria to secure independence for Prussia, but never claimed any Austrian territory. Next, in service of his plan to unify Germany's disparate principalities against a common foe, Bismarck instigated hostilities against France, quickly vanquished French forces, and then withdrew from enemy territory, without imposing draconian peace terms.

Once these objectives were accomplished, Bismarck ended aggression—utterly and forever. Despite his military leaders' persistent protest, Bismarck never struck out against an external enemy again. Bismarck had achieved what he deemed a worthy end, and stopped. Bismarck turned his strategic focus toward creating a German social welfare state that was 60–100 years ahead of what is now featured in all western nations, including the United States. No wonder Bismarck's stellar reputation for exemplary governance remains intact. The Bismarck brand continues to shine brightly throughout Germany and among knowing foreigners more than 150 years after he first began growing into his power. If you, like Bismarck, see several steps ahead and plan through to the end, you will be less tempted by emotion or less likely to improvise at inopportune moments. Your clarity of purpose should lessen the anxiety and uncertainty that ultimately lead to many branding failures.

Experience: A Leverage-able of Branding Power

The acquisition of branded positions from which professionals can ethically exercise power and persuasiveness is not like acquiring the sort of wisdom that supposedly accompanies wrinkles and gray hair. You cannot simply wake up one day and discover you have secured either power, persuasiveness, or wisdom by dint of "time served in rank." But as surely as experience eventually yields wrinkles and gray hair, the role that experience can play should not be discounted or ignored as you work to develop brand identities that imbue greater power and influence.

You must experience a good mess up, likely once or twice, but hopefully not too often, before you can really understand how to develop and deliver a powerful branding message. Insert your preferred adage about the value of experience here, if you wish. Our favorite, however, because the statement confers insights that are germane on any professional stage is:

- Good judgment comes from experience. Experience comes from bad judgment.

We are all living, playing, working and performing today on the stage called Earth only because our ancestors had the fortitude to persevere and acquire the sort of experience-based knowledge that proved necessary for the species to survive and eventually thrive. You consequently should treasure your professional branding experiences. But you also should classify and categorize your experiences. And thereafter, you should reference those experiences in all their glory or disappointment and learn from them, especially, in those situations and on those stages where you exercised less than ideal judgment.

Ancient Greek Branding Lessons

The ancient Greeks valued experience more than most other virtues. They also believed, with good cause, that three paths existed through which experience-borne wisdom could be acquired.[29] The first path involved reflection. Reflection was deemed the most noble source of wisdom. There is no question but that you should reflect deeply and persistently about the nature of the brand identities you pursue, how to sustain the value or values after attaining them, and when to shift your branding initiatives into other directions.

The second source of wisdom involved imitation. Imitation was deemed the easiest path to identify, navigate and master. The ease with which branding imitation can be successfully executed relates is inversely related to the difficulty that "imitating" professionals would experience as they sought determinant branding identities. Imitation may be the sincerest form of flattery. But imitation, trying to more like someone else, is hardly a reasonable means to successfully pursue effective branding differentiation.

The final path to wisdom involves experience. Experience was simultaneously deemed the most effective and bitter source of actionable insights. Tipping a hat to Buddha, that's because experience is a tough teacher. After all, as Buddhism suggests: With experience, the tests come first. Meanwhile, learning, if it arrives at all, only appears after. "After," is in, after you have failed the initial test.

The lessons for increasing your branding power introduced above in this chapter, more so than anywhere else in this book, were grounded in the accumulated experiences and resulting wisdom of well-branded historical leaders. Their experiences and wisdom were introduced, described, and positioned as a conduit through which actionable chunks of wisdom applicable to contemporary branding stages might be acquired. Each idea presented above is consistent with this book's premise that your ability to brand successfully depend materially on your faculty for understanding and subsequently mastering whatever professional "staging" circumstances and human nature has dealt you. Fundamental, and actionable, insights into how you might master staged circumstance and human nature are embedded in the historical experiences provided above.

The value of lessons gleaned from historical experiences should not be discounted. Following historically-grounded branding rules, no matter how distasteful or manipulative some may appear on the surface, will enhance your prospects for greater brand-based power and persuasiveness in your future. Then you can decide whether to use your recently acquired branding power and persuasion for worthy or less than worthy ends. But you know which end we hope you'll lean toward ... Right?

Notes

1 Eliot, Thomas Stearns (1958). *Introduction to Pascal's Essays.* New York, NY: E.P. Dutton and Co.

2 Bosco, Ronald A. and Joel Myerson (2003). *Ralph Waldo Emerson in his Own Time.* Iowa City, IA: Iowa University Press.

3 Swenson, David F. (2000). *Something About Kierkegaard.* Macon, GA: Mercer University Press.

4 Bennis, Warren (1985). *Leaders: Strategies for Taking Charge.* New York, NY: Harper Business.

5 Brotheridge, Celeste M. (2002). "The Emotionally Intelligent Workplace." *Personnel Psychology*, 55(2): 527–532.

6 Campbell, Mary (1986). Bob Seger to Storm into Poplar Creek with Rock Poetry. *Chicago Sun-Times.* July 25, 1986.

7 Strutton, David and Kenneth Thompson (2016). *Marketing from Scratch: The Principles You Really Need to Know.* Second Edition. Dubuque, IA: Kendall-Hunt.

8 Strutton, David (2004). "The Courtly Path to Managerial Leadership". *Business Horizons*, 47(1): 7–16.

9 Taubman, William (2003). *Khrushchev: The Man and His Time.* New York, NY: W.W. Norton

10 Scharfstein, Ben-Ami (1995). *Amoral Politics.* Albany, NY: State University of New York.

11 Brands, Henry W. (1997). *The Wages of Globalism: The presidency of Lyndon Baines Johnson.* New York, NY: Oxford University Press.

12 Nichols, Peter (2004). *The New York Times Guide to the Best 1,000 Movies Ever Made.* New York, NY: Macmillan.
13 Sobel, Robert (1998). *Coolidge: An American Enigma.* Washington, DC: Regnery Publishing.
14 Ebert, Roger (2007). American Gangster. *Chicago Sun-Times.* Retrieved March 16. http://www.rogerebert.com/reviews/american-gangster-2007.
15 Simon, John (1994). "True Lies." *National Review.* August 29, 1994: 13–15.
16 Nicholl, Charles (2005). *Leonardo da Vinci: The Flights of the Mind.* New York, NY: Penguin Books.
17 Plutarch (1960). *The Rise and Fall of Athens.* Trans. Ian Scott-Kivett. New York, NY: Penguin Books.
18 Ibid.
19 Ibid.
20 U.S. Marine Corps (2014). *Commanders Tactical Handbook.* Retrieved November 27, 2015. http://www.marines.mil/portals.
21 Greene, Robert and Joost Elffers (1998). *The 48 Rules of Power.* New York, NY: Penguin Putnam.
22 Tversky, Amos and Daniel Kahneman (1986). "Rational Choice and Framing Decisions." *The Journal of Business*, 59: 240–251.
23 The Hopes of Mankind (2003). *Wall Street Journal.* March 20, 2003: A18.
24 Seeger, Raymond J. (1966). *Galileo Galilei, His Life and Works.* Oxford, UK: Pergamon Press.
25 Rebhorn, Wayne A. (1988). *Foes and Lions: Machiavelli's Hit Man.* Ithaca, NY: Cornell University Press.
26 Strutton, David, Gina A. Tran, and David Taylor (2013). "Fighting Dragons with Dragons: Approaches for Negotiating with Chinese Partners." *Business Horizons*, 54: 561–572.
27 Parker, Geoffrey (1984). *Europe in Crisis 1598–1648.* London: Fontana.
28 Stone, James (1994). "Bismarck and the Containment of France 1873–1877." *Canadian Journal of History*, 9(2): 281–314.
29 Russell, Donald A. (1973). *Plutarch.* New York, NY: Scribner.

Chapter 9
Developing Your Brand's Creativity

"Your learned ability to solve current and emergent problems more creatively may prove your ultimate survival skill"

—David Strutton and Kenneth Thompson.

Atlantic Magazine recently published a Top-50 list ranking the most impactful new products in history.[1] The most impactful, that is, since the invention of the wheel. At #50, the list begins with the combine harvester, which was created during the 1930s. At #1, the list ends with the printing press, created during the 1430s. Forty-eight other surprising and unsurprising products flesh out the list. Each history-altering product shared one trait: Its arrival always ensued from a creative professional's development and exploitation of new and useful ideas. In their time the founding ideas from which these world-altering solutions were derived were new, different, and useful. Every time. The ideas from which each history-altering product was birthed were, in a word, innovative.

Lessons from the List

Your ability to creatively develop solutions will almost certainly prove crucial to your current and future branding success as you compete on now-global stages. Innovativeness is reflected in anyone's ability to generate creative ideas that lead to new and useful solutions.

Creativity may prove similarly critical as you brand on those same stages. Indeed, many successful attempts to develop powerfully differentiated brands can trace their origins to professional performers' strategic exploitation of one or more creative ideas. The sort of ideas one could and would only create for oneself. After all, who else would actually create great new ideas that so directly benefit you?

Creativity and innovativeness are processes. Neither is primarily process driven, however. Not on professional branding stages, at least. Success at either endeavor is more a matter of people, including professionals, caring enough to keep thinking about solving until they identify the simplest way to do it. Creativity is reflected in an ability to connect seemingly unconnected concepts and relationships.

There are people who paint portraits. Then there are professional artists. Professional artists—or artistic professionals—are able to see and perform professionally based on their ability to envision the colors inside colors. Because they are able to experience color so deeply and expansively, creative professionals are able to reveal inside "in-the-colors" hues to others in interesting, new, or useful ways.

Creativity:

- Entails the ability to produce something novel and/or original that is useful and/or adaptive.

The capacities to achieve "brand creativity" and to "brand yourself as creative" are important enough that an entire chapter is dedicated to addressing the topics.

Creativity is extremely difficult to achieve. Were things different, we presume, more professionals legitimately could be described as creative. But the cohort of professionals, in any field, who genuinely can be described as "creative" is surprisingly small. This fact alone is telling. Because when any marketplace or economy has less of any asset, the asset is valued more. Usually, much more. Creativity is an asset. One that you can cultivate. The role that creativity might play in your branding success therefore should not surprise. Because when the subject is creativity, one initiating thing always leads to newer and even more useful solutions. Especially when that initiating thing is great new idea.

One Thing Really Does Lead to Another

Examples of how iteratively creative professional processes work—wherein one good thing leads to other good things—have unfolded on global stages across history. When Johannes Gutenberg created ideas that made mass printing possible, for example, legions of people began regularly reading now more readily available books for the first time. Suddenly, many readers realized they had a problem. The theretofore largely unrecognized but pervasive consumer problem now called farsightedness. A problem that only creative professionals could solve. Awareness of this problem facilitated creation of a new solution. We call this innovation, this once-new but still useful solution, eyeglasses. Not coincidentally, *Atlantic Magazine's* fifth most important new product of all time was optical lens.

As craftsmen worked more precisely with glass and lens, telescopes soon followed. As did microscopes. Each new product facilitated huge advances in other professions. Think, for example, astronomy, and, again, Galileo, and his pivotal astronomical- and religious-altering ideas that the Sun did not revolve around the Earth; Or the microbiological, germ, and infection-related insights facilitated through enhanced optics. Germs; now there's a bigtime consumer problem. Have no fear, once the problem was known, the third (penicillin), ninth (sanitation systems), and thirty-forth (pasteurization) most important innovations in history quickly followed as creative new product solutions. Penicillin, discovered to kill germs. Sanitation, developed to remove germs. Pasteurization, created to prevent germs. Marvelous solutions, all. All worth hanging their professional progenitor's branding reputations on, forever. Each new product was birthed by a single idea, the idea for germs, or was it the idea for microscopes, or was it the idea for printing books?

Progress hardly ended here. Increasingly efficient European glassworkers soon radically improved technologies that made superior mirrors possible. More effective, widely available mirrors allowed more people to see themselves clearly for the first time. Whoops, other consumer problems emerged for other creative professionals to solve. As people examined themselves more carefully, did they become more introspective or more self-critical? Perhaps both. If so, the initial consequence may have fostered philosophical debate and progress. The second, more likely consequence, probably entailed dented self-esteem. If so, greater numbers of more effective camouflaging new products now known as cosmetics probably emerged. Or not.

And if we really wanted to extend this exercise, we could point out that all-timer new products #31 and #9 (photography and the Internet, respectively) actually did foment philosophical debate and new processes, as well as increasingly challenged self-esteem among many. Also called the Facebook Effect. Which has created more problems still for psychological, psychiatric, and pharmaceutical professionals to one day presumably resolve. Until newer, tertiary problems arise for new professional generations to solve.

Truth be sold, this seemingly "far-fetched" chain of ideas, events, consequences and the need for newly developed products as solutions to newly arising problems is imminently "near-fetched." It is happening now. All because, as 1980s-era rockers The Fixx sang, "One Thing Leads To Another."

What's Your Plan for Becoming More Creative?

Success today increasingly no longer revolves around making or moving things. Indeed, breakout professional success today is usually impossible if all you can do is provide known solutions to known problems. Because on many contemporary professional stages, previously unknown problems requiring yet to be discovered solutions are rising at, yes, previously unknown rates. On these stages, sustainable success and the long-term attractiveness of your brand identity will substantively rise or fall based on your ability to create and deliver innovative ideas. Innovative ideas that, in turn, lead to new and useful solutions to existing and emergent problems.[2] Professionals who generate the highest density and velocity of good ideas will thrive today and in the future. "Good ideas," defined as those leading to beneficial, practical, and creative solutions.

Once you strategically upgrade how you think, "ideate," and make key decisions, and grow more creative, others sharing your stage will generally view your brand more favorably. ("Ideate" means "to develop new ideas.") As many hurtle toward unknowable futures one thing is known for certain. Domestic professionals will deliver whatever problem-solving solutions they develop on shrinking and increasingly competitive global stages. In such settings, sustainable branding power will follow entirely from your ability to "stand out" from rather than "fit-in" with fellow professionals. Your ability to establish and sustain a branding reputation as a creative actor is a highly desirable way to "stand out favorably" on most contemporary professorial stages.

The performance of domestic legal, accounting, medical, engineering, architectural, manufacturing, supply chain management, and information and technological management functions is increasingly being outsourced to India, China, Brazil, Ireland, or other usual and not so usual suspect nations. More providers from more regions and nations are entering your domestic scene each month. International professionals—mostly, direct competitors—are typically as smart and well-educated as you. Fact is, many were educated at the same universities as you. Their technologies work as well as yours. And why not, they use the same tools. Your international rivals willingly work as hard and, on average, perhaps harder than you. They are, after all, up-and-comer underdogs playing catch-up who care as much about their families and careers as you do about yours'. Plus, on average they don't like you, given that in their eyes you are a "rich arrogant American", and covet opportunities to beat you. Finally, these foreign competitors are delighted to do your job for 15–35 cents on your salary dollar.

This is the up close and personal impact that globalization is imposing on many US professional sectors. As you enter or sustain your professional standing in an information-driven, genuinely-global professional marketplace, will you possess the creativity-generating skill sets that will permit you to successfully differentiate your brand? You had better. Globalization's impact will continue to expand across the arc of your career. Going forward you cannot reasonably aspire to "cheap out" your international competitors. But you can out-create and out-think them. Your learned ability to solve current and emergent problems more creatively may prove your ultimate branding survival skill.

Which raises one question: What's your plan for becoming more creative? If you do not have one consider yourself fortunate. Because this chapter teaches exactly what you should learn to become more creative.

Creativity Is ...

The term "*creative*" touches upon the human imagination. "Creativity" is related to a human mind's willingness and ability to derive original ideas. Creative professionals see and experience the same stimuli and circumstances that other professionals sharing their field see and experience. Creative professionals, however, retain or develop an ability and willingness to go beyond what their less creative counterparts see. The ability of creative professionals to "go beyond" their fellow professionals entails, first, visualizing or ideating and second, developing new and useful "things" that also have value. Those new useful "things" generally include innovative solutions that creatively address client problems.

Creative professionals are more likely to develop great ideas. Dare we call them brandable ideas? Creatives will more likely succeed during futures in which the marketplace of ideas is becoming exponentially more competitive. Creatives will more likely succeed because their branded reputations implicitly or explicitly exude greater power and influence as a consequence of their prior creative success. Innovative successes that redound to and coalesce around their brands. What about your brand?

Professional creativity entails the ability to produce client solutions that are novel, original, useful, and/or adaptive.[3] The idea-generative processes through which professionals fashion creative solutions are typically assumed to be part of a complex process. The delightful culmination of that process is often depicted as a "aha" or "eureka" moment. Experiences that are more likely to arise inside the minds of Isaac Newton- or Marie Curie-like characters than you. But you would be wrong to assume these things.

You Can Become More Creative

Nearly everyone can be taught how to become more creative. This fact hopefully reassures more than it threatens. However there is no guarantee that your creativity-learning process will unfold smoothly, easily, or in a linear pattern. The circular path that often must be traveled in route to greater creativity may prove emotionally or psychologically challenging to certain types of professionals. Engineers, accountants, or medical practitioners come to mind. But any intelligent person who does the hard work and bears appropriate risks can learn to become more creative.

As most serious people learn moving forward through their lives—and you likely are serious about your work—the pain of any extra work or risk you bear is temporary. But the cost of "your brand may suck" if you don't work hard enough or take acceptable risks may last forever.

Creative professionals excel at recognizing relationships, establishing new associations and connections, seeing things and relationships that others don't perceive or perhaps even comprehend, and seeing those often obscure things in original ways. Creative individuals usually work harder than less creative others. Likely creatives do this because they love their work and earn much more money doing it. Creative people are frequently polymaths. Polymaths possess broadly intersectional interests across disciplines. Creatives are generally more venturesome and exploratory, willingly accepting measured and sometimes less measured risks. The work that risk-taking creatives execute more likely will unfold at the frontiers of what is known. The edges of knowledge in any professional sector are precipitous and jagged. Places, in other words, where creative professionals are more likely to fall, get cut— and bleed.[4]

Screw the "cutting edge." The phrase is so 1990s. Contemporary professionals who become branded as creatives likely got there because at some point they went for broke. Gone for broke more than occasionally, in all likelihood. People who have stretched themselves to create ideas and solutions so new that they lived their professional lives on the "bleeding edge."

Yet true creatives persist despite occasional failures. After all, they believe deeply in themselves and in the value and importance of what they do. Earned creative success usually requires persistence: A commitment to stare at a particular problem until its potential causes make sense. These are dirty little simple secrets about what it takes to be creative that actually are neither dirty, simple, or secret. As suggested, the process through which one might become creative is rarely linear. Creativity—or becoming more creative—frequently entails caring enough to keep thinking directly and indirectly about a problem until they find the simplest possible way to do or solve it. In the gym, in church, while listening to National Public Radio or reading Sports Illustrated.com. Thinking persistently, but not obsessively, about the sorts of problems only truly creative solutions will resolve. Letting things flow rather than forcing things to flow.

Creative professionals are often autodidactic, teaching themselves rather letting others feed them. Consider the uber-successful college dropouts named Gates, Jobs, and Zuckerberg, three wise professionals whose collective efforts have framed the modern technological era. Creative people, channeling 1960s icon Bob Dylan, are less likely to "follow leaders." But they are more likely to become well-branded leaders themselves.

Creative thinking requires a sort of perpetual conversation with your work the thoughts thoughts of others. As well as ongoing chats with yourself. Ready to launch those conversations? Once launched, will you continue them? No excuses that you're too old, please. That your time, regrettably, has past. It has not. Because with sufficient commitment, anyone at any age can become more creative. One wonderful thing about aging is that it is accompanied by increased seasoning. Seasoning, in turn, that yields more time-tested episodes of success and failure for you to ponder. The value of pondering should not be sold short. Think about the word, ponder. Its value. Because while "eureka" moments do occur, they usually arrive only after long periods of precipitating preparation have past.

How to Grow Your Professional Creativity

Successful creative endeavors usually involve acts of recombination. The reason: Ideas have sex. And what can happen when two or more fertile ideas have unprotected sex? That's right, a new idea, a beautiful and potentially life- or career-altering baby, often results.

How can you create situations in which two or more fresh and useful ideas relevant to the problem driving the need for your creativity can be developed and recombined? Five steps should be pursued. Each is based on prior research.[5]

The order in which you execute these creativity-enhancing activities is important. Specifically, you should:

- Create intersections
- Develop multiple perspectives
- Lower associative barriers
- Avoid certain creativity-defeating traps
- Respond properly to failure

  … in your professional and personal life. The meaning as well as the "how-to" of each creativity-enhancing step is discussed below.

Step 1: Creating Intersections

You became professional only after having consciously cultivated expertise in you specific field across an extended period of time. You almost certainly earned a degree or degrees, endured or enjoyed internships, and passed various official or putative "entrance exams." This is wonderful, of course.

Your specialized expertise, combined with experience, permits you to adroitly solve known or standard issue as they arise in your field of expertise. Unfortunately, the same highly specialized, perhaps overly focused expertise and experience often degrades your creativity. This is because few professionals live, operate, or discover at intersections.

Professionals instead generally remain ensconced in disciplinary silos where everyone else usually thinks similarly about similar problems. When you operate on a specific progression stage, you are primarily capable of effectively combining concepts that already exist or arise on that stage. Most professionals are also understandably predisposed to do just that. Most people crave the familiar, the known, the comfortable. But when you consciously chose to think and operate mindfully at the intersection between two or more professional fields you are better positioned to combine concepts from those disparate disciplines. Your ability to create new ideas and develop superior solutions will then grow organically and exponentially.

Accountants, engineers, operational analysts, logisticians, human resource managers, and marketers, for example, all work in the same business world. The people performing in these roles each confront similar business or business-related problems. But these diverse professionals rarely "see" and experience the same problems in the same way. Nor are they likely to develop and propose the same solutions to those problems. Which is actually a good thing. Especially when diverse groups come together and share their divergent thoughts and ideas at a place called the *intersection*.

The intersection can exist as a hypothetical or actual place. Strategic leaders can knowingly create intersections by constructing diverse problem-solving teams. Intersections exist in any location where ideas emanating from different professional functions or disciplines can cross paths. Intersections are places where professionals arriving with differing points of view and areas of expertise can crisscross, recombine, "have sex" and consequently engender new ideas.

Intersections Already Reside Inside You

Intersections can also arise and exist perpetually inside your mind. That is, if you decide to create and sustain them. We encourage this exact choice. Create them, visit them, and reside permanently at a flux of interactions. When this happens, you might become more like the creative masters who bred waffles with doughnuts, creating wonuts; Italian with Jewish cuisine, creating pizza bagels; Mexican chili with German frankfurters, creating chili dogs; or peanut butter with chocolate, creating, yes, Reese's Peanut Butter Cups. Nothing like fast food savants discovering exciting new ideas that create new "solutions" that, in turn, make even more expanding Americans struggle to fit into shrinking airplane or stadium seats. Which leads to two additional ever-expanding problems for other creative folks to solve, one might suppose. Diet pills that magically shred the pounds, anyone?

More seriously but no less creatively, you also might become more like the architectural and entomological professionals who jointly created construction design ideas that permitted large sub-Saharan African office buildings to remain cool even when the electricity powering their air conditioning units failed. In other words, professionals who came together to solve a recurring problem common to all sub-Saharan African nations. The secret sauce for their creative success was no secret at all: An intersection.

An intersection was established from which builders could integrate core architectural principles with new ideas that entomologists learned from studying how African termites construct ventilation tunnels throughout their huge mounds that permitted cooling air to circulate. A remarkable spate of creative results emerged when a self-selected team operated, cooperated, and solved huge problems at the intersection they consciously created between entomology and architecture.

If you consciously to pursue the next four steps you should similarly become more creative. But not because you participated in more cross-disciplinary intersections. Instead your brandable creativity will grow because you will have created more intersections inside your own mind. You know, your mind. The only place where you, us, or anyone reading this actually lives.

Effective professionals, being intelligent, often feature two radically opposed personal impulses and qualities. First, they frequently combine a desire for solitude (professional privacy) with the need for social stimulation (performing publically on their respective stages). Second, effective professionals also frequently combine superior knowledge about their chosen domains with an almost childlike naiveté about their core subjects. When these dichotomous qualities coalesce (intersect!) within a single professional, he or she is more likely to derive great new ideas and subsequently execute based on those ideas.

Do these characteristics already characterize you? Or, and we're asking a lot but not the impossible, could you cultivate them inside yourself? If you can already answer yes to the first question or create a context from which you could affirmatively answer the second question, you're on your way toward establishing intersectional-like idea-generating platforms inside your mind. Then you will be the one who is better prepared to solve vexing problems. Which implies, over time, you're more likely to transform into a "creative" professional. The "creative one" toward whom others turn when big problems arise because you're the "go-to guy or gal." Two wonderful branding identities, taglines which most thinking professionals would surely welcome.

Step 2: Developing Multiple Perspectives

Professional organizations seeking greater creativity can generate it by developing diverse—or intersectional—teams. In large corporate settings these teams might feature accountants, logisticians, technology designers, and marketers. A creative team might then be asked to generate naturally arising intersectional batches of ideas leading to new products that solve pressing customer or client problems. But our mission here is to elevate your creativity for purposes of making you a "hero brand." So let's concentrate on you and your mind. How can you create intersections inside your own head?

The first step involves consciously developing multiple perspectives; that is, introducing diverse ways of thinking about pressing problems or issues, inside your mind. This can only be accomplished over time. Purposefully changing your perspective in response to nonroutine professional problems will slowly and then more rapidly stimulate your imagination and creativity. Once you own multiple perspectives in your mind, intersectional thinking becomes more natural and easier to execute. And not as a leap of faith. But as an activity based on new perspectives that are grounded in intersecting facts.

This prescription for creating multiple perspectives in your own mind is simple. Then again, the best new ideas usually are. To expand your perspectives, pursue intersectional-expanding activities such as:

- Reading both the *New York Times* and the *Wall Street Journal*, or pursuing activities similar to this. We might have suggested listening to NPR and a networked conservative Christian station, or watching Fox News and MSNBC. Similar multiple-perspective enhancing outcomes would arise. But back to the page. These two newspapers operate in the same world. Each publication addresses the same problems/issues every day except Sunday, in the case of *The Journal*. *The Times* and *The Journal* also inevitably develop resoundingly opposing views regarding next "best steps" to pursue as solutions. Or, offer diametrically opposed interpretations about the underlying causes driving problems de jure. You can "scoop out" remarkable intersectional value from the multiplicity of views that this simple, imminently doable activity will manufacture for you. Because as The Eagles drummer Don Henley sang: "There is your side, there is my side, and then there is the cold hard truth." In this nonethical context, branding professionals should gravitate toward this "middle truth."

- *Eating lunch or merely talking regularly with people who look nothing like you, as often as possible.* The fact that they look nothing like you enhances the likelihood that your conversational partners would hail from different cultural backgrounds—and view the world as different and know things that diverge from what you know and think. You can learn a great deal from them, and presumably they would learn from you as well. Our points of view are predetermined by our culturally preordained points of viewing to a far greater extent than most people realize. Continuously "intersect yourself."
- *Engaging other information sources that provide new perspectives.* If you're a current or former male jock, read about the history of fashion. If you're a female fashion maven, read expositions on the history of violence. How were apparel problems solved in the past? Problems of terrorism or zealotry? "Ponder" these questions and the creative insights that answering them would generate.
- *Traveling.* Especially to places where lots of people who aren't like you will be. Off the beaten path, unusual destinations, far away from maddeningly similar touristy crowds are preferable. Once you're exposed to difficult sets of cultural values, you can more easily extricate yourself from overly narrow self-imposed perspectives.

Avoid becoming like the radically liberal or conservative thinker who supports diversity in everything. Everything, that is, except their thoughts and thinking processes. Yet even if you actually such adopt properly open-minded perspectives while creating appropriately diverse perspectives inside your conscious being, all the good developed during Step 1 may come to naught. Unless ... which leads us to the next creative "must do;" as an absolutely necessary "next step." A stage that speaks directly to the presence of one impediment to your creativity. Yet happily, this stage also demonstrates how you can alleviate that obstruction's negative impact. Notably, the impediment primarily exists inside your own mind. However, the barrier also can arise from external sources.

Step 3: Lowering Your Associative Barriers

After his innovative ideas about a new solution to an interminable problem—what what will happen to us after we die? —were rejected by his former neighbors and friends in Nazareth, his hometown, Jesus Christ said (Mark 6:6): "A prophet is honored everywhere except in his own hometown and among his relatives and friends." Genuinely creative thinkers performing on professional stages will probably encounter similar needs to overcome the opposition of others who reject truly innovative ideas as they; that is, creative professional thinkers, summon them. And such pushback likely would emanate first from those situated closest to where the creative professional works. Most particularly, their superiors or peers.

Each of us presumably would do well to honor any true prophets arising in our midst. Yet counting upon their timely arrival is an inefficient way to ensure that you can stimulate original ideas in response to the sorts of threats and challenges that will enter your stage for decades to come. Consequently, no recommendations are offered on this front. Likely, however, no recommendations should be offered. That's because the biggest obstacles to accepting truly creative insights coming from others or, more importantly, to generating such ideas themselves that most professionals will encounter exists within your own mind. The real barriers preventing you from becoming more creative dominate thinking inside your mind.

Contemporary author Frans Johansson called these persistent, internalized obstacles "associative barriers." Associative barriers function like anchors inside your mind. Their presence drags down the creative instincts, abilities, and activities of anyone lugging associative barriers around. In global supply chains, for example, associative barriers might emanate from connections that domestic professionals have already established with existing supply chain ideas, principles, methods, or processes.

The smarter professionals are and the more they learn about how things should be executed procedurally on their respective stages, the more associative barriers will exist. "Buying into" the value of and "acting based upon" what you learn from newly created intersections inside your mind is often easier said than done—usually because your potential creativity is inhibited by associative barriers. Associative barriers are essentially guaranteed to arise in your professional life simply because you already know so much about what you know, professionally-speaking. Like other professionals you compete against or with whom you collaborate, you already understand how to solve obvious problems in your discipline. An ability that merits a big "so what?" After all, being like every other professional in your field will never meaningfully set apart the value of your brand on increasingly globalized and crowded stages.

Please understand, however, that these bonds of association are entirely appropriate and beneficial in most aspects of your professional life. Associative barriers are precisely what make you a professional. Because human minds operate learn and operate best through association, our brains typically follow the simplest path, the path that is least disruptive and easiest to navigate. We lean naturally and steeply into our professional habits, in other words. And habits can prove quite beneficial. To you! Until, on stages where genuinely creative solutions are needed, your habits become antithetical to creativity - and thus to the likelihood that you could create new and useful solutions.

When habits emerge, your brain stops fully participating in decision making. You will recall, habits emerge because your brain continuously strives to save effort. Habits themselves consist of cues, routines, and rewards. Change any one of these dimensions, and you will change habits for better or for worse. There is a problem, however:

- Even professional minds cannot always discriminate bad habits from good.

Moreover, bad habits always lurk, waiting for the right cues and rewards to kick them into action. Habits are often more curse than cure in creative contexts. Your tendency to fall back fully into can prove self-defeating, even if the habits reflect professional customs and routines, when you seek to develop the "creatively destructive" - remember Schumpeter - ideas that are necessary to solve the sorts of disruptive problems that are currently arising on now global stages. Disruptive problems such as the ones professions and professionals now confront require true creativity—intersectional thinking—and are difficult to navigate. No established path exists through which truly disruptive professional problems can be solved. In fact, disruptively creative solutions are the only solution.

Lowering Associative Barriers

The first way to lower the creativity-negating impact of your associative barriers is to remain aware, perpetually, that they exist. Now that you know, you know what to do.

The second way is to develop and exercise tools that nullify the degrading effects the presence of associative barriers otherwise will impose on your creativity. Five tools are presented below. Each is designed to lower your associative barriers. You should:

- *Learn Differently*—Employ strategies that permit you to learn as many different new and potentially useful ideas as possible without getting overly bound up in narrow-minded ways of thinking about, or judging, those new ideas.
- *Consciously Reverse Assumptions*—Assume you are a marketer. A logical assumption to make, by the way, because you are a marketer. Your perpetual task is to derive innovative ideas that lead to creative solutions that satisfy new and existing customers. Now, invert the purpose of this task. Temporarily assume your job is to develop as many new ideas as possible about how to create outcomes that would *dissatisfy* present or prospective customers. Finally, create forward by doing the reverse of these "wicked" ideas.
- *Wear Different Hats*—You are what you are until you consciously choose to be someone else. Please assume, again, that you are a marketing professional who has been assigned responsibility for creating nine innovative ideas that are intended to facilitate solutions for a particularly challenging problem. Now, adopt the divergent mind-sets that an accountant, philosopher, or a Navy SEAL would would bring to the stage were he/she charged with the same responsibility. Then create the requested ideas. Congratulations, you switched perspectives. More importantly, you defeated associative barriers.
- *Remain or Become More Open Minded*—Here, you might fake it until you make it, if necessary. The task of becoming more open minded should become more manageable once you understand the value of multiple perspectives. Professionals typically learn about objects and ideas, and then inventory and classify the resulting concepts until they are needed, usually as solutions in known situations.

Creatives, by contrast, remain open to new possibilities for new applications in new or existing situations.

- *Permit Your Mind, Occasionally, to Become a Free-Fire Zone*—This conscious choice, and behavior, would prove especially useful when you engage with audacious challenges and problems that traditional (known) sorts of thinking cannot confront or resolve successfully.

Now is likely not the time nor is your professional stage the place for you to reflexively make quick, known decisions in pursuit of "obvious" solutions to truly vexing problems. Because given the new professional realities, the best decisions and solutions—the sort inevitably requiring more creative decision making and consequent solutions—will not be obvious. Your times, your stage instead demand that you lower your associative barriers. That is, if you genuinely seek to brand yourself as "different from" and "better than" your fellow professionals by becoming and remaining more creative. Professionals who consistently lower their associative barriers across time and circumstance should earn material branding advantage. The advantage will arrive as an extension and consequence of their new-found ability to think and respond more creatively to truly vexing problems.

We wrote the preceding paragraph with certainty and conviction. The only uncertainty is whether you will have the conviction of purpose that would usually prove necessary for you to lower your own associative barriers in route to elevating the power and persuasiveness of your brand.

Step 4: Avoiding Creativity-Defeating Traps

The Noble Economics prize-winning prospect theory provides useful insights regarding how best to establish a productive balance between your natural desire to mitigate risks (primarily of a psychological nature, by the way) and your need to stimulate and identify creative ideas, to become more creative, to elevate your brand's status and relative standing. Prospect theory suggests that when humans confront risky decisions, the personal anxiety and concerns that accompany our choices surface not so much because we hate uncertainty, but rather because we fear losing. Most people innately find it easier to envision how their lots could quickly grow worse than how their lots might quickly improve. For most people, the "prospect" of loss is more vivid—and experienced more viscerally—than the "prospect" of gain.

Professionals who otherwise should be branding vigorously consequently generally hold fast to the status quo when things are going well. We remain securely inside our fields rather than thinking and choosing creatively outside the professional domain we presumably have already mastered. So does almost everyone else. By contrast, many people take huge risks when things are going badly. Or, at exactly the wrong time. Wrong because when the heat is on or the clock is running (insert your cliché here), you often lack sufficient time, resources and reasoning necessary to make the best decision. Nothing written here can change core human nature. Still, you should remain mindful of the need to accept and cultivate a balanced view of risk in good and bad times alike. Especially now that you know the need exists.

Please read the prior two paragraphs again. Every word and nuance. That you understand their true meaning and associated implications is remarkably important to whatever future branding success; heck, let's just say, SUCCESS, that you earn.

Many professionals never succeed on large scales or stages, creatively or otherwise, for avoidable reasons. Simply stated, they fail to succeed because they were afraid to try—a sad insight, this. People are afraid to try because the prospect of failure weighs so heavily upon them.[6] Human beings are wired to "hate losing more than they love winning" - a phrase one-time tennis great Jimmy Conners offered in response to a reporter's question about why he competed so ferociously. Accordingly, you might fear the "prospect" that you will fail if you venture too far forward creatively. But today you must rationally balance the prospect of acceptable risk of failure against the prospect of creative and ultimately branding success. Dare we write: No guts no glory?

Average levels of creativity will not ensure big-time success in the world stretching out ahead of you. Low-hanging, easy-to-pick creative fruit has long since been plucked. This is "go-for-it" time for ambitious professionals.

Stepping out and stepping up are challenging. Professionals tend to value certainty. Again, so does everyone else. People are demonstrably willing to sacrifice prospects for future creativity-engendered success to achieve more certainly now. As discussed, people assign more weight—more negative value—to the prospect of loss than to the prospect of gain. Truly creative people must take measured risks to generate enough ideas to succeed. Particularly, the risk of having their ideas fails more often than not.

The idea about innovation and creativity are structured processes has been taken to an extreme. If you seek and plan to achieve big-time creative success you must knowingly and willingly take measured risks. One won't become more creative by uniformly adhering to one strictly defined process. But you can become more creative by caring enough about the creative process and creative outcomes to keep thinking about how to solve complicated problems better until you develop the simplest possible idea that will lead to their solution.

Occam's Razor prescribes the simplest possible explanation, process, or idea that "captures all the data" and solves the problem is always the best solution. The ancient Greeks thought and acted similarly. Ancient Greece was responsible for remarkable governmental, democracy; architectural, Corinthian, Doric and Ionic columns and arches; philosophical, Aristotle, Plato, and Socrates; sporting, the Olympics; and theatrical, tragedy, drama, and comedy *solutions*. Each solution dominates until this day. When creating solutions, the ancient Greeks routinely sought and ultimately achieved brilliant simplicity. Why not you? And us?

Step 5: Responding Properly to Failure

Failure is no stranger on any professional stage. Professionals or professional firms generally keep doing what works until it no longer works. In other words until what once worked fails. A circumstance and description that should resonate. And what once worked inevitably crashes on many stages, because environments, customers, markets, and technologies—let's just say elements throughout your entire world—always changes. Winston Churchill wrote:

- "Success often entails the willingness to go from failure to failure without loss of enthusiasm."[7]

The great leader and still well-branded quote machine not writing about the professions. Or what is necessary to cultivate your creativity. He could have been, however.

Perhaps the best way to respond to the prospect or arrival creative failure is to fail early and often. The preceding is no misprint. In fact, comparatively few new ideas that any professional develops succeed to the point where they are actually transformed into new solutions. Remember, however: Quantity of ideas is key to the quality of any ideas that eventually make it all the way through creative processes. Thomas Edison, the inventor who created myriad once-new, still-useful innovations, failed more than 1000 times to invent a functioning bulb. Undaunted, he replied: "I have not failed. Instead I have learned 1000+ ways to not make the light bulb."

To become creative, professionals sometimes must let go of their self-consciousness. Take risks, including the risk of occasional failure and embarrassment. No one can fail his or her way to success. But beyond question many professionals who eventually succeeded big initially failed, sometimes on large scales, at various points along their path to success. They presumably learned much that was useful from their failures—and going forward avoided the same mistakes.

The entrepreneur Kemmons Wilson developed and founded the once innovative concept called the *mo*tel. *Ho*tels or *no*tels, places you wouldn't voluntarily disclose you'd visited, have existed for millennia. Wilson invented *mo*tels. "Mo" as in "motor"; attached to places of *h*ospitality. The motel was a sanctuary where travelers knew they could reliability and safely stay overnight. The innovation was developed in response to a problem that arise during the 1950s, 1960s, and 1970s as families and other travelers began making longer car trips. Car trips were made possible by interstate highways—another innovation. Again, we see how the creation of one innovation typically leads to the development of another.

The name of the motel chain—a third innovation—he launched was *Holiday Inn*. Decades after his initial success Mr. Wilson was invited to present at a prominent university about business success and failure. A skeptical student stood up and asked: "Mr. Wilson, how can you profess to teach us about failure. Look at how successful you are." To which Mr. Wilson replied:

- "Young man, I have likely failed more than you have even tried."

People usually learn more from aspiring or ambitious failures than from modest successes.[8] Buddhists learn: "We all have lives of 10,000 sorrows and 10,000 joys." Make the most of your creative sorrows.

What the entrepreneurial Wilson understood, and you should learn, is that one must develop new ideas and try new things or get "dusted" those who do. But fail only in those situations where failure is not fatal. And finally, like Mr. Wilson, you must learn to accept the losses while never embrading a forfeit. Because a forfeit means you never even tried.

Accept Occasional Impressive Failure

Two things: First, you should be rewarded when you succeed. And two, no one has ever failed their way to the top. Everyone knows these two things. But if you're seeking a creative branding reputation you should understand a failure to generate new ideas often represents your greatest failure. Naturally you should learn from your mistakes and upgrade your subsequent ideas and processes as a result. It is usually acceptable to make occasional mistakes by stretching one's vision. But repeating the same mistake is never acceptable.

To succeed as a creative professional brand, you must generate numerous new ideas. The rationale is simple: the more new ideas stimulated, the greater the likelihood that a truly difference-making new idea can be identified. Creatives will experience more ideation failure ideas because they produce more ideas. You should accept this fact as a cost of creative success.

Creative professionals should not punish themselves for occasional "impressive failures." Mistakes and false steps are part of the process for lowering associative barriers, stimulating intersectional thinking and creating new ideas. Within question, failing impressively should be acceptable. Because over the long-term useful and otherwise inaccessible; meaning never-before acknowledged solutions can result from your stretched imagination.

You May Note ...

One approach means of stimulating innovative ideas, namely, brainstorming, has not been discussed. Nor will it be, beyond this brief comment.

Many professionals assume brainstorming stimulates many useful new ideas. They are wrong. Research shows that people generate almost twice as many useful new ideas when working/thinking by themselves. The primary reasons relate to "fear rider" and "free rider" effects. Fear rider, as in: "I'm afraid to speak because others will 'ridicule' me; so I'll stay safe and let someone else take the risks." Free rider, as in: "I'll let someone else pull the creative wagon; I'll just hop in for take a ride".

Consider one bad thing, let's call it "starvation," that would arise in a situation where a small population of fear riders and free riders fail to do their "fair share." Take one desolate desert island, 25 shipwrecked survivors, and a raft. Two choices, framed in one question: Who wants to sit on the cliff under a palm tree and watch for rescue ships; who wants to paddle out and spearfish tuna in shark invested waters using our raft? We will divide all fish equally. You'll get a very crowded cliff, a near empty raft, and too few tuna. All due to "fear rider" and "fear rider" effects.

On most professional stages someone needs to take charge. Stick out their neck; take chances; expose themselves to risk. Someone, in brief, needs get in the raft, paddle to the deep water, and spear big fish like tuna. Someone exactly like you. "Fear rider" and "free rider" effects create stages on which most occupants let others do all the thinking. Professionals would do this because they are afraid to "air out" truly innovative ideas or too "lazy" to think with sufficient effort. Or just as perniciously, because someone else will willingly do the work.

Eliminate "fear riders" and "free riders" from your life—stage. To create and subsequently distinguish the power, persuasiveness, and value of your brand while simultaneously elevating the reality of your creative value, do more new things. Pull the wagon yourself. Speak up! And insist others reporting to you do the same. Once again, your professional brand will thank you. So will your family and firm.

Further Down the Creative Path

To become more creative, you could also engage in the following creativity-enhancing behaviors.

"Capturing" for Yourself

Capturing ideas requires that you nonjudgmentally preserve ideas whenever and wherever they happen to arrive. Perhaps when you are exercising or talking to a friend. Goodness knows, in a "smartphone world" many ways exist to capture new ideas.

Otto Loewi won a Nobel Prize for work based on an idea about cellular biology that he almost failed to capture. He had the idea in his sleep, woke up, and scribbled the idea on a pad. But the next morning he could neither read his notes nor remember the idea. When the idea turned up in his dreams the following night, he used a better capturing technique: He put on his pants and went straight to his lab! Lucky man, in terms of the idea reappearing in his dreams. Smart man, given that he took action right away.

Another story, perhaps anecdotal, applies. One about a Professor who used to take power naps in his office. While thinking deep thoughts about profound problems, as Professors do (j/k), the Professor would hold keys in his hand as his hand hung off the office couch he lay on as he was falling asleep. When he checked out the keys would fall from his hand, and wake him up. He would then immediately write down the last thought he could recall. The Professor did so based on the now proven assumption sometimes our best creative thinking *may* occur in the intersection between consciousness and unconsciousness. We'll leave it up to you to determine whether the story is true. But the point to be taken is the value of capturing.

"Challenging" Yourself

To become more creative, lean toward the most pressing problems. Ask by name for the toughest assignment. If you're in charge, take on the challenge yourself. You are, after all, nothing more or less than a problem solver.

Creatives persistently seek out the most challenging problems to solve. Multiple behaviors and diverse thinking are typically required to solve highly challenging problems. Ideas must compete vigorously with each other in the midst of intellectually challenging situations. This competition among ideas is good thing. Forced interconnections—think intersections—create new behaviors and facilitate new ideas. Tough times breed tough people, right? Shouldn't challenging problems breed more creatively branded people, too?

Consciously seeking challenging assignments, the sort that involve important problems, may confer other highly valued branded identities to you. Volunteer for the toughest tasks, and secure attention from your superiors. Even if you fail or fail to succeed completely, which will likely happen with tough problems, you position yourself more favorably in superiors' minds. Newbies entering the professional workplace should do this as first opportunities arrive.

Less daunting but still effective ways exist to challenge yourself to become more creative. You could, for example, read something that no else in your profession would likely read. Alternatively, you could be confident enough to think something no one else in or around your stage is thinking. Most importantly, you might do something no one else is currently doing. Takeaway:

- These activities will allow you to establish more intersections, cultivate new perspectives, lessen or destroy associative barriers, or learn how to address and recover properly from failure.

One more clear and present branding benefit can be to snatch and subsequently "own" when you step off the porch and run with the big folks. Doing shallow professional work well prevents you from getting fired. Usually. Shallow work entails managing e-mails, showing up on time at meetings, accurately shuffling information around. Doing deep professional work elevates your brand and gets you promoted. But only after the deep work you have done elevate the power and persuasiveness of your brand.

"Broadening" Yourself

Broadening oneself for creative purposes entails choosing to mindfully expose oneself to more intersections. And consequently, to more intersectional thinking that will expand and diversify your knowledge base incrementally, across time. All along you are prepping mind and spirit such that you will become better able to create more interesting, potentially more useful, interconnections. Takeaway:

- Elevate your creativity by learning interesting new stuff - ideas, principals, relationships - not related directly to your field.

This sort of learning may require burdensome activities such as traveling to new places or reading real books and articles rather than reading and sending all texts, all the time. Once broadening happens, however, you may engage more easily in mind wandering—following interesting, unexpected offshoots of the main task at hand as you prance around productively inside your own mind. Your social intelligence should expand. As should your ability to learn implicitly and readily switch back and forth between tasks. After broadening yourself, you should retain or develop the ability to remain disciplined but still open-minded enough to see other possibilities and opportunities absent the urge to reject them out of hand. And in process, defeat associative barriers.

"Surrounding" Yourself

"Surrounding" is similar to "broadening." Surround yourself with people, new ideas, and other "unusual", seemingly unrelated things that force you to elevate your professional game. That is, upgrade the quality of your thinking on a continuous, going-forward basis. "Surrounding" requires that you consciously manage your physical and social environments. The more interesting and diverse the things and people around you are or become, the more interesting your consequent ideas will be. Perhaps without realizing it, you have invested yourself in multiple perspectives.

Choose your friends and associates the best you can. No one has complete control, we get that. But do what you can. As noted earlier, more often than not, if you show us your professional or networked friends we can show you your professional future. Your tennis, basketball, or chess game never improves when you play against people who are worse than you. Translating sporting lessons to creativity games, your creativity will rarely improve if you play exclusively with people who know less than you or the same things as you. Choose carefully.

"Einstein-ing" and "Picasso-ing" Yourself

Albert Einstein knew creativity. The world-altering nature of his three major theories directly underscores this fact. The great physics theorist said: "You cannot solve problems by using the same sort of thinking that created them" [in the first place]. So, with a nod hat to Apple and its *1984* advertisement that only played once on network television, you should *"Think Different"* from how you used to think as new and important problems arise. Often it is not what you don't know, but rather what you think you know for certain that tamps down your creativity. Consequently, you should loosen your grip on certainties to expand your range of possibilities. Carefully choose what you think—or choose to not think—about.

The most creative professionals consciously engage in mind wandering; possess or grow social intelligence; remain knowingly fluid in their goal orientation; are able to learn implicitly; are willing and able to switch tasks easily; and are conscientious about the importance of branding success.

Creatives are diligent and disciplined. As is anyone characterized by a higher propensity and capacity for creativity. But "creatives" —people are already creative and those seeking the brand—should remain persistently open minded toward new possibilities and opportunities. Essentially, we would argue, in a childlike fashion.

Childlike? Yes. Aldous Huxley wrote:

- "A childlike man is not one whose development has been arrested. On the contrary, he is a man who has given himself the chance to continue to develop long after most adults have muffled themselves in the cocoon of middle-aged habit and convention."

  Pablo Picasso spoke similarly, saying:

- "It took me 4 years to learn how to paint like Rafael; the rest of my life to learn how to paint like a child."

Humans are born to be powerful and natural explorers. Yet most people grow out of this natural propensity. One primary culprit is the US educational system, but we cannot correct that. As for you, never forget nor ignore your natural childlike inclinations. Instead accept and exploit your acceptance of the fact that times will arise on your stage when you should consciously regress back toward the child's creative inclination by being a lifelong learner. Lifelong learners—you?—grow new connections, strengthen existing connections, and create new brain neurons.

Tall orders, these. But the creative giants among us routinely engage in similar thoughts and behaviors throughout their lives. Each created ideas that changed the world to this day. You enjoy the purview and power to adopt these same ideas yourself—and to become more creative as a consequence.

Identifying Your Best Creative Ideas

According to managerial guru Peter Drucker:

- "Nothing is so useless as doing efficiency that which should not be done at all."[9]

If for no other reason than to avoid pursuing "useless efficiencies," when branding yourself as "creative" you should act based only on the best creative ideas you stimulate. Your first step toward maximizing creative effectiveness; that is, after you have already acted creatively: Postpone judgment of any new ideas you generate. This recommendation is straightforward. But unless you allocate sufficient resources, primarily to the identification task, execution will prove challenging.

Postponing judgment usually proves psychologically difficult to professional minds. You possess deeply rooted field expertise that enabled you to become professional in the first place. Your mind consequently judges quickly. Your mind is trained and enculturated to mechanically degrade the value of genuinely original thinking by comparing creative ideas to ideas already known to work on your familiar stages. Likely even your profession is being challenged as never before. Yet paradoxically, creative minds—or the minds of professionals aspiring to become branded as creative because the label is their reality!—should judge more leisurely.

For good reasons, following precedent makes sense in many situations. Yet on stages experiencing threats that require dynamically creative solutions, prior experience provides a poor framework from which to evaluate the superiority of new and useful ideas emerging from unusual concept combinations. But odd, rare or previously unfamiliar idea pairings are exactly the sort that yields the most creative solutions.

How often have you derived precedent-based solutions to pressing challenges, assumed the underlying ideas reflected your best work, and then identified a superior alternative shortly after a deadline passed? The need to extend often artificial deadlines that you, a client or superior impose upon you by allocating sufficient resources to the identification task is real. The most important of these resources? Time, of course.

As you manage this "best-possible" idea-identification process, avoid conventional wisdoms or conventional thinking. Especially thoughts reflecting opinions such as:

- "If my idea was so great, someone would have thought of it already."

That's exactly the wrong way to think if you actually did live out, think though, and create innovative solutions at the place that you know as "the intersection." The fact is that genuinely intersectional ideas are exactly not what anyone else would have thought of before. The connection between intersectional concepts and myriad emerging professional threats or opportunities that had to align to expose the truly creative idea would never have been revealed to anyone who had not established and exploited the intersectional insights. Like you did, of course.

Five "creative criteria" through which the best new creative ideas follow:[10]

Simplicity

Ask:

- Is my idea simple enough to lead to a new solution that other people who share my stage will understand?

Simple new ideas improve existing value or expedite the development of new value by revealing new solutions to old or new problems. Simple ideas should be easy for you to explain. Easy for clients to understand. Eyeglasses that permit people to read or watch TV while lying flat on their back. In-wall ironing boards that double as mirrors. Dustbins that allow sweepers to scrape all the dirt off the broom. Each new and useful (i.e., creative) is based on remarkably simple ideas. The obvious question, again, is why did it take so long for engineers or product designers to identify these solutions?

Overly complex ideas represent unnecessary and thus inefficient compromises for genuinely professional thinkers. Developing complicated solutions is actually easy. But you have the opportunity and ability to coalesce complicated concepts or problems into a few simple themes. Exploit the opportunity whenever possible. The best professionals, in any field, can explain complicated solutions or ideas to uninitiated others, including clients, in a simple fashion. These professionals can truly be branded as "creative ones." In a now globalized marketplace of ideas, the virtue of simplicity usually makes "the simple" incredibly attractive.

Achieving simplicity in creative contexts is never simple, however. Simple ideas, the sorts that lead to profoundly creative and desirable solutions and enhance your brand, honor two principles. First, your new idea and any solution emanating from it should be distilled down to its essence, its most fundamental elements, and core value. Second, the core value delivered by your new idea should be sharpened to the point where the resulting solution becomes easier for anyone sharing your - but most importantly, clients - to understand and use. Your brand will thank you.

In Retrospect

Ask:

- Does my idea appear obvious, now that it has been created?

Why did it take furniture designers so long to discover the brandable idea that led them to design desks one could use while standing up or sitting down? Which is genuinely useful solution, insofar as sitting in offices in front of screens is the new smoking. Expert designers suggest, essentially as doctrine: if designs do *not* appear obvious in retrospect, get worried. Then consider starting over. Were he alive, Chief Apple Designer Jobs would agree.

Then again, were he alive, Jobs might repeat his adage that "It's not customers' job to know what they should want"—or we might add should "need." Indeed, not. Your job, as a creative or ordinary - that label does not portend well for your brand identity, does it? - professional remains the same: You exist to solve the most pressing of clients or customers. Your voluntary assignment, if you seek to develop a more powerful brand, is to solve those same pressing needs more creatively. Any refusal to accept this assignment represents a self-inflicted wound. A wound experienced most acutely in terms of what you would lose: Greater branding power and persuasiveness.

Seemingly Out of the Blue?

Ask:

- *Is my idea unexpected?*

New and useful ideas are usually more unexpected to the extent that they arrive from unexpected sources or unusual combinations. PepsiCo, who owns Frito-Lay, asked a team to cut the salt in some new products while retaining the salty taste that customers crave. The Frito-Lay team obtained the idea that solved this problem from a group of osteoporosis researchers. The medical professionals had created nanoparticles by smashing calcium into tiny pieces and regrowing them into eatable particles that tasted sodium-like or salty.

This type of unexpected sourcing is actually common. Proctor & Gamble professionals recently identified an idea for reducing wrinkles on clothes just taken out of dryers by sourcing a polymer idea invented by European computer chip professionals. Creative people should step outside whatever "boxes" currently constrain their creativity. Routinely release your constraints, as well. What a great habit to break.

Credibility

Ask:

- *Is my idea credible?*

If you still believe in the potential of a new idea 72 hours after it was developed, the idea is probably credible. Credible, as in believable, convincing, worth trusting. But what if critics assail your idea or ideas' credibility? To begin with, you should anticipate that criticism from others will arrive if your idea is genuinely creative. Criticism, then, is often a good sign. So hang in there. Welcome criticism for the opportunities to change, upgrade, and correct that it may provide. Studied and diligent responses to disapproval frequently inspires a new idea or an improved version of the original creative idea. The criticism of others might force you to engage more fully with the work and ideas of others. Aforementioned "intersectional-like" effects will more likely arise when this happens.

You might also secure both solace and strength from reviewing what 19th century German philosopher Arthur Schopenhauer wrote about substantial new ideas: First, the idea is ridiculed. Then it encounters outrage. Finally, the truth of the idea is acknowledged to have been obvious all along.[11]

Walking in Their Shoes

Ask:

- Will clients or customers, or other professionals sharing your stage feel an empathic connection with your idea and any solutions emanating from it?

Empathic connections are important. The presence of empathy lessen the gap between you, one who is presumably developing creative ideas, and clients or other audience members presumably benefitting from the resulting solution. To enhance the prospects that empathic connections can be established, you should solicit and secure feedback from intended or actual customers. Then actually listen. The listening act confers all manner of noncoincidental relational benefits to listeners. Really, truly, actually listening; listening without formulating your next response in your mind; listening sans prejudice or bias demonstrate regard, respect, or even love for the speaker. Once speakers realize this is happening, all manner of affirming value will flow back toward you and your brand as a "listener."

Speaking Generally about Specific Creative Professional Brands

This chapter was written to help you develop creativity as a platform from which to expand your brand's power and influence. Successful professionals generally organize and execute their working lives according to repetitive, disciplined routines. Steady routines, pursued by intelligent people, signal focus and ambition. Learned routines, along with your successful execution of known processes and delivery of established solutions, are substantially what makes you a professional.

Routines also necessarily function as prerequisites to your ability to develop creativity. This is because the order, structure, and discipline you impose and exercise during your professional life also function as a prerequisite to your daring. Order, structure, discipline furnishes you with both a learned willingness and the opportunity to bear and take the risk of occasionally ambitiously failing. Discipline buttresses your baseline professional brand every bit as much as cultivated creativity will elevate it to heights your competitors cannot possibly achieve. Professionals lacking the discipline to govern their own behaviors and appetites cannot creatively govern, influence, or solve the problems of others. Paradoxically, this is because they lack the ability to respond innovatively to pressing problems experienced as they arise on contemporary stages.

Creative professionals can be classified into two broad categories: artists and engineers. Genuinely creative people generally think like artists and work like engineers. As noted time and again about most well-branded professionals they think like people of action and act like people of thought. Even if the professionals actually are engineers or artists. The intersection that unifies action and thought, wrapped inside a single brain, surely should contribute to winning brand identities.

Disciplined professionals, after having been branded as a thinking person's action heroes, have combined inside themselves:

- The liquid and the container, "liquids" solve problems, "containers" keep solutions in-bounds.
- The star performer and sage director, on any stage.
- The dreamer and the doer.

Competition, overt or not, exists in every great pairing of artists, engineers or artists, and engineers. Every creative mind needs another to push against in order to achieve its full potential. People who compete inside their own minds with themselves and others, even when collaborating with them, should be more creative.

Artists are kite flyers, floating good and not so good ideas into the air. Artists develop great prototypes; see big pictures; experience impending or existing problems as whole things ... and constantly lash things together that frequently don't work out well at all. They're intuitive—and creative, featuring expansive imaginations. Artists seek to apprehend the full sweep of what's happening. But artists can be untidy. Realistically, often benefitting from the order and structure engineers provide. Engineers who function as strings or supporting forces. Or as craftspeople who identify good ideas and create practically useful solutions from them.

Behold the professional as artist: He creates good ideas. Behold the professional as engineer: She identifies and then makes the best of those good ideas useful by creating new and marketable solutions. To become more creative inculcate these complementary creative perspectives into your professional life. Become more creative, and you discern the nuance inside the nuance; pick out the value inside the value; identify the differentiation inside the differentiation; and, ultimately, create the solution within the solution to the most pressing problems in your field. When this happens you will inevitably become as "the one brand-identified as the most creative problem-solver around the most creative." On troubling or merely challenging stages, whose brand will other stagehands, directors, actors, and most importantly clients turn to first?

Notes

1 Fallows, James (2013). The 50 Greatest Innovations Since the Wheel. *The Atlantic. November.* 56–68.

2 Beatty, Jack (1998). *The World According to Peter Drucker.* New York, NY: The Free Press.

3 Strutton, David (2009). "Horseshoes, Global Supply Chains, and an Emerging Chinese Threat: Creating Remedies One Idea at a Time". *Business Horizons*, 52: 31–43.

4 Strutton, David and Kenneth Thompson (2015). Marketing, from Scratch: The Principals You Really Need to Know. Dubuque, IA: Kendell-Hunt.

5 Johansson, Frans (2006). *The Medici Effect.* Cambridge, MA: Harvard Business School Publishing.

6 Kahneman, Daniel and Amos Tversky (1979). "Prospect Theory: An Analysis of Decision under Risk". *Econometrica*, 47(2): 263.

7 Shanahan, John (1999). *The Most Brilliant Thoughts of All Time (In Two Lines or Less).* New York, NY: Cliff Street Books.

8 Surowiecki, James (2014). Epic Fails of the Start-up World. *The New Yorker.* May 19. 36.

9 Drucker, Peter F. (2001). *The Essential Drucker.* New York, NY: Harper-Collins Press.

10 Health, Chip and Dan Heath (2007). *Made to Stick: Why Some Ideas Survive and Others Die.* New York, NY: Random House.

11 Magee, Bryan (1998). *Confessions of a Philosopher.* New York, NY: Random House.

Chapter 10
Exploiting Paralanguage

"As I grow older, I pay less attention to what men say. I just watch what they do"

—Andrew Carnegie (1835–1919).

To develop his branded identity as a powerful leader, World War II U.S. General George Patton practiced domineering facial expressions in the mirror. General Patton apparently understood the value of non-verbal communications. He consistently and strategically sought to leverage his insight to secure interpersonal advantage and additional power. All for purposes of elevating the power of his brand. Although the concept we call "professional brand", as a designation and source of power, did not exist during this era.

Further case in point: Patton had a not so discrete photo taken of him urinating in the Rhine River. The Rhine has historically existed as Germany's primary line of defense against attack from the West. Patton pulled all possible strings to ensure that the evocative photo was distributed as widely as possible through all media of the day.

Purpose one: To communicate visceral disdain to his German foe. Your land is my land, now, Nazi bastards! That picture was worth more than a thousand words to his intended German audience. Identifying branding message send. Compelling branding message received. Patton was pissing, and metaphorically, on Germany's leg. His enemy surely viscerally recognized that the "damp feeling" they were experiencing had nothing to do with any rains falling during the spring of 1945.

Purpose two: To signal to a second and third audience that Patton and his mighty Third Army was first to cross the Rhine.' Audience one was the world's media, who had the rest of the world as their audience. The second audience was Patton's fellow allied officers. This group was concurrently comprised of Patton's superiors, subordinates, and peers. In fact, especially Patton's peer group, often fierce rivals who competed internally to acquire more than their fair share of always limited material resources and command attention from their superiors. A diverse set of peers, all wrapped up in one often pissed-off package. Pissed-off because they had not been so aggressively creative in their non-verbal presentation of self.

Or something close to this.

Unexpected Places and Practices

Anyone reading this believe he or she would not benefit from learning how to manifest similarly masterful images on strategically selected stages? We doubt it. Do you now sense how opportunities to effectively leverage similarly creative nonverbal branding management tactics might crop up in unexpected places, ways, and practices? "Leverageable," in terms of your ability to exploit nonverbal tactics for purposes of enhancing your brand's power and persuasiveness.

You Say a Lot When Saying Nothing at All …

… as lyricists and poets have understood forever. For example, songwriter/performer/singer Alison Krause recently wrote:

> "It's amazing how you can speak right to my heart; without saying a word you can light up the dark;
> Try as I may I could never explain; what I hear when you don't say a thing.
> The smile on your face lets me know that you need me; there's a truth in your eyes saying you'll never leave me;
> The touch of your hand says you'll catch me if ever I fall; you say it best when you say nothing at all."[2]

Lyrics from "You Say a Lot When Saying Nothing at All" by Alison Krauss.
Reprinted with permission by Hal Leonard Corporation.

Ms. Krause, of course, was opining beautifully about putatively permanent love. As for your authors, we're writing mundanely about the branding power that could migrate your way once you understand paralanguage, and how to exploit it.

Paralanguage flows from how messages are sent, rather than the words used to convey your branding missives. Were the use of language compared to the how a guitar playing singer might perform a song, paralanguage is embedded in the music rather than the lyrics. Paralanguage is another brand identity-making tool through which you can purposefully (for the better) or inadvertently (for the worse) communicate your relative strengths or weaknesses to audiences around them. Or for matter, your relative weaknesses.

You generally should use paralanguage to convey an image of strength or authority to audiences. When professionals lack confidence or are anxious, they usually speak more softly. For a while, renowned pediatric surgeon and 2016 Presidential candidate Dr. Ben Carson proved an exception to this rule. But unsurprisingly, his once powerful branding appeal quickly lost steam.

Insecure people exhibit more speech disturbances. Failures to complete sentences, leaving out parts of words, or taking exceedingly long pauses between words also illustrate paralanguage's negative nature. Professionals striving for branded images that bespeak confidence, truthfulness, or power—as most professionals surely hope key others perceive them—should avoid signs or distress or weakness in their voices. If you have nothing to hide; have faith in the values and solutions you are offering; or genuinely are confident, your voice will not betray you. Fall short along any one of these dimensions, and your voice might squeal on you like a pig on steroids.

- Old school communication philosopher and public intellectual Marshall McLuhan remains well-known today for having said: "The medium in the message."[3]

But since his utterance experts have coalesced around the idea that the critical medium is the human being who actually delivers the message. Your voice, poise, presence and appearance materially contribute to or detract from your communication capital. The more you invest in improving each, the larger branding return you will earn. Perhaps this counsel strikes you as threatening. Perhaps as opportunity. But this advice should strike you as fact, because it is.

From Front or Back: Just Lead

Middle Eastern sheep are led from the front by the voice of the shepherd. Sheep are dumb (sorry, but this is true) and easily distracted. But even so, they are able to distinguish the voice of one shepherd from other. Meanwhile, throughout the rest of the world—for example, in New Zealand—these restive creatures are driven from behind by a combination of the shepherd's voice and sheep dogs. Lead from behind, lead from the front, lead with or without sheep dogs—or Dobermans. The pasture or stage doesn't matter. Professionals who seek to lead audiences by dint of carefully cultivated power should always leverage the value or mask any deficiencies associated with their voice.

Powerless speech features questioning voice tones or conversational hesitations. Questioning voice tones arise when raising one's voice at the end of declarative sentences as if a question was being asked. Conversational hesitations arise when those cursed "uh's" and "you knows" that pop up when otherwise mellifluous professionals present without their Teleprompters or deviate from focus group-approved talking points. Hedging phrases such as "kinda," "I guess" or "maybe" also undermine others' perceptions of the power, authority or decisiveness that you might have conveyed. "Might have," now there's a sad phrase. As would any demonstrated reticence to take strong stands or stake out turf on dicey stages. Think the opposite of Lame Beaver. Your seeming reticence to commit or firmly state "yes or no" might also contribute to an aura "suggesting" you are less than straightforward or completely confident about your ability or a decision you have made.

Powerfully persuasive presenters exhibit none of these qualities. Powerful presenters never beg or plead. Well, rarely. Instead, they assume or implicitly demand. Or directly command through initially mindful but ultimately instinctive word choices, voice tones, and uninterrupted goal-directed speaking styles.

Even the pace of your speech has more to say about what you say that most suspect. Modulate and vary the pace at which you speak, rarely speaking too quickly, especially when issuing formal presentations to others. On your stages these "others" include individuals, small groups, and auditorium-sized assemblies. At times the spaces between words are as important to great presentations as the spaces between played notes are to great music. Thing about this notion, and draw valuable presentation-related insight from it.

Professionals who believe in themselves and govern the value of the values they create and/or deliver should do these things, as well. A great presenter, just like a great instructor, teacher or professor, takes control of the room. Any room or stage becomes their room or stage.

There is a reason why, when people have done well as presenters, they say they have "killed," as suggested earlier. Making people pay attention is, at its essence, an act of domination. Your ability to convince or make others pay attention, to you of course, often proves a prerequisite to their learning, your persuasiveness, and the degree of branding power you acquire or sustain.

Ace Your Space

All professionals are or should view themselves as marketers. Because all professionals have something valuable to sell. The "something valuable" features and delivers value becomes it is associated with a solution that you presumably are uniquely positioned to provide. The "somethings or value" you are poised to sell might include ideas you have created, products you have developed and could deliver, or yourself as a solution to whatever taxing problem afflicts prospective or current clients.

Many of your professional "marketing" activities will occur in spaces you choose. Your office, boardroom, building; your favorite restaurant or golf course. Places over which you should take ownership. We've just described a controllable opportunity that anyone seeking more power and persuasive ability might strategically exploit. To surprising degrees, spatial arrangements can be controlled in ways that permit you to exercise more control over branding impressions that audience members develop about you.

Arranging Furniture

Furniture arrangements in any office where professional–professional or professional–client interactions occur should involve more than just the aesthetics of interior design. Seating can be arranged to influence the amount of communication that occurs, who talks with whom, how much each person speaks, and who appears most dominant. For example, individuals who occupy central seats or places are positioned either to dominate or manage conservations, depending upon the ends sought. People seated on the periphery, on the other hand, are often excluded from conversation.

The mythical King Arthur famously used a round table in his office. Arthur purportedly did because he did want status differences to influence meetings with his knights.[4] Unless you lead or are primed to lead flatter, less hierarchical organizations that promote equalitarianism we don't recommend round tables. But if round tables are used, people who on the branding make should establish or leverage power by occupying prime spots next to or directly across from the actual leader.

Interpersonal cooperation can be encouraged through side-by-side seating arrangements. More successful conversations can be promoted by seating key players corner-to-corner on one end of a rectangular table or by placing them directly across from one another along the table's sides. Preset table nametags will do the trick. This is your space, after all. Manage your stage!

Other professionals who you manage or know and might seek out as partners or allies may be the sort who cannot live together or apart. Assume these potential adversaries want to work out their differences and minimize the likelihood of further conflict. As initiator of the conciliatory effort (a branding act that would strengthen your power and influence), employ seating arrangements that encourage cooperative conversations. And, believe it or not, your branding identity might be a prime benefactor of the right seating arrangement.

Designing Women and Men

Good office design should feature a perfect marriage of performance and purpose—think function and form—in ways that implicitly suggest meaning (usually, at a sub rosa level) to audience members as they experience your space. Effective design reflected within how an automobile, smart device, apparel item, or office space brand is purposefully arranged, outfitted, and constructed. Good design, generally playing out "quietly" on any brand-able stage or context, also speaks directly to quality. In this scenario, of course, speaking to any number of key audience members presumed perceptions of your professional "quality." Or, stated more efficiently, the quality of your professional performance.

Quality may be described as freedom from defects. Quality is directly proportional to efficiency, meaning fundamentally that quality and efficiency rise and fall in lockstep. An earned reputation for quality (your own) also drives quantity. In this context, quantity of clients or other vital relationships. People who earn the reputation as high quality professionals almost inevitably can charge higher prices while maintaining their share of audience minds and wallets. Which should prove motive enough to inspire brand players to learn more about how to manage the spaces they "own."

Effective design makes it possible for you to connect more easily with others. A discussion of exactly what this sort of design would entails extends beyond the scope of this book or the expertise of its authors. However, to the extent that establishing genuine connectivity with key others, including clients, is crucial to your success you should consider engaging the professional services of an interior designer. He/she presumably can deliver exactly this sort of value. Assuming the professional you hire understands your primary designing goal, of course. Which should be driven more by the goal of elevating power of your brand than the aesthetics of the design.

Exploiting Nonverbal Branding Signals

Imagine that representatives from a potential alliance partner firm recently you to present your organization's ideas for streamlining their firm's information management functions. The presentation is today. Professional that you are, you've thoroughly prepared. You're confident the ideas you plan to present are worthwhile. And indeed they are. Your proposal, if implemented, clearly would complement the efficiency with which your presumably soon-to-be partner manages information.

The time arrives to deliver the presentation. You begin by speaking rapidly and profusely, waving your hands and arms for emphasis. When you sit, you do so stiffly, smiling wanly and looking anxiously at other people seated at the meeting. When the meeting ends, you're surprised to learn that almost nobody remembers your ideas or is enthusiastic about the ones they can recall.

As this staged illustration implies, first impressions are important. A principle you already understand. Professionals have traditionally made their first impressions with audience members within about 90 seconds. Those impressions are then the ones targets carry away and on which they base future branding evaluation of you. Of course, in today's Internet-mediated impressions at the speed of the Web, these impressions are likely formed much quicker still. The ways you gesture, sit, and smile or scowl may contribute materially to any branding professional's success or failure. Dozens of subtle, but important, nonverbal cues affect how other perceive and interpret your brand. Will your brand be deemed weak or strong? Credible or untrustworthy? Aggressive or passive? To a degree that may surprise many, various nonverbal branding-impression behaviors that you project and impart to others will radically influence how each branding question is answered.[5]

A well-known Chinese proverb pronounces that a picture is worth a thousand words. A useful insight, this. It implies that when you get eyeball-to-eyeball with target audiences, you can finally unleash the entire, unadulterated version of yourself. For worse, or we hope, for better. Wise professional branders know this, have already inserted a wide-ranging set of nonverbal weapons into their branding impression toolkits, and learned how to use each to create positive branding identities for themselves.

Using Nonverbal to Empower Verbal Branding Messages

When we encounter human beings face-to-face; the look in their eyes; their facial expressions and body lean, how closely they are willing or seek to approach you; and the tense or laid-back nature of their gestures and entire physical being are revealed. Their tone of voice and speed of their speech become unmistakable, easily read. Yet many professionals are not fully aware of the influence this sort of information exercises on others' impressions of them as they interact with those others. But anyone attempting to brand anything, particularly their professional self and thus their value, should understand how this process works. Nonverbal cues that you emit play crucial roles in determining the sorts of brand-impressions audiences that will develop about you. Nonverbal communication styles can decisively break through the verbal clutter and convey brand-related imagery far more meaningfully than most specific words you elect to speak.[6]

The effective use of nonverbal behaviors can enhance positive verbal messages. Unfortunately, the misapplication of nonverbal cues can undermine otherwise favorable verbal branding messages. Suppose, for example, that you attempt to ingratiate a key audience member by saying: "I appreciate how you gave me enough time to describe all the advantages of our [prospective] partnership." Suppose further, however, that you do so with closed, crossed arms and/or a smirk on your face. Positive branding effects that otherwise might have eventuated from the positive aspects of the oral message would be lost on your target.

Branding professionals should align themselves with the nonverbal tone and signals send by key audience members. Your body's language is conveyed through your posture, gestures, hand movements, presence or absence of longer eye contact, and the direction of your eyes' movements. Your rate of speech, inflection, tone and voice also contribute materially to favorable or undesirable branding outcomes. Each element influences how any audience perceives you.

Facial expressions are especially influential. If professionals consistently arrive on any stage for various purposes looking angry, intentionally or not, they may cultivate a branding aura that evokes annoyance or irritation. Of course, an irritated, annoyed or generally threatening appearance might enhance or degrade your power or influence, dependent on stage and context. The outcome depends upon the specific branding identity you aspire to cultivate in the moment or in your specific professional role.[7]

When interacting with dramatic and/or effusive counterparts who sustain eye contact and speak rapidly and expressively (perhaps these are powerfully branded individuals, maybe they're merely manic), you might accelerate your speech rate, gesticulate more than normal, and vary the tone of your voice. Whether you do these things should pivot based on the comparative power status that separates you from or bonds you to the audience member being targeting through your paralanguage. Conversely, when interacting with a monotonous speaker who rarely makes eye contact, you might elect to speak more slowly and suppress your gestures. Either nonverbal brand management tactic should enhance your audience member's receptivity to other brand-related overtures that you have initiated.

To project hard-core branding power, hold eye contact. Alpha brands do not look away. But about 3 seconds is right for men during initial interactions with males or females. Stare longer and you quickly enter creepy territory. Your behavior would generally suggest one of two things: either "I want to kill you" or "I want to have sex with you." Neither outcome would redound favorably to your branding identify unless, perhaps, you're a professional action movie hero or porn star.

Messaging through Unwritten Codes

Nonverbal branding management behaviors exist as part of elaborate unwritten codes. Especially when you render these behaviors at individual levels. "Unwritten," because essentially by definition such codes cannot be captured in words. "Elaborate," insofar as those professionals who are able to exploit them successfully must perform in sophisticated and nuanced ways. Yet the power of nonverbal branding communication is implicitly or explicitly understood by nearly everyone you encounter and interact with on your stages.[8]

The way you move, sit, or stand may provide the single most power-enhancing brand impression that some professionals ever make. Who is the Big Kahuna on this stage?

Yet other nonverbal behaviors and nonbehaviors exist that most professionals could pursue to make solid, credible, and lasting good first, last, and in-between branding impressions. But first, let's examine what many branding actors may be doing wrong.

Experts suggest, other things being equal, the fewer hand and body gestures you make, the more powerful, deliberate, credible, and intelligent you're perceived to be. As a rule of thumb, in a videotaped study of how professional women and men entered a room where an important meeting was about to begin, women displayed on average 27 different major movements. Men brandished only 12 movements, on average.[9] This is not gender bias. This is an observed and empirically investigated fact.

The average woman might remove her jacket, set down her files, adjust her hair and clothing, pull items from her bag, and so forth. The test subjects observing this videotape believed that women took materially longer to get composed than did men, distracting attention from what they said in the meeting. Women are more likely on average to "hand dance" when making a point. They may feel that are simply being expressive. But observers were more likely to perceive they were leaking emotions. Trust us:

- Leaky emotion distracts from the power and persuasiveness of branded messages as they are conveyed.

All professional messages are "brandable." The messages may be branded well or poorly, but they will be received as part of your brand. Post-reciept, the manner in which audiences interpret your verbal and nonverbal—stated and unstated—messages will strengthen or degrade your power and persuasiveness.

Your authors are sufficiently experienced and cautious enough to not enter a gender dispute, here. But one reason why men are more likely than women to be perceived as leaders may follow from the fact that men, on average, employ fewer, lower, slower movements. Indeed, many women who emerged as global leaders throughout the past took the same less-is-more approach. Did they knowingly engage in effective brand-building body language? Catherine the Great literally took no prisoners. This hard-core stance was directly reflected in her physical stance. Think about current German Chancellor Angela Merkel. Watch her give a speech. Mrs. Merkel is solid, and direct, as in "in-your-face", in her presentation style. Consider the Iron Lady, Mrs. Thatcher. Or more distantly, Indira Gandhi. All four women knew how to pose and present themselves and their ideas in ways that spoke directly to and of their power. Each leader knew how to forcefully stand her ground and quickly earned reputations for tolerating neither fools nor excessive dissent.[10]

Less is more when listening. Listen more. Especially if you are concerned about your brand. As discussed, one of the purest ways to demonstrate regard, respect and, depending upon the setting, even filial love one for another is to listen attentively and uncritically to that audience member. And to do so without formulating your next response or question for the speaker. Listening more, inevitably, requires speaking less.

Professionals branding for power should not qualify key conversational points. "Qualify", as in the excessively using words such as "maybe," "perhaps", or "might happen." What does this mean? Speak directly. Get to your point quickly. Make it. Then stop talking. Or leave.

Professionals branding for power should not be intimidated by supposedly awkward periods of silence that often arise when tough subjects, typically the most important subjects, are initially introduced. Be or become "comfortable" with the silence that frequently also follows when you pose tough questions to, or impose challenging expectations on, others. Times will arise when you should not speak at all. As a general rule, you should not speak unless your words improve the silence—as an adage suggests. Figures no less luminous than Winston Churchill and Lao Tzu frequently spoke about speaking. Churchill, by the way, also spoke about writing when writing about speech. Churchill:

- "Broadly speaking, short words are best, and old words, when short, are best of all."

Tzu, more mysteriously but no less meaningfully, as noted earlier, wrote:

- "Those who know do not speak; those who speak do not know."

Managing Your Body as a Brand

Powerful messages about your relative dominance or submissiveness flow naturally from your body. Most people believe they can tell in a near-instant whether their professional counterpart, questioner, or presenter is a warrior, worrier, or wimp. In this context, with apologies to operatic 1980's rocker *Meat Loaf*, "two out of three IS bad" for branding professionals. And least as so far as those audience member's first and current perceptions represent their entire "imagined" reality, they are right. Use this human propensity to your advantage.

Specific body postures and movements confer powerful branding impressions. You will be perceived as more dominant and higher in status when your bearing is erect rather than stooped. Movements that are dynamic, brisk, and purposeful rather than slow, strained, or aimless facilitate the same branding outcomes. Display relaxed rather than edgy movements, when possible. Avoid extending your arms and hands toward an audience in a palms up position. This gesture insinuates weakness or even begging.

Staring eyes, in particular, are thought to exude power. Count Dracula supposedly froze victims through the power of his intimidating stare. Of course, we are not advocating staring at individual audience members to a degree where they might become overtly intimidated, or worse still, assume something is wrong with you. But remember, eyes project power. Hold eye contact. As noted, alpha brands do not look away. But alpha brands never stare so long that they disturb others and consequently diminish their own branding power and persuasiveness.

Looking down, rather than directly at someone, is universally signals either conciliation, agreement, or civility. Like canines, human brands lower their eyes when admitting or feeling defeat, or seeking forgiveness. Not for nothing did the phrase "to err is human but to forgive is canine" enter the domestic cultural lexicon. But there is more. When people are embarrassed or, perhaps most disturbingly in myriad contexts, feeling guilty, they generally avoid eye contact with others. On professional stages, looking down should generally be avoided. The potentially positive or negative power of your eyes, as part of your branding gestalt, should never be sold short. Empathy is born through eye contact and body language. And many a powerfully persuasive brand has been born out of professionals' genuine or "contrived" projections of empathy. Again, the preceding statement is hardly uplifting. But it is surely useful.

The world we share features seven human wonders. These wonders are embedded in our opportunity to touch, see, feel, laugh, hear, learn, and love.

Touch is one wonder that can be easily managed by knowing professionals who have the mind to do so. Touch, as a physical gesture, universally connotes warmth, closeness, caring, and intimacy. The ultimate connotations of touch, of course, depend on the stage and circumstances involved. The act of human touch, particularly its initiation, also can be wielded subtly as a symbol of branding power. Professionals can employ touch to make, underscore, or reinforce power differences, or to delicately signal one's current or impending career progression. High-status professionals, or those steadily moving toward that brand identity, generally can initiate touch without impunity. By contrast, subordinates can rarely touch higher standing professionals without some sort of invitation. Yes, invitation; an extended open right hand comes to mind. (Across millennium, open right hands, normally the bearers' dominant appendix, signaled to ally, foe, friend or stranger alike that their "strong hand" held no weapons. And thus posed no threat.)

Professionals playing power games should use these insights to their branding advantage. Especially professionals who currently occupy subordinate positions but plan to the power and prestige of their brand.

You can also manage your personal space to positively influence impressions made by your brand. Leaders take up more space than followers, or at least they should. Aspiring leaders should follow suit.

In group settings where people are seated, the powerful professional, or whoever aspires to be perceived as such by key others, should tilt forward slightly, with elbows on the chair or table, appearing relaxed. By inhabiting more space, you emanate the impression that you are in charge, even when you are not. Professionals who feel less powerful or perhaps who have learned helplessness upon particular stages tend to draw up their bodies, sit too upright, hold their arms closely to their bodies and keep their legs together (if they are male). Such players also would generally either initiate too many motions or none at all. Either extreme should be avoided.

Practice being asymmetrical. When photographs have been taken of powerful world leaders are cut in half, one half of the photographed figure almost always differs from the other. Such leaders, for example, might rest their hands on one leg, not both. Or cross their legs at the knees, not the ankles. Leaders are almost always photographed gesturing with one arm, not two. Disgraced former President Richard Nixon was one exception. But the exception may speak more to the treachery of his now-known leadership—the media branded him as "Tricky-Dick" —style than of the "rule" we report above. Asymmetrical body positions create the impression, among mindful or mindless audiences, that you are relaxed, confident, self-possessed, credible, and competent. Consequently, asymmetrical body positions create the impression that you're in charge.

Another cliché-alert:

- Learn and subsequently remember that your actions often speak louder than your words.

Stage-managed actions of the sort outlined above require substantial and deliberate practice to master. But people as intelligent and motivated as you can learn how to project their best first- and most-lasting impressions by judiciously applying these nonverbal branding tactics.

Never Forgetting Little Things

The topic may appear too self-evident to discuss. But the subject is too important to ignore. You may be displaying an authoritative vocabulary. A prepossessing or powerful personality. You're even rocking fabulous kicks (shoes). But wet spaghetti handshakes will degrade your brand, every time. There is a direct relationship between the qualities of a firm handshake—its strength, full-hand grip, and duration—and favorable branding impressions. Never forget that.

Correspondingly, the intrinsically human action called a smile, says, simply, "I like you. You make me happy. I'm glad to see you." Their innate ability to continuously display similar sentiments through their behaviors makes dogs the world's only animal (besides cats, perhaps) that typically does not work for a living. Because dogs are always thrilled to see us, we are naturally happy to see them. Abiding relationships bound up in love, loyalty and affection seemingly intrinsically follow. What branding professional would not desire that sort of relationship?

Professionals rarely experience the luxury of doing only one thing at a time. Consequently, they can easily permit negative emotions attached to one activity to spill over into other activities. When a big deal just went bust, it is difficult to avoid communicating some aspect of disappointment to other audience members with whom you must deal. So what. Smile anyway. Actions may appear to follow emotions, but actions and emotions actually work together. By self-regulating actions that can be directly controlled through conscious willpower, you can indirectly influence your emotions. "Smiling,", yes simply smiling, is one such self-regulating action.

The act of compartmentalizing entails leaving the negative baggage locked within the confines of a particular situation. Compartmentalizing is something we can logically and easily advise you to do. Yet we find compartmentalization extremely difficult to do ourselves. As will most readers. But forcing yourself to smile pushes the compartmentalization process along. The act of smiling generally improves human moods and outlooks.[11] Audience members are almost always more favorably impressed by us when we arrive on our stage bearing a "honest-to-goodness" "happy-to-see-you" smile. This, as opposed to the response you would would earn if you lived-out your brand in any other manner. "Live out," or is it "act out"; okay, we would say "perform!" On your stage, of course.

Words Matter, Too

Times will arise when you should honor "not-to-do" lists as much as "to-do" alternatives. This is true of the words you use or choose not to use. Thinking professionals and nonprofessionals constantly edit their lives. You should also constantly edit your words; the ones you actually speak. Because, words, once they are out ... Well, you know the rest. As the New Testament Book of James pronounces:

- "Huge horses are controlled by putting small bits in their mouths."

Behold the power of the tongue, watch your words; what you say or don't say truly matters. Because once words leave the tongue they aren't coming back. And, yes, we discussed this same notion previously. But the underlying lesson, and its implications, is so nice that its appropriate to say them twice.

Criticism puts audience members on the defensive. A place where many clients already feel they reside when interacting with professionals. Criticism frequently compels targets to justify and defend themselves. Either externally, or more likely and more damningly, though internal and thus nondiscernable means. Nondiscernible, that is, until after your brand identity has been degraded.

The transformational late 19th century-era Philadelphia retailer John Wanamaker wrote: "I learned long ago that it is foolish to scold. It is difficult enough to overcome my own limitations without fretting that God did not distribute the give of intelligence evenly." Somewhere during his life, the retailing icon apparently learned how futile criticism can be.

Yes, times arise when your criticism of others, implied or direct, is appropriate and necessary. But unjustified or noncompulsory criticism; that is, in situations where you could have broached the issue differently, can prove dangerous. Criticism can wound pride and spur resentment. President Abraham Lincoln purportedly never directly or publicly criticized his enemies, allies, or acquaintances. Acting "with charity for all and malice toward none," Lincoln always held his public or written peace. As soon as you learn how to do yourself tell us. We could probably make a lot of money together by writing a book about the topic. But if you believe your branding interests are served by stirring up controversy, building resentment in others, or leaving audience members with the logical impression that because you are saying this about "them" you must also be speaking ill about "me" to others, unleash the hounds of criticism. Like us, you're probably good at it. Perhaps we both can even ignore that fact that the the resulting harm to our brands may take years to overcome. At the same time, however, we should similarly each own the fact own the fact that situations could arise where such censure or disapproval might actively promote the brand identity we are seeking.

Professionals who must deal successfully with other people in order to succeed, a list including nearly all of us, should remember they are frequently dealing with less than completely rational human beings. Instead, we interact with audience members often unconsciously driven by emotion; burdened by biases, like us, they are often influenced more by prejudice than principle; motivated by inordinate pride and excessively high self-regard; and "gifted" with elephantine memories when the subject turns to gossip-like information that contemporary folks typically spread at the speed of Internet.

Young Ben Franklin, the entrepreneur, was known for his rapier-like critical thrusts. Mature Benjamin Franklin, the statesman, became so skilled at managing branding impressions that he was appointed as fledging America's first Ambassador to France – America's most important global alliance partner at the time. Moreover, as a 70+ years old, married, not terribly attractive man Ben was able to charm the pantaloons off numerous decades-younger ladies living at the royal French court. The Ambassador's secret branding formula: "I speak ill of no one … and speak of all the good of everyone. Any fool can criticize, condemn, and complain, and many fools do exactly that." To ensure that the wrong branding impression is never made, avoid such foolishness yourself.

By avoiding such foolishness, you also may sidestep an otherwise dreadful murder-suicide scene. Stages on which professionals knowingly assail other professionals' or even clients' reputations, in the process actually diminishing their targets' brand equity, but who themselves end up getting covered in blood themselves. That's because, in the process, hypercritical professionals damage or even destroy their own good names. Experts agree that two people bleeding emit more blood than only one bleeder does.

Demonstrate respect to subordinates, superiors, peers and clients by listening to them as much as reasonably possible, given the situation's parameters, without interruption, without concentrating so diligently on formulating responses that it becomes self-evidently obvious that you are not listening. Listen uncritically to what your conversational dance partner is saying. Acknowledge your conversational partners' response without further comment and restrain any impulse to offer negative commentary—unless, of course, it is your job to criticize, correct, sanction, and possibly terminate.

Hold Up a Mirror

Your manageable ability to understand brand-impression management behaviors and the effects your staged behaviors impose on targeted audiences will allow you to see yourself more clearly in metaphorical mirrors. The reflections should permit you to assess where you are and subsequently improve the images that others hold about you. Take advantage of this opportunity.

Few people ever examine their images in a mirror with indifference. With good reason, we might add. Mirrors may function as partners in our vanity. They may function as theater-like stages on which we act out certain fantasies. Mirrors may even help professionals by leading them to useful self-knowledge by enhancing their self-awareness.

One certainty: Many professional actors play out substantial portions of their working lives in front of mirrors. Mirrors reflecting back to professionals the likenesses/re-projected impressions that audience members project or radiate as they interact with their brands. Two simple questions that mirrors can answer for professionals: Is the branding identity you're seeking to project working, or not? Are you largely ignorant about how others perceive your nonverbal and verbal appearance.? Hope not, if your brand matters to you.

Style

Style points matter. As does dressing not so much to impress, but in ways that leave zero doubt you mean business even though you quite likely perform on a non-business stage. Look the part for the stage role you are acting out. Dress in ways consistent with the stylistic norms established in your particular sector. And at the least, even if you perform on the "coolest, loosest, most anything goes" in terms of what you wear onstage, you still should dress and act like a prospect rather than a suspect. Of course, this means dressing consistent with what represents a "prospect" as opposed to a "suspect" look on your particular professional stage. Our point being: a "prospect" look in a "white-shoes law firm"—an evocative branding appellation, by the way—would be deemed "suspect" in agencies managing the affairs of pop stars. This point is important. After all, as historical wit and bon vivant Oscar Wilde insightfully wrote:

- "Only shallow people do not judge others by their appearance."[12]

Hope you read Wilde's statement carefully. It clearly underscores the extent to which appearance matters on performance stages.

Appearance

Apart from your attire, appearance is largely the consequence of your fitness. Even in an America where about 1/3 of citizens are overweight, with another 1/3 actually being obese, this standard still holds.[13] Fitness plays a huge role, for better or worse, in your branded identity. The world's reviews can be harsh.

But your confidence also plays a major role. Confidence is reflected in your projected but presumably genuine sense of self-assurance, particularly in terms of your proficiency. Confidence would similarly project forward into your branded identity in ways that elevate the power and persuasiveness of your brand.

Your confidence level is partially a consequence of your appearance. Clearly, you should undertake reasonable and appropriate measures aimed at improving your physical appearance to the best of your ability and to the extent that time is available to be allotted to the task. As far as finding the willpower to and remain on top of this mountain goes; that's yet another topic for another book to address.

Attire

The way you choose to dress forms an immediate, powerful, and lasting impression among crucial audience members. Your dress, your attire, provide direct and indirect signals about who you are and what you stand for. Be careful what you stand for. Because, as the Reverent Dr. Fred Cassell taught, "if you don't stand for anything you will fall for everything."

First, dress first to look competent. Competent-appearing people are hired and promoted more easily. This has long been true, despite the fact that appearance is not linked to improved performance. Yet as you surely realize the notion of exactly what constitutes "conservatively competent dress" will vary wildly across professional ranks. This is an issue you must manage for yourself on your particular stage. Still, professionals generally should dress conservatively. This recommendation is likely more germane among younger, presumably up-and-coming professionals.

Second, dress for the job you want, not the one you currently occupy. If you believe that you can tell a lot about others by the way they dress, it appears reasonable to assume others to whom you are emphatically branding your new or enhanced value are drawing the same conclusions about you. The more conservative your attire, the harder you are read. This condition should subsequently make it easier for you to lead audience members to the branding impressions you seek to develop. As a general rule, serious branders should aspire to have their attire say nothing about them, other than perhaps that their clothing is well-tailored and fits them nicely.

What you wear is another business card. You visibly represent your profession to others with whom you interact. And dependent upon that profession what you wear or your fitness level may speak as boldly about you and any values your brand "promises" to deliver as your LinkedIn profile. Ascertain what you want say to others sharing your sphere, or stage. Then dress accordingly.

Style versus Substance?

You've read that professionals often engage in self-promotion to increase the chances that they will receive more credit for successful outcomes or to make one's strengths more apparent, and better known. You've likewise learned that ingratiation, by contrast, is a more subtle tactic. Ingratiation, you recall, might include agreement with targeted others on major issues while intentionally disagreeing with them on minor ones. Or, more duplicitously, complementing a key target on, say, an idea well-presented when reality suggests this is not true.

Each tactic likely will be used by knowing professionals as they attempt to earn branding "style points" in important audience members' eyes. Unfortunately for professionals who genuinely work diligently and succeed as a consequence, purely stylistic brand-driven renderings sometimes trump more substantive value. But one fact remains: despite the potential effectiveness of such branding tactics, self-promoting and ingratiating professionals always face substantial pitfalls.

In fact, as discussed, professionals who promote style over substance always face the same paradox. That being, the exact stages on which the potential branding benefits of self-promotion, ingratiation, or apparel/appearance-driven style points are greatest are the same stages on which use of these tactics and their underlying motives are most apparent.

To succeed, be skilled, cautious, and fortunate enough to not arouse suspicions regarding your true motives. Otherwise, you might find that your projected brand identities are bluntly or covertly rejected by the objects of your scripted branding affectations. Client trust, at that point, might just not be lost. Future trust might likewise would prove difficult to restore on that stage.

The stages on which you work and perform are shrinking due to the ever-extending reach, power, and velocity of Internet mediated communication. Moreover, only so many stages exist on which many professionals—say, academics, athletes, or salespeople—can create and deliver their values. So nothing could ever be gained while quite a bit might lost by missteps on any stage.

Judging Books by Their Covers: Everyone Does It

"You cannot judge a book by its cover" is an enduring cliché. The associated implication is that one should not evaluate books or other objects on such a shallow basis. The adage offers sound advice in many settings. But it assumes special relevance on and around professional stages. There, many audiences actually do judge people, certainly many professionals, by their covers—often to the branding detriment of the "judged."

But, evoking another platitude, what about "the other side of the coin?" Does a positive side exist to this human tendency to judge others at very surface levels? The answer is yes. An upside definitely exists for professionals seeking to intentionally brand themselves as having the most appealing "covers." At this point, we should admit something: Most people already do these things. We're already concerned about our outward appearances. Likely because even naive brand-impression managers generally understand that how our brands are perceived by others can be influenced by things or events to which our actual performance is only loosely connected.

Brand-impression management tactics have existed since the beginning of mythical time. Eve's presumably metaphorical acceptance of the forbidden fruit in the Garden of Eden resulted in part from the Serpent's skillful employment of ingratiation in pursuit of his own goals. All the serpent had to do was appeal to Eve's vanity. Nasty, yes. But professionals do and should use nonverbal and artifactual brand impression behaviors for the same reason as the serpent—when exercised properly, they work. If you are going to do it anything, why not learn how to manage your branding impressions more effectively?

We hope you do not interpret the preceding question as an endorsement or condemnation of the practice. Most professionals will try to manage their branding identities regardless of what we write here. Consequently, we encourage you to examine your own brand image and to make sure the one you are purposefully pursuing or unintentionally developing is worthwhile.

You enjoy the opportunity to construct a more appealing branding "cover" for yourself by making proper language choices, displaying appropriate manners, employing prudent body language, and judiciously selecting which brand-impression management tactics and power enhancing rules to use. Rightly or wrongly, your success depends, substantially, on the skill with which you manage the perceptions and attributions that key audiences develop about you.

Learn more about your current brand-impression tendencies; the identities and images those actions project toward others, along with the reaction those others project back; and, ultimately, the positive or negative consequences of your behaviors. Better for you that you approach important audiences armed with a fuller awareness of any "chemistry" opportunities or problems inherent in the relationships you enjoy or endure with targeted audiences. Good or bad chemistry, after all, may facilitate greater audience trust and respect for your brand, or contribute to the absence of each. Better still if you recognize that most branding problems are not grounded entirely in chemistry, but instead partially based on negative audience perceptions and attributions. Then you'll less likely experience the predicament that befell the serpent. He was, of course, cast out of the Garden of Eden.

Poor devil. Satan's brand has suffered ever since!

Notes

1 Keane, Michael (2014). *George S. Patton: Blood, Guts and Prayer*. Washington, DC: Regnary Publishing.
2 Whitburn, Joel (2011). *Top Pop Singles 1955-2010*. Gold River, CA: Records Research, Inc. p. 500.
3 Carr, David (2011). Marshall McLuhan: Media Savant. *The New York Times*. January 6, 2011. Retrieved February 1, 2016. http://www.johnralstonsual.com/wp-content/uploads.
4 Geoffrey of Monmouth and Lewis Thorpe (1988). *The History of the Kings of England*. New York, NY: Penguin.
5 Demarrias, Ann and Valerie White (2004). *First Impressions*. New York, NY: Bantam Books.
6 Stubbs, Kevin H. (2003). *Can't Get Through? Eight Barriers to Communication*. Gretna, LA: Pelican Publishing Company.
7 Barsade, Sigal and Olivia A. O'Neill (2016). "Manage Your Emotional Culture." *Harvard Business Review*, January/February, 58-68.
8 Driver, Janine (2010). *Your Say More Than You Think*. New York, NY: Crown Publishers.
9 Anderson, Peter (2004). *The Complete Idiot's Guide to Body Language*. New York, NY: Alpha Publishing.
10 Massie, Robert K. *Catherine the Great: Portrait of a Woman*. New York, NY: Random House.
11 Messinger, Daniel S., Alan Fogel, and K. Laurie Dickson (2001). "All Smiles Are Positive, But Some Smiles Are More Positive Than Others." *Developing Psychology*, 37(5): 642-653.
12 Epstein, Joseph (2006). *Yale Book of Quotations*. New Haven, CT: Yale University Press.
13 Levy-Navarro, Elena (2008). *The Culture of Obesity in Early and Late Modernity*. New York, NY: Palgrave Macmillan.

Chapter 11
Communicating More Powerfully

"There is only one thing in the world worse than being talked about, and that is not being talked about"

—Oscar Wilde (1854–1900).

"The West" is comprised of native son nations born of European stock. By name, "The West" has traditionally included namely, the U.S. and Canada; more recently, Australia and New Zealand; and naturally the 30-something European nations themselves. (The vague description "30-something" applies because unresolved disputes exist regarding whether Ukraine or Turkey and a handful of lesser nations are European.)

Regardless, Western culture dominates the world. Despite occasional rattlings about Asian culture possibly growing into this role, this statement remains true. Without pause, when push came to shove, as is so often the case, West has largely dictated to other global regions from around 1492 until the present time. Despite some occasional "elbowing" for space from other regions, Western cultural dominance is poised to continue.

The West has not successfully lorded over the globe due to the superiority of its "enlightened" ideals, ideas, or principles. The increasingly more democratic or Judeo-Christian values that proliferated and ultimately prevailed throughout the West during the last 500+ years were generally good things. And remain so. But the presence and preponderance of these values and ideas are not directly responsible, either. Instead, the power and persuasiveness of Western culture won the day, long ago, and holds sway today, due to the demonstrated superiority of its violence. As well as its repeatedly communicated willingness to wield either the reality or threat of violence "through whatever means it deemed necessary." "Through whatever means necessary;" a branded phrase that Malcom X forcefully promoted as he fulminated against Western dominance during the 1960s—until, ironically, he was murdered by rival members of his own Black Muslin party.

Violence, or the threat of its imminent arrival, is the special sauce that Western nations have historically and strategically communicated, and ultimately leveraged, as solutions whenever potential or actual problems arose on global stages. The threat or reality of fierce retribution has been and remains the primary source of hard-edged differentiating power that traditionally made and still positions the Western brand as the most dominant regional brand in the world.

Somehow, however, even highly-educated Westerners often forget, ignore, or never learn about the role that hard-edged branding-power played in elevating their culture's global branding stature and reputation. Meanwhile, well-educated African, Asian, Indian, Middle-Eastern, or Latin/South American natives always learn and never forget. Each audience nation knows by heart the propensity of Western nations to communicate the threat of or actually exercise violence when pursuing their strategic goals or preserving their strategic interests. Nor, for that matter, do Russians forget. Most topically, a group that includes President Vladimir Mr. Putin, notably, has branded himself as a true "kick-ass" power-playing professional during the last 30 or so years. And Putin's Russian audience largely loves—or, at least, fears and respects—him due to his strongman branding identity.

Even today, during less violent times, "The West" continues to punch above its weight. Yes, you read "less violent times" correctly. It is true. Despite two brutal World Wars and three epically-scaled nationally-sponsored genocides (Nazi Germany-, Soviet Russia-, and Communist China-induced events) the percentage of Earth's citizens who died violently during the 20th century is lower than any other 100 year period in history.[1]

We live, however, during a 24/7/365 era in which Internet-mediated media promote their respective self-interest by ginning-up the perception of violence. "If it bleeds it leads" is not media myth but rather historical reality. The media, logically, put their best interests first by communicating information that is "sticky" and "contagious" (more about what each term means later). As should you. Especially when communicating hopefully determinant messages to key audiences.

The West also punches above its weight because this "loose coalition" has become increasingly sophisticated in its ability to communicate brand power through softer messaging. Substance generally does prevail over style. Western culture has evolved into an extremely attractive product. A brand-able product featuring values, benefits and yes, solutions, that are simply not available in any other regional bloc in the world. Hundreds of thousands of refuges never clamor, genuinely risking lives, fortunes, or freedom, to enter China, India, Russia or Japan, or African, Middle Eastern or Latin/South American nations. But legions continue to sacrifice fortunes and health, leaving loved ones behind, as they struggle to enter Europe, the United States and Canada, or Australia.

By Any Ethical Means Necessary

The West and western culture has clearly earned and sustained a reputation as an exceptionally powerful brand. Whatever it took or takes; whether the route to power was more or less responsible—western nations long ago committed individually though not communally to doing the right or even the wrong things right to build, sustain, and communicate the power, persuasiveness, and attractiveness of their collective brand.

The value of this branded power thing—or game—is real. Were this not true, the best way to sustain peace would not be to prepare for war. Struggles driven by the goal of earning and maintaining dominant branding reputations by communicating hard and soft power unfold perpetually across the world. Should you similarly struggle—or at least work—to achieve to achieve the same outcomes?

The answer is a clear yes. Plan to do whatever is necessary and ethical to develop, strengthen, and sustain hard-edged or soft-edged methods through which to communicate your branding power more effectively. Arguments supporting this exact point were presented earlier and will not be repeated. But even had the case not been made, your innate desire to achieve greater branding power likely would still have risen to the top. The desire to stand out more powerfully and persuasively than others around us is apparently biologically predetermined.[2]

Male peacocks, for example, boast spectacularly gaudy tails. All male peacocks. Their tails function as differentiating branding symbols that favorably distinguish peacocks from all other aviary associates. Their female counterparts' tails? Well, lady peacock tails are nice but far less extravagant. Yet females enjoy the privilege and purview to choose, from among many potential suitors, with whom they will mate. Who does she choose? The partner with the "good enough tail?" Or the "boy" peacock with the best, the persuasively powerful, tail? You know the answer. No, you are not a peacock. Your goal, nonetheless, should be make your brand (tail) stand out from other professional peacocks because it is perceived as or genuinely is "different from" and "better than" your rivals' "tails."

The Professional Will Speak to You Now

Your primary goal should be to deliver "best possible" "need-satisfying" values to clients. You do this in order to solve client problems. Execute this task successfully and your clients benefit. You, your brand, and other entities—your family or organization—whose fortunes rise when you perform successfully will also benefit.

When professionals communicate to various audiences, their primary goal should be to develop desirable branding messages and deliver the messages efficiently to precisely targeted recipients. Professionally branded messages should inform, remind, and/or persuade prospective or actual clients that the particular value delivered by the "professional product"—you, of course—represents the most logical choice to make. Professionally branded messages also might be designed to create new relationships between with clients (or other audience members) or to strengthen relationships that already exist with clients (or other audience members).

Clients always chose the "alternative" (product) that they believe will deliver the most problem-solving value to them. Being highly self-interested, it is only logical that clients act in this manner. Client choices, of course, might relate to which provider to engage with, disengage from, or endorse or denounce. Never communicate anything to anyone, branding-wise, until you appreciate the implications that these facts of professional life exercise on your brand communications.

Basic Professional Communication Principles

Principle 1: Treat Branding as an Action Item

Take a product (you), a professional yet still personal "entity" about which most people entering or sharing your stage know little or nothing. This description is certainly accurate when your first enter a new stage. But even people who do know you as a "professional product" often could care less. Caring less, that is, until and unless you convince them think differently and care more.

Your job is to elevate this product; that is, you and your brand, to a position where you become the temporary center of other people's world. Become the "temporary center" of their world on cue, as it were, when problems of the sort that you are uniquely qualified to solve arise in their personal or professional. Only highly creative or absolutely exceptional professionals could produce this result, right?

But this ambitious result is exactly the communication outcome that you, operating under and for the auspices of your brand, should routinely aspire to achieve. This is also more or less how the daunting action item of communicating your branding power more persuasively unfolds. Branding is an action word. This means "brand-ing" is a gerund. Any word ending with "ing" used as a noun that also conveys the meaning of the verb, as in "to brand," is a gerund.

Branding, then, is something you should engage in—or do. But you can never "do branding" well unless you also "do communicating" well.

Principle 2: You Are the Message

Marshall McLuhan and his principle that the "medium in the message" was referenced earlier. McLuhan's message infers that you are and should be the originating source and primary purveyor of your branding message. Each reality further implies that your voice, poise, presence (your aura), and appearance (your look) might be wielded as difference making parts of your brand. Your appearance, in particular, contributes substantively to the level of power you project as a communication "medium" through which your professional branding messages are sent. Appearance is important in most communication settings. The fact that human appearance matters greatly is also probably biologically-predetermined—witness the peacocks. Indeed, a strongly felt yearning to classify, categorize, and eventually stereotype anything and everyone as being more or less desirable appears innately human. Humans perpetually classify, categorize, and/or stereotype people or brands (or even cities, states or nations) as attractive or unattractive; as good (i.e., benign, beneficial, appealing) or bad (i.e., malignant, harmful, threatening); or as more or less powerful.

Some power communication principles are largely self-evident. Let's discuss them anyway.

First, the more you invest in improving key elements of your appearance, including physical attributes, the larger branding returns you can expect to earn. How to achieve improve physical attributes, however, is a subject addressed by numerous other books. Moreover, one can never discount the harsh reality that when it comes to brains, brawn, or beauty, some people actually have won the genetic lottery. Yet don't we professionals still face what is essentially a moral obligation to do "best we can" with whatever talents God, some other higher being, or fate itself deemed us worthy of receiving? The answer, we believe, is yes. People should do the best with whatever assets they have been gifted. If only to advance the interest of the family for whom you work.

Second, your perceived credibility is likewise crucial. Again, this is because you are the brand-able message. Your personal credibility elevates or degrades the likelihood that targeted audiences accept or reject your message. Absent acceptance of your messages, your brand will never sway anyone.

The extent to which any source is deemed credible is directly related to the source's perceived expertise and trustworthiness. Trustworthy reputations, for you, will emerge as a function of your perceived objectivity, honesty, and integrity. Because these are the exact characteristics that drive others' perceptions of your believability.

Third, your branding power will wax or wane, like phases of the moon, based on how much trust you develop or fail to develop among audience members. Trust is reciprocity flavored by emotion. (Reciprocity, best described as the fact that, over time, one gets-back [good or bad] what one gives-out [good or bad].) When you behave in trustworthy fashions during tough times, you earn regard and self-respect that becomes invaluable as good times return. Messages delivered by expert sources whom others believe are genuine—professionals perceived as credible, honest, sincere, and buzzword of all contemporary branding buzzwords, as "authentic"—would inevitably be more persuasive.

Your reputation as a credible, trustworthy, and authentic (real!) "actor" will generate greater branding power. The quality of your reputation will rise and fall directly with the amount of loyalty you capture and sustain from clients and other audience members. You can typically charge higher prices for those services (your solutions), particularly over time. Successful client management, as well as successful client acquisition, involves making people "like" or "trust" you. This is human nature at its most natural. Knowing these things, some advice follows.

The first thing to say when meeting someone, even and perhaps especially when they've made an appointment to meet with you, is "thanks for making time for me." The second thing to do is to ask them about themselves. The third thing to do is to make them laugh, unless laughter is absolutely inappropriate or unachievable in the moment.

These are not tricks. The trick is understanding there are no tricks, just a world full of rich, poor, and in-between folks hoping to get treated better than dirt. As a professional you occupy a stage from which you can elect to gift them that present. Meanwhile, the ultimate beneficiary of said "gift-giving" will be you.

Remember "enlightened self-interests?" Or, "doing well for yourself by doing good for others." Trust is the most important currency in all relationships, cultures, business, or professional settings. An earned reputation for trustworthiness and credibility will contribute materially to the power of your brand messages, in both the near term but especially the longer term.

Principle 3: Ensure That Messages Sent Are Messages Received

For successful communication to occur, the "intended branding message" must be received and understood by the "intended client target" in the manner in which the originating/initiating professional sender—you—intended. This principle applies to branding messages and all communication processes. Messages are depicted bilaterally, or two-way, in traditional communication models. Senders; here, you as professional brander, develop messages and initiate the messaging effort. Messages are conveyed through various media, also called *communication channels.* You are the primary communication channel on your stage. In turn, on the other end of this "dyadic" communication exchange process, receivers—generally clients—respond in reaction to their receipt of your branding messages. Dyadic means two persons or two parties. You must package, or encode, the central ideas that you are seeking to convey through your messages such that receivers understand your messages in the manner you intended.

Absent effective encoding, successful communication cannot occur. At the exact time they receive messages, receivers *decode* them. *Decoding* is the process by which an audience receives, interprets, make sense of, and assigns meaning to your message.

Encoding or decoding processes frequently go awry. What happens next, as the prison warden infamously said to the inmate character played by Paul

Newman in the 1967 movie *Cool Hand Luke*, "... a failure to communicate." Due to this "failure to communicate" the warden proceeded to hit Luke in the head with a whip handle.[3] Luke, in retrospect, probably had too much noise, too many distractions, in his life. As the warden likely did as well. You almost surely do, too. So what? The "so what" is that branding professionals must learn to communicate successfully through the noise. If not, you'll experience the longer-term pain associated with having two-few happy clients.

Noise impedes successful communication. Noise is any physical/psychological barrier, distraction, or interference that impedes recipients from successfully decoding a message. Your message. In today's congested traditional and Internet-mediated media markets "noise levels" and information overload are higher than at any point in history. This the profusion of noise worsens the communication challenges that professionals face as they seek to differentiate their branding messages.

Principle 4: Master Brand Encoding

You must master four vocabularies to successfully encode branding messages. In descending order of "difficulty to learn," the vocabularies are: Reading, listening, speaking, and writing. If you're still reading this book you've mastered purposeful reading. So we'll attemd to the other three tasks. To increase your proficiency in professional brand-related listening, speaking, and writing, the following rules of thumb are useful. These "rules" are also time-tested and experience-based.

When conveying branding messages to others, whenever possible, you should display a self-deprecating humor; an unpretentious demeanor; and an unaggressive conversional style, all while listening carefully. Hopefully, you can muster the discipline to complete this not-so-simple mission. Never forget: knowledge, particularly about clients and their problems and how best you as "their professional performer" might solve them, is obtained by the ear rather than the tongue. Often you should defer, or signal deference, to others.

Pursue sincere listening. Sincere, in this context, means you do not presume to understand what your communication target will say next. Sincere means you do not think about what you will say next while purportedly listening. Especially when the subject is important, listen, even if you do not understand. And it is okay if you don't understand the client's intent or meaning. Your task is to keep listening intently until understanding and an opportunity for either rapprochement or advantage-building arrives.

"Rapport" arises and is necessary to establish empathic connections with key people. "Empathic connections" can be created and nourished when professionals understand the other's point of view; feel what the other feels; and/or have demonstrably exhibit concern for the other. No surprise to follow: the first and most important ingredient for establishing rapport as well as the key to achieving empathy is listening. Even manifestly displayed compassion, if compassionate displays are appropriate on your stage, begins with listening. Listening uncritically to what s/he is saying exemplifies regard and respect to your conversational other. When you demonstrate consistent empathy, respect, regard, or even appropriate love—agape, again from the ancient Greeks—for others on or orbiting about your stage, only good would result for your brand messaging, identity, and power.

These tasks are easier described than achieved, of course. Indeed, as soon as you learn how to achieve these simple yet challenging and wondrous results, write us. But just because professionals generally struggle to achieve these delightful outcomes doesn't mean they shouldn't try. Especially when branding.

Professionals who talk too much rarely fail to incite resentment from those around them. The only thing amusing about professionals who speak too much or for too long without taking a metaphorical breath is watching what happens when two souls sharing this inclination encounter one another. Seeming uninterested in what others have to say; speaking excessively about your personal life; prying for others' secrets, telling long, essentially pointless stories; contradicting or disputing someone directly, or rebelling against ideas of others, except in small witty doses. Spreading scandals; dishing dirt; criticizing others behind their backs. Engage in any of these behaviors only to the extent that you seek to degrade your ability to successfully encode powerful branding messages.

When writing to key audiences ensure each phrase is subject to only one interpretation. Meanwhile, communicate an adult enthusiasm about the value of the issue about which you are writing. Few people have ever earned power in their chosen fields absent an acute enthusiasm for the ground they voluntarily chose to cultivate.

When writing ensure that sentences are not too long. Write your audiences' ears as well as their eyes. Do the words and sentences sound appropriate, proper, and interesting to your ear as you read what you wrote out loud? If either your words or sentences sound too much like writing, keep writing. Finally, cribbing the late crime novelist Elmore Leonard's writing advice: Take out parts people don't want to read.

Principle 5: Be FABulous When Messaging

You are the product being branded. You already knew this. But the notion is so important it bears repeating. As such, when you message about your brand you should emphasize Features, Attributes and ultimately Benefits (FAB) associated with you that are also deemed valuable by clients or perspective clients as they decide to engage with you, stay with or leave you, or talk you up/put you down.

There's more: if you fail to communicate your key "product" values to targeted audience members, they are unlikely to appreciate them. Or, likely, even know that your hopefully uniquely desirable values exist. Clients generally live in low involvement, low information consumption worlds. Your best communication option, then, is to directly targeted clients exactly how and why you are "different from" and "better than" other professionals who provide similar services or solutions. But quickly!

The best branding messages focus doggedly on emphasizing a unique value proposition. On your stage, these "value propositions" entail a combination of promises of value acknowledged and promoted by you and the beliefs emanating from clients that the values you promise actually will be delivered (by you) and experienced (by them). In traditional market environments, research is often used to determine exactly which product values ("solutions") are most important to clients. Different target segments (audiences) usually assign higher values to different sets of Features, Attributes, and Benefits—as those three "product" elements coalesce into solutions.

Presumably, professionals operating on stages they control or at least manage are already able to discern which solutions are most important to most of their clients. You should also be capable of artfully or materially altering the degree to which you emphasize one or another feature, attribute or benefit (i.e., values, all) in branding messages targeted at different clients.

In some ways, everyone reading this is like everyone else on earth. We're all human beings. Meaning, in brief, everyone wants to be loved, fed, clothed; feel safe and for that matter "cool." In some ways, everyone reading now is similar to fellow members of their cultural or subcultural group, gender category, social class, professional association, age cohort, and so forth. Meanwhile, those same folks are substantively different from others not belonging to their gender category, social class, professional association, age cohort, and so forth. And in some ways everyone reading right now is unique.

The omnipresent nature of these human similarities, differences, and uniquenesses is why you must tailor branded presentations of your FABulousness such that the messages address clients' unique wants, needs, and preferences. That is, if you plan to grow the power of your brand messaging efforts.

Principle 6: Differentiate Messages by Emphasizing Determinant Distinctions

When messaging, emphasize the personal or professional Features, credentialed or experience-based Attributes, and/or practical or psychological Benefits that you are uniquely equipped to deliver. Always emphasize *"determinant"* branding differences when communicating to clients. Determinant differences would materially differ from the values that professionals you are competing against can or do offer. The word determinant means "decisive." The differences that you emphasize also should *be important; that is, decisive to clients* as they decide which professional to select, retain or reject.

Let's exit our normal professional context to illustrate what determinant means. During most promotions it initiated during the last 10 or so years Southwest Airlines emphasized the branding tagline "Bags Fly Free." Flyers almost always enjoy saving money when traveling, right? Consequently, most travelers view "Free Bags" as an important difference; important enough to "determine" their airline choice. By promoting this difference relative to legacy airline competitors such as American, Delta, or United, Southwest effectively grounded its ongoing communication efforts in genuine, effective, and determinant brand differences. "Bags Fly Free" proved a difference-making message that provided a distinction. A branded line of demarcation that clearly distinguished Southwest from the airlines it competed against.

Your ability to elevate your branding power is predicated on your ability to "stand-out-from" rather than "fit-in-with" whatever "crowd" of professionals you compete against on your particular stage. Your branding power might similarly grow based your ability to make "old-things-appear-new", if you and your brand are the more established and experienced option. Finally, your ability to cultivate branding power may turn based on your ability to "make-new-things-known", if you and your brand are the "new things" on your stage.

Your branding power is always grounded directly or indirectly in your ability to create perceptions or the reality that the right sorts of differences exist, and you are uniquely able to deliver them. When identifying the differences you plan to communicate for purposes of establishing, enhancing or sustaining branding power, choose carefully.

Principle 7: Manipulate, But Only for Ethical Ends

Your communications effort will grow more persuasive if you "intentionally" accept that you perform and compete in the real world—rather than some idealized version of the world that never has or will exist. Sometimes your messaging will manipulate others. Accept this reality, and respond accordingly. Here's why:

- Your clients need to feel unique at the same time while believing they are part, or could be part, of something great. Because being your client, partner, associate or subordinate indeed should be great. You do believe this, right? If not, this book surely cannot help you.

Promoting your branding value in a persuasive fashion need not entail describing to clients how much they will benefit from working with you. Instead, a more persuasive messaging approach entails framing your message negatively. This is actually easy to do. Simply emphasize how much "value" clients will lose if they don't begin or continue working with you. This message might be construed as manipulative. But when the premise is accurate; that is, clients actually will lose material value if they don't engage with you, the messaging tactic is ethical, powerful, and persuasive. The message is driven, as should be the case, by your ability to satisfy or solve clients' needs or problems. And if you don't believe the solutions you deliver to your clients are superior to what competitors offer you should either step-up your current professional game or pursue a new profession in which you can excel.

Be judicious when executing manipulative messages. In the end, clients always decide whether your messages mostly make sense or mostly make noise.

One should not discuss manipulation without also addressing the issue of sincerity. The secret to success in various; for example, Hollywood, leadership, political, ministerial, and professional settings may depend in part on the ability to affect an appearance of sincerity in one's communication efforts. After all, once you can "fake sincerity" in your communication efforts you've got it made—as French diplomat Jean Giradoux once argued. Right?

We'll leave it up to you to decide whether we just manipulated you? Or if we delivered another useful branding valuable tactic by introducing the notion of "fake sincerity"? Your call.

Other Keys to Persuasive Brand Communication

The baseline communication principles introduced above are useful. But while necessary, these principles are not sufficient to ensure that you'll communicate more powerfully. To achieve breakout branding power, also honor the following communication keys.

First Key: Begin Branding Mindful of the Communication Outcomes You Seek

You should always "understand" the outcome that you are seeking to generate through particular branding messages. This understanding, when present, should "inform" you about the type of messages you create and send.

Branding messages, communicated by branding professionals, should always generate one or more of the following communication outcomes. Every branding communication should be "informed" by a desire to either remind, inform, persuade or influence and/or incentivize message recipients. When you perform mindful of the fact that when brand messages efforts achieve one or more of these communication outcomes over the longer or shorter run, your prospects for sustainable branding success grow. You certainly will be better prepared to create new or strengthen existing relationships with clients and core audience members.

Remind

Reminder branding messages should remind targeted recipients why and what they once loved or feared/respected about you as a branded professional. Reminder messages, in effect, admonish clients: *Don't You Forget about Me.* This simple message should be delivered with the same memorable spirit that Irish rockers *The Simple Minds* did as the band sang that memorable phrase as the classic 1985 *The Breakfast Club closing credits were rolling.*[4] The new, as espoused during the first season climax of the television show *Madmen,* "is a glittering lure." But the allure of the new never lasts long. Clients should be periodically reminded that whatever value they once loved or admired about you—but now, given the passage of time, have grown accustomed to, is still there!

Reminder branding messages generally prove more useful on stages where your value is already established and well-known. Most people, including clients, need to be reminded more often than they need to be instructed or motivated. People generally know the right thing to do. Say, remain loyal to you and your brand. Sometimes clients simply require some prompting from you to remain in your camp.

Inform

Informative brand messages create awareness that something new, special, different, or better is now happening or available. Ideally, the new, better, different thing should be you, or innovative values you now deliver and on which your new brand power is based. No one ever purchased any new "product" or participated in any special experience until s/he was made aware that the "special" thing and its new value now existed. Informative branding communications are appropriate as you enter your professional field, embark on a new stage, or have created a new and useful client solution.

Persuade

Persuasive branding messages motivate, encourage, sway, induce, and influence. Persuasion has material value. After all, persuasion is this book's *raison d'etre.*

In one form or another all prospective or actual clients with whom you interact and potentially engage live out their lives as a series of problems. So does everyone else. But as either a well-established or neophyte professional brand you occupy a special stage from which you should do whatever is necessary and ethical to ensure that you become viewed by your clients or prospective clients as "one" who is uniquely qualified to solve whatever problem aligns most closely with your specialty. To develop more powerful brand, demonstrate, through carefully designed messages, how and why choosing you and making choice that you are advocating will help clients achieve their goals. This branding identity depicts you as a "need satisfier" and "problem solver."

Problem solving and persuasion are two centerpieces of all professional activity. Each activity drives professional success and power. Learn how to persuade others that the values associated with the solutions you are uniquely prepared to provide are superior to the value associated with alternative solutions that other professionals could concurrently provide.

Clients must be motivated to buy your solutions. Employees must be persuaded to agree with or contribute to strategic scripts you author. Investors must be convinced to invest, perhaps directly, in you. On classic business stages supply chain partners must be motivated to partner and participate collaboratively with you in relationships that prove mutually beneficial. The behaviors of these clients, employees, investors, or supply chain partners will each tilt in your favor or best interests to the extent that your message delivers one thing:

- A perception that your audiences are taking away more value from an exchange with you than they are putting into the relationship.

Nearly everyone seeks more power and wants to believe they are winning. Nearly everyone wants to be more persuasive. Everyone wants to be listened to and to feel they have been treated fairly. Your demonstrated ability to develop genuine or perceptual values through the solutions you provide to clients will provide the core foundation of your persuasive branding power.

The existence and unique nature of your values should be disseminated to clients through your brand communication efforts. After persuading audience members they are "winners" who've been listened to and treated fairly, you may not know whether it was message or how you delivered it that generated your branding power. While the answer does not really matter, you should still attend carefully to each success criterion as you develop and deliver branding values.

Incentivize

Clients or prospective clients almost always respond to incentives. That is, if they are rational. But not everyone is "logical" in the same way. Consequently, the targets of your branding efforts won't all be incentivized by the same values. The need for you to engage in targeted, or selective, branding efforts is revealed. Targeted branding efforts will grant you the opportunity to position, develop, and deliver uniquely designed branding values, or solutions, to each targeted client or customer segment. You should provide incentives, create new incentives, and/or emphasize incentives specifically designed to enhance the value of your brand in the eyes of those who receive your branding messages. Good things come to those who bait, professionally, by dangling the proper in front of the right audiences.

An incentive is anything that inspires decision makers to action—generally, the specific response you are leading them to take. When doing something or buying something becomes more or less costly (is more or less incentivizing) in terms of, say, money spend; risk endured; time expended; stress experienced; inconvenience encountered or avoided; or prestige gained or lost than doing or buying something else, which "something" do you believe rational people are going to do? Pop singer Taylor Swift and her marketing team clearly understood the power of communication incentives. When releasing her album, *1989*, Ms. Swift offered three extra songs on the album to fans who purchased the whole thing as opposed to downloading songs individually. Any guesses regarding who sold the most albums during 2014?

Incentives can function as powerfully good or bad communication tools. The imprudent use of incentives may trigger unintended undesirable consequences. Consider the incentives (i.e., huge price subsidies) that the Affordable Health Care Act initially provided to people who earn barely enough—or actually, not quite enough—money to qualify them for health care subsidies. Consequently, Obamacare customers who receive such financial incentives may be incentivized to not work harder or longer hours to make more money. If they did, their subsidies would disappear.

Second Key: Frame Messages Properly

When brand-messaging, frame choices you present to actual or prospective clients as decisions that potentially lead to losses, rather than gains, if decision makers choose poorly. This point was made earlier. Gains or losses might be related to money, efficiency, or time. Or, to social standing, companionship or love. As you have learned the prospect of loss is far more motivating than the prospect of gain for most people. Fail to engage with Fidelity Investments and its Green Line counsel. You risk losing money and a happier future. Fail to wear Old Spice and blow your chances with the ladies. Eat a cereal other than Wheaties. No championships for you.

The ease with which information is recalled and thus the probability that it will influence client behaviors is influenced by the impact said information makes as it enters minds. Human minds respond instinctually to and consequently are highly influenced by three factors: fear; extreme tension or stress; and/or novelty, "the new."

Human brains are hardwired to allocate more attention to things that appear threatening. These instinctual responses account for the disproportionate impact that fear and stress exercise in our lives. In the distant past, strangers, starvation, or sabre toothed tigers actually existed as real-time threats to our ancestors' survival. Those instincts were passed genetically from generational survivor to generational survivor up to contemporary times. Negative information, communicated through marketing or other media (e.g., interpersonal or socially networked sources) consequently is stickier and more viral-like than positive information. Bad, depressing or scary information, once communicated, is difficult to dislodge because it is stickier and spreads quickly–again, like a virus.

Human behaviors, when viewed collectively, are rather predictable. Positive emotions, for example, make people more vulnerable than negative emotions. Largely because positive emotions are more future oriented. Negative emotions, by contrast, often resolutely adhere humans to the present. Gratitude and joy, over time, yield better health and deeper human connections. But in the short term, positive emotions expose us to greater risk of rejection and loss. Why? Because negative emotions tend to insulate and isolate. Meanwhile, positive emotions expose us to the big bad world with all its heartbreak. Fear or sadness, by contrast, generates immediate defensive responses, largely because they protect people from emotional attack. Fear and sadness also motivate people to acquire shielding resources in response to times of stress or threats of the sort that would invoke fear. Fear spreads quicker than viruses. The preceding statement is not hyperbolic, by the way. As noted, the fact that "if it bleeds it leads" on television, newspaper, and website front pages is grounded in this knowledge.

Smart professionals often understand these human tendencies and may them when messaging. We'll hold our noses too. But consider, for example, the proportion of negative to positive messaging that politicians employ in their branding initiatives. Watch television during election season. You'll quickly discern sense the huge role fear plays on contemporary political stages. Political branding efforts routinely feature ominous background music; quick cuts highlighting shadowy and shady figures; and/or sonorous-voiced narrators offering alarming assertions about our "side's" vulnerability to myriad threatening possibilities, if the wrong choice is made. More often than not the core political message boils down to one "big idea:" be scared, actually, be very afraid unless you are smart enough to choose me and my brand.

Or consider how vigilantly teenagers and 20-somethings work to enhance or maintain their online reputations? Do these cohorts engage in these activities driven more by their fear of falling behind others' putative enjoyment of better stuff/experiences? Or is it simply FOMA or the fear of missing out? Actually, a combination of each motive is involved.[5]

Fear, for most Americans, often represents little more than False Expectations Appearing Real.[6] But fear unsurprisingly remains the most powerful human emotion. Stress is a huge motivator, as well. Few people have ever awoke at 2:35 AM, unable to return to sleep, because they had experienced happiness or peace of mind. Smart communicators exploit their awareness of this, too. Hopefully, however, not on you. Because by now, you should understand that while well-grounded fears protect people from real dangers, our tendency to over-fear the prospect of failure often prevents people, including professionals, from pursuing genuine opportunities.[7]

These descriptions of presumed client behaviors are generally unflattering. They are accurate, however. Leverage these insights about human nature as you communicate your brand to key audiences. That is, so long as you message in concert with appropriate ethical standards and remain socially responsible. You should do the right thing because it is the right thing, not because the doing gives you something to brag about.

Strategically choosing to do right for and by others offers the "branding you" the opportunity to do better for yourself. First, your reputation will be enhanced. And second, because the same technological advances that currently threaten your hard earned welfare has simultaneously made your stage too smart for anything but your branding truth. Remember Tony Coach Dungy's observation that "what happens in the dark usually comes to light."

One more acutely felt and generally negative human emotion exists. One that you should consider when communicating on any stage. The emotion is anger. Our counsel: when angry, communicate as little as possible. Why? Again, stated simply:

- Speak, write or, in perhaps the worst possible case, e-mail or text while you are angry. And more likely than not, you will give the best speech, construct the best narrative, or transmit the best message that your brand will ever regret.

Third Key: Honor the "C's" of Good Communication

When brand messaging, explain your brand and the core determinant differentiating values that your brand delivers as clearly, concisely, and compellingly as possible.

Communicate clearly, so your message is better understood. Branding messages, almost all messages, should be built to be understood rather than deciphered. Decoding problems? When confronting, they magically dissipate. As renowned North Carolina auctioneer and one-time preacher Jeff Eanes counsels:

- "Put the candy low enough on the shelf that even children can reach it."

Communicate concisely. After all, "brevity is the soul of wit." Really. It. Is. There is a reason why "TED Talks" are limited to 18 minutes. When possible, branding messages should feature both soul and wit. Wittiness, or humor, is frequently used and quite useful in messaging. Humor provides clients with needed intellectual exercise. Humor engages their brains. Engaged clients brains are always a positive for effective branding, where one universal communicative goal is to structure and deliver messages that preclude you from essentially having to "beg for" audience attention. Humor concurrently provides fleeting yet welcome moments of escape to client brains that themselves are frequently overworked and highly stressed.

Communicate compellingly:

- Compelling brand messages are either attention-worthy, memorable, persuasive, or some combination of these three characteristics.

Compelling messages also provide solutions. Do otherwise, and, you're taking from audiences rather than giving them something worthwhile. Don't deliver solutions, and say goodbye to the prospects of developing more powerful brand identities and more sustainable relationships.

Creating compelling messages is rarely easy. But one universal guideline is useful. Compelling messages differentiate. Meaning, at their cores, the "big ideas" that drive compelling messages deliver value propositions based on fulfill-able promises that are different-from and better-than analogous propositions being promised in competitors' messaging or non-messaging. Deliver this sort of message, and then you can begin the task of building memory structures inside client's minds about the foundational value proposition that you, as a clear, consistent, and compelling branding actor, are uniquely prepared to deliver.

Attention span is the amount of time one can allocate to a task without becoming distracted. The average human attention span traditionally was about 30 seconds. By now, in an age where Internet and satellite television surfing is rule rather than exception, attention spans have dramatically shortened. Internet users, for example, spend less than 1 minute on the average website.[8] A popular Calgary, Canada radio station only plays songs that have been edited to half their original length.[9] The station boasts "twice the songs." Perhaps, however, the station should also promise half the music. Technology driven multitasking has made many people feel far more time-pressed. Consequently, you should make your key branding point or points quickly in whatever messages you construct. That you do this is more important now than ever.

Four other keys should also contribute directly to your branding communication success. We call these the "4C's" of professional branding.

Comprehensible Brand Communications

Our first key entails instant comprehension. What does it say about Americans that we eat so much fast food so fast? We actually have no clear answer, either. Presumably, Americans often simultaneously feel hungry and hurried. But this fast food analogy clearly suggests that professionals should deliver instantly understandable messages.

In "Thinking, Fast and Slow," Nobel Prize winning economist Daniel Kahneman describes two frameworks through which people usually make decisions. The first framework is called "thinking fast." The second, "thinking slow."[10]

"Thinking fast" occurs when people make decisions without being aware of how they are making them. Fact is, absent substantial mental effort, people don't "think" about the decision. Sounds like us, and probably you, a lot of the time.

"Thinking slow" would arise when clients are highly attentive to, and thinking hard about, any decision you have set before them. Similar to solving calculus equations—something most people are loathe to even try to do.

Human brains generally default to largely automatic and subconscious decision-making processes. So most decisions involve "thinking fast." When "thinking fast" happens, client decisions are based on the quantity and depth of memory structures *they have already created* through prior exposure to communications related to your brand. We humans have evolved to the point where we usually make simple, fast decisions when evaluating either new or known information. One messaging takeaway: When communicating your brand, make your key messaging point, comprehensibly, and get to your key branding point, quickly.

Connective Brand Communications

Our second "C," or branding communication key, is connection. To influence others or to be memorable, messages should resonate with and trigger positive responses from targeted recipients. The term "resonate" is routinely used in contemporary speech. For example, a particular political message might "resonate with voters." Or a new song's "sound might resonate with young people."

What does "resonate" mean on your professional stage? Resonate implies your branding messages should be specifically designed to logically-influence, personally-affect, or emotionally-appeal to targeted clients. Messages, in brief, should strike "resonate chords" with clients exposed to them. Turning-clients-on, not turning-them-off. Or, motivating clients to lean toward rather than away from your specific values.

Credible Brand Communications

The credibility of branded messages is our third key to your communication success. Worth noting: branded messages also include "branding messengers," or you. Our value proposition is simple. For your branding messages to be effective, recipients must believe what you are saying. Otherwise, they will rarely purchase the solutions you are selling in any staged situation where alternative solutions exist. Yes, everyone reading this is selling something, even if only yourself! Successful branding, and thus successful communication, depends in no small measure on the presence of trust.

Trust is reciprocity flavored by emotion. Clients trust you when they know or believe they will get back more or the same amount of value that they give out, over time, if they engage with you. Trustworthy professionals can be counted on to tell the truth and honor branding commitments. Professionals who consistently behave and message in credible or trustworthy ways earn regard and respect from message recipients. Do this, and watch the power and persuasiveness of your brand grow.

Credible messages, like trusted brands, are powerfully but properly coercive. Good reputations deliver direct value to professionals. The more trust you earn, the more business, loyalty and favorable world of mouth endorsements you can capture and retain. As you earn trust you can also raise prices over time, without substantive customer loss.

Contagious Brand Communications

Their contagiousness gives branding messages "legs". Contagiousness diffuses; that is, spreads messages around, and quickly. In the process, contagiousness can enhance the trustworthiness and credibility of branded messages. When messages are contagious people exposed to them often "talk them up," effectively endorsing messages as they pass them along to others through interpersonal, traditional or digital means. This contagion process generally lends even more credibility to your brand messages.

Such people are sometimes described as evangelists. Evangelists, or evangelicals, are not bad words, although contemporary American media often appears inclined to designate them as such. The terms "evangelist," or "evangelical," are simply ancient Greek words that mean bringer, or spreader, of good news. The good news could be about anything, including branding messages, you as the product, or your experiences. If you, as a branding professional, routinely satisfy or exceed clients' expectations; honor all branding promises made; or engage quickly in service recoveries when things go wrong (as inevitably happens), client endorsements will be or, at the least, their endorsements will not be negative. This latter outcome is, at net, a win. This is because clients are far more inclined to evangelize about negative than positive experiences they had with you. Consequently, the news, for professionals, should be very good.

There's more, however. Potential or actual clients can opt to trust and believe what other clients tell them, or to trust and believe what you tell them. Clients might also choose to trust neither. Which outcome, however, do you believe is most likely?

Here's the deal: clients who spread the "good news" as evangelists speaking on behalf of you and your performance are not selling something for profit. Evangelical clients are endorsing you, your performance, and ultimately your brand because they actually like you or believe in the value of what you have done for them. Client evangelists "endorse" you because they actually believe in the value that your brand demonstrably has delivered. Evangelists advocate your professional acumen knowing that their advocacy will never benefit them financially. Clients or prospective clients who receive this second-level brand advocacy messages therefore realize that what is being said, good or bad, must be credible.

Client-initiated WOM, when positive, absolves you from having to say what you need to say "for the money." And many professionals, as many clients suspect, indeed will say anything to gain green. By contrast, clients or customers say what they say about brands or companies—or your professional brand—because they really believe it. And you and your professional brand may be the beneficiaries.

Tread carefully, however. WOM endorsements from evangelical clients truly can be your best branding friend. If the word is good, that is. The converse also applies: when the word is bad, negative WOM can prove your worst enemy.

WOM: Powerful Enough to Earn Its Own Section

Word-of-mouth is commonly brand-identified by the acronym WOM. WOM entails informal person-to-person communication between a nonmarketing communicator and potential or actual clients or customers about the ownership or characteristics of a brand, product, service, organization, or marketer.[11] Product, service or branding information obtained from family members, friends, associates, and neighbors is more influential than information received through marketer-controlled communications, for reasons just explained. The initial source of power for WOM communications derives from the fact that somebody whom the message recipient knows and likes becomes a credible, believable and trustworthy face of the brand. Ideally, the face of your brand—when their "word" about you and your brand is positive. The second source of power for WOM follows from the fact that individuals who engage in WOM, as opinion leaders, do so absent "marketers'"—or in this context "professional branders'".

Yes, original sin. The original sin of every marketer or professional brander is that every audience member knows everything they say or do may be driven directly or indirectly by a profit motive. We are adamantly not against profits or the pursuit of profits. WOM endorsers or detractors, however, are absolved from that stain. Because they clearly aren't saying what they say for the money. When the associated message is positive, WOM endorsements would generally prove your most powerful branding image maker.

Many things in life, however, exist as good news/bad new stories. And unfortunately, the bad is absolutely more prevalent, powerful and influential than the good in WOM communication settings. This tendency is especially apparent in online settings, which are rife with e-WOM and where most clients (and potential clients) check online reviews before buying anything. These de facto social networking sites integrate the "social" (peer to peer) with the "search" (key words) through the "D" ("Digital" communication transmission). When using social media, clients expect negative posts or tweets. Consequently, they often discount the negative effects in favor of judging how effectively the purportedly offending brand—possibly you—handled the issue; that is, the quality of your "recovery" response. The prospect always exists that effectively branded professionals can convert "injured" clients into brand loyalists. Such loyalists, once created, will more likely emerge as evangelists who advocate on behalf what is good about you. After all, who is most likely to campaign most aggressively about the "evils of smoking?" One who never smoked? Or former smoker who once was lost but is now found; one who saw the light and now has "kicked?"

Bad news or potential or actual threats are more memorable than good news or soothing circumstances. Messages that create "better watch out" effects in the minds of recipients will grab more client mind-space. This is the "sticky" concept, again.

Most people, as you know, simply find more negative information more interesting. Mid-twentieth century American poet, storyteller, and satirist Dorothy Parker once quipped: "If you don't have anything good to say about someone come sit right by me."[12] She was right, and Ms. Parker was hardly unique in revealing this ironically humorous observation about human behavior. Too often for your liking, these third parties may function as the real voices of your brands and messages. Negative WOM, which is hard to resist and perhaps more difficult still not to spread, is akin to marketing gossip. And truth-be-told most people enjoy gossip. Gossip, akin to receiving sexy stolen goods. Gossip, the thing happening when two or more people tell stories about a third person that the third would prefer not be told. While gossip features fascinating speculation, professionals would rarely want clients gossiping about them. So don't give them any fodder.

The potential threats that negative WOM will impose on your brand communication efforts have heightened exponentially during the last 15 or so years. This period, of course, roughly corresponds with the years during which Internet-mediated messaging has truly come of age. The Internet makes scale-free, low-cost connectivity possible between (a) professionals and clients, (b) clients and professionals, and (c) clients and clients and prospective clients. Wherever scale-free, low-cost connectivity exists, huge numbers of networked users also exist. Within these networks, good and bad messages about messages and brands flow back and forth in quick, transparent, and largely unfettered fashions. For you, e-WOM exists simultaneously as a communication opportunity and threat. Realistically, you have no other good choice but to manage its effects on your brand.

E-WOM communication, like traditional WOM, entails any positive or negative accounts offered by potential, current or former customers about products, brands, or marketing organizations. The impactful difference, however, is that these beneficial or harmful endorsements are potentially made available to whole herds of humans through Internet-mediated communication channels. These communication channels include various marketing media. These media consist of instant messaging, Twittering, Websites, blogs, social networking sites, Instagram, e-mails, and text messaging.

Text messaging, for example, is a contemporary, largely customer-driven channel through which e-WOM is widely disseminated. The average US teenager sends about 2,000 texts per month. For teens and increasingly for people in their twenties and thirties, texting is their default communication mode. More than 97% of texts are read, and 90% are read in the first 3 minutes of receipt. This percentage is about four times higher than the rate at which e-mails are read.[13] Baby Boomer parents of Millennials and Generation X children are slowly or suddenly realizing their texts were read, even if there was no response. This same parental cohort has mostly given up hope that phone calls would be listened to in a similar fashion.

A No Longer New Communication Reality

These are the contemporary stages on which you perform and must communicate. Stages that are in certain critical ways more difficult to manage than at any time during your profession's history. Yet this is stage on which you must build and manage your reputation.

You must remain ever-vigilant for signs of trouble. Bad news, after all, bad news spreads at the speed of light in this now longer new Internet age. Watchfulness alone, however, will not ensure that the levels of professional service quality and problem-solving value you promised to clients are actually delivered. Try as you might, things occasionally will go wrong as you deliver values and solutions on contemporary stages.

You should attend constantly to the client satisfaction or dissatisfaction that results you deliver solutions. Do this, and you will be better prepared to engage in quick response service-failure recovery efforts or other brand restorative practices when things don't work as scripted. Being constantly observant and quickly responsive will permit you to preempt much of the havoc that otherwise damages brand reputations when negative WOM and e-WOM is transmitted from or between clients—or, for that matter, prospective clients.

Final Communication "Don'ts and Do's"

P.T. Barnum, 19th century entrepreneur and principal partner in the Ringling Brothers and Barnun and Baily Circus, famously said, "There's a sucker born every minute."[14] So true, unfortunately. By now, however, you've learned enough to not willingly take advantage of said suckers. Because you've also learned to value the longer-term benefits that your enhanced reputation will confer to your brand more than any short-term exploitative takeaway you might secure. You've likewise learned that whatever value or problem-solving ability you are showing or telling, demonstrating or explaining, and communicating or promoting had best emanate from a place of truth. There is no substitute for honesty. Because in the Internet world, far more so than any past worlds, the world has grown too small for anything but truth.

The 1st century Apostle Paul, writing in the Book of Romans, offers several useful insights related to professional brand communications. Particularly in situations and on stages like yours'. A place where we presume you have a message that is great to tell because you have provide a solution that is great to sell—and receive. Or, at least we believe you should!

Paul pronounces: "How then will they call on Him in whom they have not believed? And how are they to believe in (a new professional solution or idea) of whom they have never heard? And how are they to hear (about the professional product or idea) without someone preaching (disseminating, communicating the good news)? And how are they to preach (inform, remind, persuade, and ultimately build lasting brand-driven relationships) unless they are sent? As it is written, "How beautiful are the feet of those (including you, the professional communicator) who preach the good news!"[15] These verses from Romans represent a terrific historical shout-out and strong endorsement for the importance of powerful professional branding communication. Especially when a worthwhile message, developed about a professional who performs-out solutions that deliver determinant value to others, is being communicated honestly and yes, powerfully... By you!

Notes

1 Harrari, Yuval Noah (2015). *Sapiens: A Brief History of Humankind.* New York, NY: Harper Collins Publishers.
2 Jacobs, M. (2014). *A New Look at Darwinian Sexual Selection. Natural Science* (9/14/2014). http://naturalscience.com/ns/articles/01-11/ns_mej.html.
3 Grant, Barry Keith (2007). *American Cinema of the 1960s: Themes and Variations.* East Rutherford, NJ: Rutgers University Press.
4 Gora, Susannah (2010). *You Couldn't Ignore Me If You've Tried.* New York, NY: Three Rivers Press.
5 Anderson, Hephzibah (2011). Never Heard of FOMO? You are So Missing Out. *Guardian.* April 16, 2011.
6 Strutton, David and Kenneth Thompson (2015). *Marketing from Scratch: The Principles You Really Need to Know.* Dubuque, IA: Kendall-Hunt.
7 Kahneman, Daniel (2011), *Thinking Fast and Slow.* New York, NY: Farrar, Straus and Giroux.
8 BBC (2012). Turning into Digital Goldfish. *BBC News Article* on how the internet affects attention span. February 22. http://www.bbc.co.uk/2/hi/science/nature.
9 NPR (2014). Your Favorite Songs, Abridged. *NPR All Things Considered,* August 7, 2014. http://www.npr.org/2014/08/07/your-favorite-songs-abridged.
10 Kahneman, Daniel (2011). *Thinking Fast and Slow.* New York, NY: Farrar, Straus and Giroux.
11 Strutton, David, David Taylor, and Kenneth Thompson (2012). "Investigating Generational Differences in e-WOM Behaviors: For Advertising Purposes, Does X =Y?." *International Journal of Advertising,* 30(4): 559-586.
12 Meade, Marion (1987). *Dorothy Parker: What Fresh Hell is This?* New York, NY: Penguin Books.
13 Conversational Advertising. A Report from Mobile Squared. *Totango,* June, 2010, Retrieved April 26, 2015. http://www.docstoc.com/docs/119372644/Conversational-Advertising---Mobile-Squared#
14 Kunhardt, Philip B. (1995). *P.T. Barnum: America's Greatest Showman.* New York, NY: Knopf.
15 Holy Bible (1999). *Holy Bible: New Standard Revised Edition.* Nashville, TN: Thomas Nelson Publishers.

PART III

Keeping Your Brand Fresh

Chapter 12

Once Your Story Is Told: Renewing Brand Vitality

"Dreams can come true again, when
everything old is new again"

—Peter Allen and Carole Bayer Sanger (1944–?; 1947–?).

Ever watch what happens when newly failed trees or pruned limbs are sucked into wood chippers? If the answer is yes, you have seen previously viable things enter grinders at one end and exit the other utterly transformed. Hopefully, should the need arise, something similar may one day happen to you. An utter transformation, that is. Absent the obviously painful chipping and grinding experience, of course.

Ever think about the challenging processes one would have to create and manage successfully in order to reincarnate, reenergize, and revitalize the formerly living but now lifeless material that entered "the machine?" Probably not. But this chapter does. As should you.

Professional Branding: To End Is to Begin (Again)

This book was written to produce transformational effects for your brand. Having read it you now enjoy the opportunity to upgrade your brand's persuasive power. But what should happen next after you have initially transformed the power and persuasiveness of your brand? This final chapter answers that question.

Professional Branding, from Scratch began with a story. The story behind the story revealed a knowledge gap—about professional branding—that existed in most readers' minds. The story we told then showed readers how to bridge this gap. This narrative structure made sense. The preceding storyline enlightened, revealed, and informed professionals and offered instructions about what they should and should not do to increase the power and persuasiveness of their brands.

Every brand, after all, as rocker Rod Stewart passionately sang: "Tells a story." Especially yours. Or at least it should. Every good story usually features a powerful or interesting (often, both qualities are present) beginning; an ofttimes middling middle (but audiences must pass through it); and a resounding, redemptive, revelatory, and/or emotionally satisfying or frustrating end. This specific storytelling tradition dates to ancient Greek theater. Theater, naturally yet another Greek word, means "gazing forward in a highly focused manner into one specific direction." Something that all professionals should do, for a while, until the time comes to shift our attention, and consequently the attention of our clients, into another realm. That time will come for all professional branders. Especially those professionals who have successfully branded themselves and the uniquely desirable value they deliver.

Most contemporary scripted plays or movies still devotedly follow practices established by the Greeks. Sometimes, however, staged and scripted endings—to movies, plays, or branding initiatives—prove renewable. Previous and new audiences then can experience recontextualized theatrical, cinematic, or branding sequels. But unfortunately these renewed efforts often fail to live up to standards established by the original highly successful works. Remember later generation Star Wars movie franchise character Jar Jar Binks? If you don't, no worries. You're better off. Jar Jar was no R2D2.

Whatever ending you initially conjure and ultimately create for your professional branding story should be renewable. But not through some lukewarm or insipid version that undermines the standards for quality and determinant differentiation established by your original branding story. Instead, professional rebranders, including you, should seek true renewal, genuine rebirth, possibly an utter transformation of the branding identify and values you initially created to enhance your brand's persuasive power.

All professionals who brand themselves successfully eventually confront the need to renew the vitality of their brands. A confrontation that often arrives sooner than later. Because, riffing Bob Dylan, the environmental times that once were "a-changing," and demanded that you step-up your branding game or get left-behind, still continue to change at unprecedented speeds. Environments would rarely halt their dynamic ever-changing natures at the exact moment when you perfect the persuasive power of your brand. Okay, this will never happen. Instead, the technological, client base, competitive, and global changes that initially prompted you to re-tool your brand keep rolling and roiling forward, always evolving. Sometimes in favor of, sometimes against, the best interests of your current brand. Consequently the value and vigor of your brand should evolve as well.

Rocker Neil Young first bellowed "Rust Never Sleeps" during the 1970s. The thing is, entropy never sleeps, either. The word entropy synopsizes the notion that any idea's, thing's, or brand's value and power unceasingly declines over time. Entropy is inevitable unless someone or something purposefully intervenes to prevent, well, the entropy from occurring. Because entropy exists, and always imposes its will, the need to continuously renew the power and persuasiveness of your brand never ends.

Don't Let Your Story Grow Old

As the branding story told through this book began (Section I), we explained why and within which strategic and ethical constraints you should endeavor to expand the power and persuasiveness—the *vitality*—of your brand.

During this story's middle part, we explained how you can directly expand the authority, power, and persuasiveness, again, elevating the *vitality* of your brand. The five stage approach we used likely appears logical, almost inevitable in its self-evident value, now that the proper actions to take have been explained to you. During Section II, we encouraged you to power-up your brand by (a) managing audience impressions, (b) integrating seven power rules into your professional life, (c) developing the creativity of your brand, (d) exploiting the power of your brand through paralanguage and artifact, and (e) communicating your newly earned branding power more persuasively.

This story about how to vitalize your brand power is ending. But ending, logically, with a story about how to renew the persuasive power of your still newly revitalized brand. You may thinking: Brand renewal? Time for that already? Yes, renewal of your newly powerful brand will prove necessary. You should learn more now about how to resolve a future problem that you must resolve to sustain your branding success.

The problem that you and every other successfully branded professional will eventually confront is synopsized by lyrics lifted from a love song that bluesman Boz Scaggs wrote and singer Rita Coolidge made famous during the 1970s. Boz wrote: "Once a story's told, it can't help but grow old."

"Growing old" is a genuine problem on many contemporary stages. There is no way that your professional value being perceived as stale, less relevant, and basically yesterday's news will not suck for you. As you've learned, the ability to develop sustainably renewable branding power on professional stages is fundamentally predicated on your ability to "stand out" rather than "fit-in"; on your ability to make "new things known"; or on your ability to present "old things as new and vital."

The "new thing" is, or once was, you as a professional. The "old thing" is, or one day will be the professional you, if you do not successfully re-vitalize your brand. Politicians know this "old song and dance" quite well. Election cycle in, election cycle out, politicians perform on stages. Although there, their branding success rises or falls based on the skill with which they make the novel, generally their ideas, appear familiar—and thus safe and secure—and make the familiar (or old), generally themselves, appear novel and vital.

Renewed Vitality

Vitality absolutely will impose its way and have its say on today's professional stages. Especially, in today's professional world. Vitality is an elixir known to define youth. Vitality is also a necessary condition for positive change. Vitality enables choice. Choice enables change. Changes enable growth. Growth, usually through not inevitably, facilitates improvement. Here, tellingly, of the power and persuasiveness of your brand.

The unappealing alternative to renewing or sustaining vitality in your personal life is passive aging. Passive aging entails the acceptance of a slow but steady decline in one's health and physical appearance after, say, age 50. Age 50 presumably and hopefully the new 40, right? Notwithstanding ill-fate, every professional reading this now either is or one day will be 50+. Are you willing to accept passive aging? Didn't think so.

No reason exists, then, to suspect you would accept the passive aging of your brand, either. Especially if and after you have successfully engaged in your own personal branding-renewal project. This project specifically requires that you reimagine, restage, reinvigorate, revitalize, and ultimately, renew even your new brand; that is, as it inevitably ages.

The Talmud offers a story about how Old Testament Israel King Solomon found a magic ring. This ring had the power to make happy men sad and sad men happy. The plain gold ring had words "this too should pass" inscribed on it.[1] Change is the only certain inside any profession. Or, for that matter, any species. Wall Street financiers and Galapagos Island beasts alike, it does not matter. There are no exceptions to this rule.

History is littered with the wreckage of professions and professionals who refused to adapt. Entire sectors have collapsed when burdened by myopic leadership and a refusal to change even when all signs underscored that purposeful change, often of the whole profession's branding identity, was not just necessary to succeed. Worse still, change was necessary to merely survive. Ask a 17th century Dutch tulip trader. A 1st century scribe. Or, a 21st century coal mining engineer trying to find work in the US.

Everything Old Should Be Made New Again

In the song lyrics that introduce this chapter, Peter Allen and Carole Bayer Sanger wrote about romance. During the 1940s/1950s Joseph Schumpeter expressed similar thoughts about professional organizations. The great economist and business thinker suggested that nothing mature enterprises could do would deliver more sustainably differentiating value to them and their brand then becoming new, again. But fashioning the new again from the well-worn cloth of mature or maturing organizational brands counters the natural order. As is similarly true of mature or maturing professional brands.

Schumpeter demonstrated how even the most successful organizations typically calcify over time, become institutionally inflexible, and view new ideas suspiciously. Those organizations would usually include firms whose obviously successful founding day had actually stemmed from their founders' creative visions and values. Schumpeter was not writing about brands when originally expressing these thoughts. He could have been, however. Because his insights apply directly to your professional stage and brand and what you should do or not do after you have created a successful brand.

Exacting creative ideas, ideals, and behaviors that once made your brand great often succumb, over time, to inertia. After the creative passion and energy that once drove your renewed or new brand diminish, your branding fortunes may similarly shift for the worse. As may the branding power of an organization you founded, now lead, or merely serve. For example, once upon a time, its Board of Directors forced out Steve Jobs. In shockingly quick order the once dominant Apple brand essentially become a market afterthought. Upon his return, however, the founder and brand powerhouse that was Steve Jobs renewed Apple's then stale branding vision. He quickly re-transformed the Apple brand into the most powerful name and symbol in the world. The value of your grand branding vision is difficult to overstate. The difficulty of rekindling the creative spirit that originally engendered your new branding power, especially as your once-new stories grow older and mustier is similarly difficult to overstate. But the task can and should be done.

What Schumpeter Said Then Matters Now

In his genuinely paradigm-shifting book *Capital, Socialism, and Democracy (1950)*, Joseph Schumpeter was first to correctly identify innovation as the core driver of most professional success. The overused phrase "paradigm shift" is purposefully employed here. That's because the principles offered in his book split managerial practice into before/after eras. Schumpeter also asserted that mature firms that failed to innovate would fall victim to a "perennial gale of creative destruction." Schumpeter called the professionals who "fanned" this creative gale entrepreneurs. He popularized the term entrepreneurship. Please take the preceding text and substitute the phrase "mature brands" for the phrase "mature firms." There, this is your key takeaway. You never want to be or become a "mature professional brand." Here, at the end, we characterize branding professionals who strive to recreate similar gales on their particular and perhaps "maturing" branding stages "re-branding professionals."

Schumpeter described the entrepreneur's role as moving any firm's assets to where those always finite resources—you might relate this notion to your own limited time, talent and treasure—will do the most good. He argued that organizations of all types, sizes, and life cycle stages can behave entrepreneurially. Entrepreneurs, he argued, can exist anywhere. We argue further, as can entrepreneurially-oriented branding professionals. Especially on stages where entrepreneurial behaviors are welcomed, cultivated, and rewarded. You should embrace and continue to implement re-entrepreneurially re-branding changes, even to your recently renewed brand.

Like nations, formerly entrepreneurial but now mature professional brands are seldom murdered. Instead many mature professional brands commit prolonged suicides. Your brand, for example, might outlive your original branding vision. Once this happens you subsequently slowly or quickly lose the entrepreneurial edge that once drove your original branding success. At that point, you would inevitably experience a gradual diminution of your branding power and persuasiveness. A simple recommendation:

- Don't let this be you.

Re-Entrepreneurial Re-branding

Re-entrepreneurial re-branding efforts ideally would unfold on stages where professionals initiate thoughtful actions designed to integrate redefined and reenergized entrepreneurial branding values into their now mature brands. Re-branding professionals will succeed by rediscovering, rebuilding, or reigniting an entrepreneurial spirit as they endeavor to make their mature brands *new, again*.[2] A "reignited" entrepreneurial spirit would undoubtedly enhance your brand's focus, energy, intensity; ultimately, your brand's vitality.

Re-brandin professionals should expect to confront and must manage various obstacles as they seek a middle path between honoring their "old" brand's heritable best and reenergizing the rest in route toward their renewed brand. Key takeaway:

- A renewed brand should permit you to present more of your best and less of your worst as you communicate anew with key audience members.

Obstacle 1: Check Your Ego at the Door

If you elect to engage in re-entrepreneurial rebranding, a "not to do" list may prove more crucial to your eventual success than a "to do list." Shortly before or after you've launched your rebranding initiative, you may be tempted to announce a new sheriff—okay, your killer new brand—is or soon will be arriving. After all, you already mastered this branding thing, once. Otherwise you would not be experiencing the need to re-brand, again, now. Don't. No need exists to meet with every client, send letters to every partner, or necessarily cultivate or issue real or metaphorical press releases, at least not at first. Avoid "I," when possible, as you began re-branding. People who share your stage as clients, subordinates, peers, or superiors rarely want to wade through your "branded ego" in route to your re-"branded info."

Issuing "here I am, again" types of re-branding pronouncements may make you feel good as you issue them." Remember, however: This is not entirely about you. Even the most radical re-entrepreneurial re-branding transitions begin with assuring your old brand's continuity to audience members. Former JC Penney CEO Ron Johnson might have benefitted from such advice. Then you might not have implemented everyday low prices in lieu of persistent price discounts without first bothering to ask his customer base about they felt about Penney's re-branding initiative.

For most audience members any change represents a threat, and will be received cautiously on whatever stage you command. This is certainly what happens with Penney and its predominately female customers. Similarly, on your professional stage former colleagues or direct reports, partners, or clients who knew you as the old brand do not know you as a renewing brand. In no way or form do current or potentially new audience members - think clients - have any obligation to accept your new brand. Remember or learn:

- Demonstrated humility rather than hubris or haste will earn you the space, respect, and insight that may crucial as you slowly baste re-branding decisions before pursuing potentially or actually disruptive changes.

As you begin re-branding, avoid being a falsely humble egoist. Never play "'ah, shucks, little ole me'" games. This particular re-branding foray may prove more persuasive than you thought possible. During any re-branding effort, however, one particular playground rule should resonate: Nobody likes bossy or conceited little children. Fine power lines divide professional leadership and self-confidence from personal authoritarianism and arrogance. Run toward the former. Brand away from the latter. Cross those lines, and see the power and persuasiveness of your renewed brand wane. Luke 14:14 offers relevant thoughts about how a paradoxical mix of "confident-humility" (not an oxymoron) might confer renewed power in any professional's branding life: "For all who exalt themselves will be humbled and those who humble themselves will be exalted."[3] One more time we confer Biblically-grounded, and thus politically incorrect, advice. Once again many readers may be uncomfortable accepting the source. If you count yourself among that group, how would you feel had the same counsel arrived from another source. There, perhaps you can accept it... now.

Obstacle 2: Don't Let Inertia Erode Your Will to Change Your Brand

Ironically, as you tap the brakes on your ego, the undertow of your old branding comfort zone may become harder to resist. Facing new challenges and decisions, human nature may draw you toward those you are already most used to making. Weaker-minded professionals may freeze, holding things constant in the comfort zone of familiar issues and expected outcomes.

Inertia arrives in other forms. Don't judge new situations through the lens of stages, client bases or competitors that now are old and gone themselves—or through familiar criteria. There are few new branding problems, only old branding solutions which for you, if you need to re-create your branding identity, are no longer working. Avoid trying to understand or solve new problems using default processes or past solutions. Instead, analyze each new situation on its terms and future impact on your current and prospective branding success.[4]

Changing your re-branded self may lead to sub-rosa conflict. Subtle conflict of the sort that arises inside the most important place—your mind. You may be tempted to cave and allow your brand to return to or remain in old places to maintain peace with bosses, subordinates, or clients who appear irreplaceable—at the time. Don't. Take the time to parse out the importance and consequences of the specific re-branding decisions that most need to be made, before changing anything about your current brand. Only then can you create and sell new branding solutions to others who share your stage. And do so unencumbered by any intensely felt need to compromise what you really need to do to your current brand.

Obstacle 3: Don't be Impatient

You may have visualized the re-branding directions you should pursue for months, perhaps longer. One not so casual observation: Everyone realizes patience is a virtue. Everyone also knows waiting sucks. But the re-branding act is one that paradoxically rewards patience and action. When re-branding think like a person of action but remain patient enough to act, at opportune moments and on suitable stages, like a person of thought. And yes, this original branding and now re-branding advice is so nice that we have presented it to you twice.

Three bad things may happen if re-branding professionals take their new identities to public stages too quickly. In this context, "too quickly" means without fully evaluating success prerequisites and securing genuine buy-in rather than just resentful acquiescence, from all places, yourself. The first "bad thing:" re-branding professionals would forgo opportunities to learn what they don't know about their putative new branding identities that they may really need to know. Here, we might reference former Secretary of Defense Donald Rumsfeld's dreaded "unknown-knowns".[5] The second bad thing: re-branding professionals would secure less insight about whether the needs of key clients or other audience members that they thought were unsatisfied with their current brands actually remain up for grabs. A third potential downside, re-branders may sacrifice, on the altar of expediency, the opportunity to rally valuable audience support behind their fresh future branding vision.

While it is widely lauded, patience actually can be virtuous or vicious. Judicious patience, however, the sort followed by brandable action when the time is right is rarely wrong. Paraphrasing John Wooden, again: When rebranding move quickly, but with patience.

The preceding three re-branding "don't–dos" are accompanied by, yes, two re-branding success-facilitating "do's." These do–do's follow.

(Do) Know Where to Stop

If you brand plan ahead, visioning through toward compelling ends, you will be less distracted by emotion or desires to freelance. Clarity of purpose minimizes uncertainty, lowers anxiety, and quells intellectual discord. Endings are critical to successful rebranding efforts.

Naturally, when the branding ends you envision are achieved, you can envision new, more challenging goals. Always designate the point where you should stop, declare victory, and advance renewed toward other, now more relevant branding goals. This is also the time to reinvent steps and processes that are now necessary for your brand to become new, again, *again*.

Professional re-branding efforts have no end. That is, unless environmental change somehow came to an end. But re-branding initiatives should have bounded beginnings.

Move Deliberately

As any re-entrepreneurial branding visioning begins, successful re-branders require ideas bigger than new merely for the sake of new to focus upon and rally around. Given today's disorderly stages, materially new and different rebranding visions may prove crucial to sustainable success. Yet you still should proceed deliberately when developing a new branding vision.

Move deliberately, first, based on an understanding that the need to craft your renewed branding vision carefully is more important than hitting ground running. Second, by understanding no delete key will be available to tap if early mistakes occur. Third, after accepting the faith of key audience members that may have been lost or gone wobbly may need to be restored before you can develop and execute new branding visions.

Rebranding Re-Visioning Guidelines

Three brand re-visioning guidelines appear useful.

Guideline 1: Crystalizing a new vision good enough to successfully drive your rebranding initiative will require you to simplify and clarify. At the least, simple and concise brand visions are less bad than complicated and long-winded brand visions.

Guideline 2: When creating a new vision, remember that are not married to any initial vision that you elect to pursue. You are, instead, merely dating, or renting the vision. If your new branding vision is not working, end it.

Guideline 3: Begin the re-visioning process knowing that audiences you target through your re-branded messaging may be unmerciful, apathetic, or uninterested in the new "you." If your clients are generally mature, highly experienced or both, proceed cautiously. An audience's maturity and experience strips aways its illusions like thinner strips away paint. With that, your ability to thrill or fool clients or other audience members whom you seek to serve and influence through your renewed brand's branding power may melt away, as well.

(Do) Promote Your "Re-branded Future" Relentlessly

The accelerating velocity of professional life on various stages that have been acutely impacted by technology and globalization threatens to overwhelm some professionals while making others less efficient. Studies have shown that the more advanced the modernity of the country becomes, the quicker the nation's citizenry's strides and pace![6] Implying that even the simplest activities in more advanced countries, that is, walking down sidewalks, speed up. But we still advocate deliberation even as you relentlessly re-vision your rebranded future. Specifically, live and plan intentionally on the horizon. Horizons offer vantage points from which you can look back to understand the past and forward to determine what should be done branding-wise in your future. On the horizon, you will understand as much about your branding past and what worked well or poorly as you do about rebranding directions you should seek in the future. Winston Churchill: "The further back you look, the further ahead you see."

Allocating sufficient time for reflection may prove crucial to your rebranding success. Re-branding initiatives demand, as a success prerequisite, that you make accurate bets about future human behaviors. To enhance your acuity, ask and as importantly answer the following three questions:

- Which new branding ideas that I could act upon will yield more profitable new revenue?
- Which new branding ideas that I could execute will succeed?
- What new story should my renewed brand tell in the future?

Future versions of your re-branded story should be refined as necessary. As long, that is, as you continue to honor your original brand's core principles. The path just outlined is based on principles offered in *Built to Last: Successful Habits of Visionary Companies*. Specifically, this advice is consistent with the *Built to Last's* core imperative: "stimulate progress, preserve the core."[7]

On professional stages, however, we recommend further that to stimulate re-branding progress you should preserve the best of your original branding core. In many and perhaps most professional sectors nothing will age quicker than the future. Consequently you will confront the need to execute this re-branding process, again and again, throughout the upward arc of your career's progression.

Future branding stories should be circulated through whatever communication channels, foremost yourself, and message forms that important internal and external audiences are most likely to know, use and trust. Branding messages should always be delivered with the candor and transparency that prove indispensable to sustainable success on contemporary stages. After all, where and how well we begin often dictates where we end up.

Ending this Story—So Your Rebranded Story Can Begin, Again

The people most crucial to your success will usually respond more favorably to your branding reality as opposed to your branding rhetoric. The people most crucial to your success, lest any doubt remained, are your current and future clients. Because nothing happens and no one gets paid until and unless somebody - you - successfully sells something having value to someone. Given these three related facts, two final brand re-visioning recommendations follow.

Recommendation 1: When visioning re-branding efforts, step outside your professional life. Doing this requires you to consider and answer eight fundamental questions:

- What client needs do you and your brand currently satisfy?
- What prospective or actual client needs could your renewed brand satisfy in the future?
- What is the gap between the client problems that your re-branded self could satisfy in the future and the client problems you currently solve?
- Can you bridge this gap through your renewed branding values?
- What competitive advantages does your current brand possess?
- What new competitive advantages could your rebranded values create?
- What old branding competencies, if any, should you deemphasize?
- What new re-branded competencies can you create?

Call this eight question process outside-in brand re-visioning. Answer these questions in the order presented and the resulting insights generally will drive your brand re-visioning efforts toward desirable results.

The questions are understandable, sensible, and answerable. But while Michael Porter would likely approve, this form of visioning is hard to master.[8] Well trained and highly educated professionals naturally think inside-out; remember associative barriers. And you should and must continue to think inside-out; after all that exact proficiency, when executed on your specific stage, is what makes you a professional, so long as you also adopt an outsider's cold, calculating eye. Answering each question successfully will make you "colder and more calculating." Sounds harsh, yes. But this exact perspective is necessary to clarify your vision for any renewed brand identity that seek to create.

Recommendation 2: Another historically based visioning alternative is available. One that involves following an opportunistic rebranding path. While no slam dunk (final basketball reference), this re-branding approach alternative should prove easier to pursue.

The approach entails identifying opportunities that may yield huge payoffs at manageable costs that you can pursue, at opportune moments. Even if your long-range branding vision remains cloudy, you can seek such openings, identify one, and develop right-now re-branding visions and goals appropriate to the opportunity. Martin Luther King followed this path, circa 1955–1956, as he opportunistically exploited unanticipated bus boycotts in service of Dr. King's overarching vision for equal rights. The boycotts were precipitated by Mrs. Rosa Park's apparently spontaneous protest in Montgomery, AL. As a consequence the already-mature branded enterprise called America, a nation that turned 188-years old as the Civil Rights Act passed during 1964, became *newly rebranded, again.*[9]

One argument bolstering this recommendation that you engage in "opportunistic brand re-visioning" follows from fact that often what appears new or daring when first introduced is usually just a creative re-combination of familiar elements introduced or reintroduced to one another at opportune moments or stages. Throughout history there was only one first arrowhead, wheel, printing press, Protestant Reformation, steam engine, computer chip, and so on. And only one first professionally re-branded you. Everything else derives from some original version—or as Coke's old school branding masters would have had you perceive, "the real thing." Even you. Somewhere Joseph Schumpeter, champion of entrepreneurism, creative destruction, and the perpetual need that professionals face to rebrand routinely, is probably smiling.

A conclusion might be a place where you go when you get tired of *thinking*. But not here, please. As this book ends we trust you'll *ponder* the motives and means that should empower and steer your efforts to build, strengthen, sustain or renew the value, power and persuasiveness of your brand. *Think* about these things, understanding that while the race you are running is long, in the end it is mostly with yourself—and against your brand. But on the rapidly changing professional stages where you now perform you likely will need to re-run and re-win your professional branding race, again and again and again.

Notes

1 Rimas, Andrew and Evan D.G. Fraser (2008). *Beef: The Untold Story of How Milk, Meat, and Muscle Shaped the World.* New York, NY: WR Morrow.
2 McEnany, Robert and David Strutton (2015). "Leading the (R)evolution: Succession and Leadership Rules for Re-entrepreneurs." *Business Horizon*, 58: 401-410.
3 Holy Bible (1999). *New Revised Standard Version.* Nashville, TN: Thomas Nelson Publishers.
4 Hamel, Gary and Bill Breen (2013). *The Future of Management.* Cambridge, MA: Harvard Business Books.
5 Rumsfeld, Daniel (2013). *Known and Unknown: A Memoir.* New York, NY: Harper and Row Publishers.
6 Gleich, James (2011). *Faster. The Acceleration of Just About Everything.* London: Vintage.
7 Collins, James C. and Jerry I. Porras (1994). *Built to Last: Successful Habits of Visionary Companies.* New York, NY: Harper Business Essentials.
8 Porter, Michael (1980). *Competitive Strategy: Techniques for Analyzing Industries and Customers.* New York, NY: Free Press.
9 McQuire, Danielle (2010). *At Dark End of the Shoe.* New York, NY: Alfred Knopf.

CPSIA information can be obtained at www.ICGtesting.com
Printed in the USA
LVOW10s1449190816

500988LV00008B/13/P

9 781465 299994